Additional Praise for *Striking Gridiron*

"Greg Nichols couldn't have written it better if he'd been on the sidelines with us."   —Chuck Klausing, coach of the 1959
Braddock High Tigers

"If you wish to read a heart-warming story, I recommend you read Greg Nichols's story of how a football team helped heal a town in Western Pennsylvania. Chuck Klausing was the football coach at Braddock High School at the very early stage of his coaching career. I had the opportunity of working with Coach Klausing while I was head football coach at West Virginia University. He was probably the best hire I ever made. I will say he was the wisest coach I ever had. Read this story and you will see what America is all about!"   —Coach Bobby Bowden, NCAA record holder for
most career wins and bowl wins by a Division I FBS coach

"I was rather unsure of myself when I started out in the scouting department for the Pittsburgh Steelers. Someone recommended I talk to Chuck Klausing. He was one of the greatest coaches in Pennsylvania, and it didn't take me long to figure out why. We'd watch game film together and he would spot every mistake every player made. Chuck saw the details, and so does Greg Nichols. This book puts you down on the field and takes you out to the streets of Braddock, Pennsylvania, a gritty mill town that faced long odds during the steel strike of 1959. This is the way a sports book should be written."   —Art Rooney Jr., vice president, Pittsburgh Steelers

"Can a team make a town forget defeat? There is tragedy in *Striking Gridiron*, but much more importantly, there is also glorious triumph. Greg Nichols takes you back to 1959, on the banks of Monongahela River in western Pennsylvania, and puts you on the cinder-covered field with the Braddock Tigers as they set records and win games against the backdrop of a devastating steel strike. Nichols has crafted not only a richly detailed chronicle of that memorable season but also the tale of a team's heroism and a town's redemption."   —Mark Beech, *Sports Illustrated* staff writer and
author of *When Saturday Mattered Most*

"Reading Greg Nichols's *Striking Gridiron* will make you forget all about Joe Paterno and Jerry Sandusky and remember a time when football in Pennsylvania was a matter of national import for all the right reasons. Not since *Friday Night Lights* has a writer portrayed a powerhouse high school football team and its coach as vividly as Nichols does the Braddock High Tigers; but Nichols tells a larger tale as well, that of the mid-century American working man whose livelihood may not last the season. The combination is unbeatable."

—Megan Marshall, Pulitzer Prize–winner and author
of *Margaret Fuller: A New American Life*

"If it is possible for a town to die of a broken heart, Braddock is it. Ninety percent of our population is gone, along with the amazing, true story of the Braddock Tigers, if not for the scholarship of Greg Nichols. Braddock, conceived in struggle, was built by the heroic sacrifices of tens of thousands of immigrants. There is so much history here—history that literally shaped our nation—from the French and Indian War to Andrew Carnegie. In *Striking Gridiron*, Greg has painstakingly related (thereby, preserved) one of Braddock's most accessible and relatable historical struggles: football. As mayor, I am humbled and grateful for what Greg has achieved with this important book."

—John Fetterman, mayor of Braddock, Pennsylvania

"Greg Nichols has written a phenomenal account of a football team on the eve of a national winning record, set in a Pennsylvania steel town during a calamitous 1959 workers' strike. A deeply inspiring story of a coach who knew how to win not just on the field and in the locker room but in the community, how to overcome racial prejudice and treat all as one. *Striking Gridiron* is a compelling read with characters that won't let go."

—Douglas Whynott, author of *The Sugar Season*

STRIKING GRIDIRON

STRIKING GRIDIRON

A Town's Pride and a Team's Shot
at Glory During the Biggest
Strike in American History

Greg Nichols

THOMAS DUNNE BOOKS ☙ ST. MARTIN'S PRESS NEW YORK

THOMAS DUNNE BOOKS.
An imprint of St. Martin's Press.

STRIKING GRIDIRON. Copyright © 2014 by Greg Nichols. All rights reserved.
Printed in the United States of America. For information, address St. Martin's
Press, 175 Fifth Avenue, New York, N.Y. 10010.

www.thomasdunnebooks.com
www.stmartins.com

Photos courtesy of Chuck Klausing.

Designed by Steven Seighman

The Library of Congress Cataloging-in-Publication Data is available upon request.

ISBN 978-1-250-03985-9 (hardcover)
ISBN 978-1-4668-3534-4 (e-book)

St. Martin's Press books may be purchased for educational, business, or promo-
tional use. For information on bulk purchases, please contact Macmillan Corpo-
rate and Premium Sales Department at 1-800-221-7945, extension 5442, or write
specialmarkets@macmillan.com.

First Edition: September 2014

10 9 8 7 6 5 4 3 2 1

For Nina,

for every moment

CONTENTS

AUTHOR'S NOTE

My research began with a simple question spoken into a computer microphone: "Do you remember the 1959 game against North Braddock Scott?" On the other end of the line, sitting in his apartment in an assisted-living facility in Indiana, Pennsylvania, Coach Chuck Klausing said he remembered. Did he ever. For the next hour I sat riveted as the former coach of the Braddock High Tigers brought that Friday night fifty years earlier back to life.

My challenge was to capture the gusto, vividness, and intimacy of Klausing's telling on the page. Material from this book is based on interviews, newspaper clippings, books, magazine articles, and my own observations. Lines of dialogue are based on recollected snippets of conversation and on quotes mined from newspaper articles. Where all other avenues of research were exhausted, I used educated guesses and my own imagination to maintain the animating spark.

Klausing's participation throughout the project was vital. Over a marathon three months in 2012, he obligingly subjected himself to near-daily interviews; he shared hundreds of personal documents spanning a lifetime in football, helped rally enthusiasm among former players, and was always available to answer urgent questions about piddling details from decades earlier. He is an extraordinary man, and it has been a joy traipsing through his past. Special thanks to Klausing's children, and especially to daughter Patti and son Tommy for their kindness and support.

Early on, John Zuger declared himself my assistant coach for this project. He proved every bit as indispensable to me as he was to Klausing and the Tigers back in '59. I'm grateful to the dozens of former Braddock High players I interviewed, and especially to John Jacobs, Larry Reaves, Ray Henderson, Vernon Stanfield, and Mark Rutkowski for their recollections and their trust. I'm also grateful to the Braddock Elks, who offered their lodge for an unforgettable reunion that had Klausing whooping it up with his old players in the room where they once ate pregame meals.

Several experts helped me in my quest to resurrect Braddock of the 1950s. Tony Buba knows the town better than anyone, and he generously shared his insights and memories. Excellent research by local historian Joe DeMarco made it possible to re-create Braddock Avenue brick by brick. Marilyn Schiavoni at the *Valley Mirror* granted me access to the archives of the now-defunct Braddock *Free Press*, where I found exceptional material. John Smonski, the sports reporter who covered Braddock High games in the 1950s, passed away just before I started my investigation, but he left behind an outstanding body of work that includes power rankings, game analysis, and in-depth coverage of the old WPIAL teams. A good deal of the game-day action in this book derives from his original reporting.

I relied on several great books to tell this story. Jack Metzgar's *Striking Steel: Solidarity Remembered* helped me understand the events leading up to the 1959 steel strike and gave me insight into the mentality of American steelworkers and their families. *Legends and Lore of Western Pennsylvania* by Thomas White provided an excellent accounting of regional superstitions. The book *Never Lost a Game (Time Just Ran Out)* by Bob Fulton and Chuck Klausing helped me grasp the connective threads running through Klausing's rich store of anecdotes. *Paul Brown: The Man Who Invented Modern Football* by George Cantor is an outstanding testament to Brown's influence and was a valuable resource for me. *Out of This Furnace* by Thomas Bell is one of the brilliant novels, and it deserves a place on your shelf. If any trace of Bell's grace and grit seeped into my style, then this book is better for it.

Joel Rice, a good friend, was the first to tell me about Klausing and his Braddock High Tigers. Not convinced that I grasped the full power of the tale, he came back the next day and dropped a big pile of research in my lap. I'm grateful for his insistence. John Fetterman, the mayor of Braddock, and his extraordinary wife, Gisele, gave me a free place to crash on countless trips to Western Pennsylvania, and I'm indebted to them both for their hospitality and generosity. I got my first chance to tell this story in a feature for *Pittsburgh Quarterly,* and I thank Doug Heuck for that opportunity.

It would take far too long to list the many ways that my agent, Laurie Abkemeier, has helped to shape and shepherd this project. She is an exquisite collaborator and a testament to everything that's great about the art and business of writing books. For taking a chance and giving this book a home, I'm grateful to my editor, Rob Kirkpatrick, and to all the hardworking folks at Thomas Dunne Books.

You need great teachers. I found two of the best in Megan Marshall and Douglas Whynott. My research on Braddock began under their guidance, and they helped nurture this book and my prose in wonderful ways. I'm also grateful to dozens of my fellow students in the creative writing MFA at Emerson College, where talent flows from the taps. Two colleagues in particular, Jodie Noel Vinson and Sebastian Stockman, helped me shore up crucial sections of this book with their meticulous edits and insightful suggestions. Enormous thanks to them both. For the gift of his encouragement and humanity, the writer Teddy Macker is thanked now and forever.

Finally, and most important, thank you to my family. Mom, Dad, Torrey, Garrett, Marc, Nancy, Brian, and Scott, your love and support mean everything. And to Nina, my first reader, I wake up next to you every morning and thank the universe for another day of this sweet dream. Your patience is a miracle, and your laughter and love sustain me.

STRIKING GRIDIRON

PROLOGUE

NOVEMBER 1958. THREE GYPSY FIDDLERS appeared on the sideline at Scott Field. Under the lights, the fiddlers improvised a slow, haunting rhapsody, a departure from the cymbal crashes and peppy oompahs of the high school marching bands. This new sound brought the crowd to an uneasy hush.

It was a cold night in Western Pennsylvania, but the temperature had not deterred the nine thousand football fans who stood shoulder to shoulder in the concrete bleachers. They had come from all over the region to witness the meeting of undefeated high school rivals. One group was from as far away as South Bend, Indiana. Notre Dame would be playing the University of Pittsburgh at Pitt Stadium the following day, and Coach Terry Brennan had brought his Fighting Irish to watch the Braddock High Tigers take on the Purple Raiders of North Braddock Scott High. All over Pittsburgh, helpful residents had assured Brennan it would be the only gridiron contest that week to feature *two teams* worth a damn.

On the field, the fiddlers followed one another through a melancholy arrangement, each taking his turn building on the bittersweet thread that held the piece together. Braddock's gypsy musicians, descendants of the Romani people who had emigrated from Eastern Europe in the late nineteenth century, didn't read music. They were guided by mood alone, and fans from the adjoining towns of Braddock and North Braddock—their nerves frayed after more than three quarters of bruising football—read portents in their sad melody.

Huffing during the time-out, the Braddock High Tigers kept their eyes on their coach.

"Don't go for the quarterback," Chuck Klausing was telling his defensive linemen. "Stay in your lanes and stop the run."

The players were too wrapped up in the game to pay any attention to the ruminative music behind them. Scott High had moved the ball to the Braddock High 10-yard line. With less than two minutes to play in the fourth quarter, the Tigers were holding on to a three-point lead.

"Mark," Klausing said, addressing his defensive corner, "you have double duty. Cover the pass first, but if the quarterback tries to run, you come up to meet him."

Spit flew out of the thirty-three-year-old coach's mouth along with his instructions. Catching the bright stadium lights, the droplets looked like sparks to his players.

Senior Mark Rutkowski nodded. He knew his assignment. The starting defensive corner had seventeen tackles on the night. Earlier in the fourth quarter, with Scott High on the Braddock 5-yard line, he had made the crucial stop to end what would have been the go-ahead drive. Under normal circumstances, Rutkowski might have been a top defensive recruit for any college team in the country. But as good as he was at stopping passes, he was even better at throwing them. Rutkowski was the best high school quarterback in the state. Klausing hated to play him on defense, where he could get hurt, but no one could read the pass like he could.

The time-out ended, and the boys ran back to the line. A swell of crowd noise engulfed the somber fiddle music, and the musicians ducked out of sight.

Braddock was ahead 9–6. It had been a bare-knuckle game so far. In the first quarter, Tigers fullback Wayne Davis had felt a sharp pop in his shoulder after barreling into the defensive line. Hobbled and in pain, the tough-as-nails senior stayed on the field when his team took over on defense. After landing a clean hit on a Scott High running back, he got to his feet and trotted to the sideline. His collarbone was poking clean through the skin. There was no love lost between Braddock High and North Braddock Scott. Whenever the teams shared the field, scrappy boys from the heart of steel country pushed their bodies to the edge.

Rutkowski took his position at left corner. He watched Scott quarterback Tom Fantaski in his peripheral vision. The two had been close growing up, had attended Catholic elementary school together. As boys, they played pickup football. In summer they commandeered skiffs to surf the wakes coming off the paddle boats that delivered coal and coke to mills along the Monongahela River. But Rutkowski was from Braddock and Fantaski was from North Braddock. Like generations of best pals who grew up in the neighboring towns, their close bond wilted before high school. Now they were rivals.

At the snap, Fantaski dropped back. The Scott High quarterback gunned it to his streaking offensive end, but he put too much on it. The ball missed its target and skidded harmlessly across the grass. Both teams jogged back to scrimmage. The crowd took a breath.

Braddock High hadn't lost in forty-four straight games. In each of the previous four seasons, Klausing's boys had captured the Western Pennsylvania Interscholastic Athletic League title. This was the last game of the regular season, and the Tigers would need to beat Scott High to have a chance at a fifth title. For seniors Mark Rutkowski and Wayne Davis, a loss would be a bitter bookend to a spectacular run.

Rutkowski lined up in the left corner position once again. He'd had a storybook three years. He was loved in town, and in the eyes of Braddock residents, he could do no wrong. Working at a summer camp before the start of the season, the senior had shaved his head into a Mohawk. The haircut stopped traffic on Braddock Avenue when he returned home, but Rutkowksi didn't care. He had a pocketful of dough and a reputation forged out of Mon Valley steel. He could get away with a lot worse than an unusual haircut. Now he had college to look forward to. He had a stack of offer letters in his bedroom and no reason in the world to doubt that he would be a star once again. For as long as he'd been playing organized sports, that's all he ever was.

Fantaski dropped back. Rutkowski watched his old friend's eyes. He saw the play unfold even before the quarterback wound up to throw. Hanging behind his man, he stayed out of Fantaski's line of sight. At the last moment, timing the explosion precisely, he leapt forward. The receiver never saw him, and he was surprised when the ball didn't arrive. Rutkowski had snatched it with both hands out of the air. Cradling the deciding interception to his chest, he fell to the ground.

A familiar noise broke through the din of colliding bodies and heavy breath. Nine thousand fans—some of them cursing, some of them screaming their lungs raw in the cold air—let loose a howl that sounded like the gale-force gusts that occasionally barreled through the Mon Valley. It was a sound every Tiger knew intimately.

Braddock High had extended its unbeaten streak to forty-five and would go on to win its fifth WPIAL Class A title two weeks later. Seniors would graduate without ever having lost a high school football game. With the 1959 season on the horizon, people started to whisper about a national record.

Chapter One

IN THE SHADOW OF PAUL BROWN

From a distance, the corrugated overhang outside the hotel lobby looked like the folds of a paper fan, or like the charted performance of a volatile stock. On the lip of the overhang, yellow cursive letters formed the word *Kutsher's*. Coach Chuck Klausing and his wife, Joann, were tired after their nine-hour drive from Western Pennsylvania, but the excitement of arriving at the Catskills resort revived them.

"Gee whiz, it's something!" Joann remarked, taking in the grounds.

"I'll say," Klausing said, stretching his legs and twisting to loosen up his compact, muscular frame.

He had done all the driving, and it left him stiff and tunnel-sighted. The two stood a moment while the sun and the fresh air played on their faces. Before heading inside, Joann wrapped her arms around her husband and hugged him.

When they pushed through the glass doors, the pair found the lobby buzzing with activity. Middle-aged men in charcoal or chocolate slacks talked in loose circles. Other men sat in the hotel's modern, pastel lounge chairs, gesticulating and discoursing in brassy tones. With excesses of charisma or sternness, each man seemed to command the three or four feet in front of him. The passing impression was of a convention of off-duty police officers, or of a lively wake packed with career politicians. These were men of power and deep humor, and they had gathered in the lobby under the mantle of mutual respect.

It was Chuck Klausing's second trip to the famous coaches' clinic at Kutsher's Country Club. Every June, the swanky resort in Monticello, New York, became the center of the sporting universe. A major symposium attracted the best basketball and football coaching talent from around the nation. *Sports Illustrated* covered the event, and college teams on the lookout for new staff often trolled the hallways for prospects. For four days, big winners like Pennsylvania State University football coach Rip Engle and the University of California, Berkeley, basketball coach Pete Newell would preach success to packed auditoriums of trophy-case aspirants. For up-and-comers, head and assistant coaches at all levels, the speakers were prophets. Men who had driven all night from the Farm Belt, the Rust Belt, and the Bible Belt would be scribbling nuggets of wisdom in the margins of their programs. In off hours, the coaches would find comfort in the relaxed bullshitting congenital to their breed. It was sleepaway camp for the whistle-blowing set. Even with his wife on his arm—"vacation" had a different meaning when you were married to a coach—Klausing felt right at home.

After checking in, Klausing and Joann followed a bellhop to the elevator. In the room, their feet sank into carpeting a mile deep.

Joann turned to her husband. "This will do just fine," she said, smiling.

A picture window, which the bellhop revealed for them behind heavy curtains, overlooked the golf course and acres of trees. Farther back sat the purple humps of the Catskills. Immediately below them, a huge swimming pool reflected the sky. Guests, some of them well burned by the June sun, lounged on deck chairs beside the pool. Klausing thought he might swim later that afternoon, and Joann couldn't wait to start her tan. They had five children at home, the youngest less than a year old; Joann couldn't remember the last time she had stopped to enjoy the sun. After tipping the bellboy, they unpacked quickly. There was only a brief window for them to enjoy each other's company. Joann knew that her husband, despite his noblest efforts, would soon be irretrievably drawn into weighty conversations about football and coaching.

At thirty-four, Chuck Klausing had a chance to make history. He had led the Tigers of Braddock, Pennsylvania, an iconic steel town on the banks of the Monongahela River, to five straight undefeated seasons. On the eve of a sixth season, Braddock High was primed to pass the national high school record of fifty-two consecutive games without a loss—a record set seventeen years earlier by Massillon Washington High School in Ohio. Massillon's name was legend, and its former coach, Paul Brown, a football god. Klausing's Tigers had already racked up forty-six straight games without losing. Their only blemish had come in a 1954 regional championship game, which had ended in a tie. Braddock had eight regular season games on its schedule in 1959. Klausing and his boys would need to win the first seven of them to take the crown.

Later that evening, the revitalized couple walked to the dining room at Kutsher's Country Club. Large and softly lit, it had nearly filled up. More than six hundred attendees had registered for the clinic. Klausing scanned the faces to see if he recognized anyone. He doubted anyone would recognize him. He was the only high school coach on the program. If a few of the attendees knew him by reputation, they wouldn't know his face. Not yet, anyway. The coming season could change that.

After consulting a seating chart, the pair walked to their table. As they approached, Klausing immediately recognized one of the men already seated. He ought to have. Red Auerbach, head coach of the Boston Celtics, had won his second NBA title one month earlier. Concealing his excitement, Klausing whisked Joann over and pulled out a chair for her, strategically choosing one two spaces from Auerbach. Then, bidding his tablemates hello, he took a seat next to the Celtics coach.

"Good evening," he said, hardly able to believe his luck.

Joann settled in for a long dinner. She knew she had already lost her husband for the weekend.

Klausing had trouble sleeping at night. The coming football season had now fully encroached on his peace, and a decent night's rest was unthinkable. For an elite group of coaches, a shot at a record-breaking unbeaten streak came around once in a lifetime, and then only when fate intervened. Unlike single-game records—records for the most points scored or the most offensive yards racked up in a game, which coaches boasted about at booster club meetings and banquets—unbeaten streaks made national news. Playing against a weak opponent, any pitiless coach might run up the touchdowns or pile on hundreds of yards of offense. Even single-season records, like the still-unbeaten 8,588 offensive yards that a high school in Arkansas had tallied in 1925, could be chalked up to ephemeral talent—a few star players peaking at the same time. But players eventually graduated, and then teams came back down to earth.

To go undefeated in league games, regional playoff matches, and championship bouts year after year took something more. It took a coach who could squeeze excellence out of any group of athletes, a coach with the nearly inhuman ability to make the correct call on each down for seasons on end. And it took luck. Streaks didn't last. Football had too many moving parts to keep perfection up for long, and no coach had ever managed a second run at a record like Massillon's. At thirty-four, Klausing knew he was staring his lone opportunity in the face. In the coming months, sleep would be scarce.

It was early still when Klausing edged out of bed, and he tried to be quiet so he wouldn't wake Joann. As a mother of five and an adoptive mother to fifty football players, she deserved her rest. Joann ran the mothers' club at Braddock High. She raised funds, orchestrated rallies, and had attended every game Klausing ever coached. She baked enough to feed an army. Her Jewish apple cakes, which flew out of the oven at an astonishing pace during football season, were in especially high demand. Klausing hoped Joann would enjoy herself here. The coach's wife had long ago made peace with the fact that even her free time would be spent in proximity to football.

Klausing rode the elevator to the first floor. A few early birds were getting started on breakfast in the dining room. Klausing noticed a man sitting alone and asked if he could join him. Jim Owens, the head football coach at the University of Washington, was just going over a presentation he would give later that day. Sliding his notes to the side, Owens said he would welcome the distraction. Klausing glanced at his neatly printed index cards, which were scarred with last-minute revisions. He could sympathize. He would be giving his own speech in two days, and he'd been tearing his notes apart and stitching them back together again for weeks.

Owens's presentation would be about the Double Wing-T offense, a variation on the popular Wing T formation that Klausing used at Braddock High. In the straightforward Wing T, a single wingback lined up outside the offensive end and one yard off the line. With a fullback lined up four yards behind the quarterback and a halfback beside him on the weak side, the formation lent itself to inside runs and shifty quarterback options. In the Double Wing T, the halfback became a second wingback on the weak side. Diagramed on a chalkboard, the balanced set looked like a bow firing the shaft of an arrow. Reverses out of the Double Wing T could effectively nullify larger defenses, and with a skilled quarterback, speedy running backs could more easily release on passing routes. Klausing had been toying with the Double Wing T himself. His offensive line would be undersized in 1959, but he'd have some of the fastest running backs in the state. The Double Wing T could be a good way to use them to their fullest.

Klausing loved the way football kept evolving. He loved its legacy—the great dynasties, like Massillon Washington High, that stretched the bounds of excellence—and loved how it marched forward, each generation adding new elements. Football was closer to chess than people knew. Within the confines of a narrow set of rules, the masters developed new strategies. Klausing's father, a lay preacher and the mayor of the small town of Wilmerding, Pennsylvania, had been a passionate football fan all his life. As a young man, the elder Klausing had often taken the train to Ohio to see professional clubs like the Canton Bulldogs play in the Ohio League, a loose confederation of teams that later became the American Professional Football Association. Back then, attrition was the game's reigning philosophy. Leatherheads made fierce runs into a wall of waiting tacklers. Football had changed in the years since—the forward pass alone had revolutionized the sport. Klausing's new friend was helping the game evolve even further, tweaking and experimenting with an offense that many coaches had never played against. A new generation was leaving its stamp.

The two coaches finished breakfast together. Then, bidding Owens good luck, Klausing returned to his room. He took out his cream-colored notebook and a blue pen, which he used for revisions. It had been difficult for him to put five undefeated seasons into words, to condense his best strategic thinking down to a pat thirty-minute talk. Much of what he'd written sounded hackneyed to him now, like the empty jargon in bad movies about sports:

"You never win football games, you only lose them."

"Most all of it falls under hard work. Never found any substitute for work—no magic formula for winning."

"Do not accept anything short of perfection."

These clichés would be no more inspiring to a crowd of coaches than a campaign slogan would be to a politician. Klausing had been culling as many false-sounding phrases as he could find. The trick was to not cut the good stuff while he was at it, the biting truths masquerading as platitudes.

"Never cut a boy who wants to play."

He'd dress any boy who could survive his hellish summer workouts. He would take guts over talent any day—"intestinal fortitude," he called it. It was the single most important trait a ballplayer could have.

"Don't ever fear your assistant knowing too much," he'd scratched in his harsh, saw-toothed script. "Be happy and learn and direct his knowledge."

He had had excellent personnel in the previous five seasons. One of his early assistants, a man named George Hays, had even played in the NFL. Klausing was always learning from those around him, and he had no qualms about seeking answers from his subordinates. His ability to lead had grown out of that thirst for self-improvement.

"Tradition of boys," he wrote elsewhere in the notebook. "We are constantly talking about the '57 team, the '56 team, etc."

Klausing was building a dynasty at Braddock High, and he expected every boy who wore Tigers red and white to buy into it. The momentum of dozens of wins carried his players onto the field every Friday night, made the crucial difference in otherwise evenly balanced contests.

No single piece of advice Klausing was considering for his talk was groundbreaking, perhaps, but taken together they showed a rough path toward becoming an effective coach, one who cared deeply about his players and his personnel. Klausing had won games by working harder than his opponents and by knowing how to draw talent out of those around him. Those pillars made him kindred to Paul Brown, the legendary coach whose record he was now chasing.

Two years earlier, before anyone in Western Pennsylvania dared to mention Braddock's chance at the record, Klausing had interviewed for the head coaching job at Massillon Washington High

School. It would have been a tremendous honor to take the reins at a place made famous by his idol. He would never say so out loud, but Klausing envisioned himself following Brown's trajectory, parlaying a storied high school career into a top college job, perhaps moving into the NFL after that.

In the weeks before his Massillon interview, Klausing stayed up half the night editing game film and drafting talking points. Joann made him pot after pot of coffee—it was the first time she had ever seen him touch the stuff. They talked guardedly of moving to Ohio. In the end, it didn't work out. An ally on the hiring board called Klausing the following day with bad news. He had done a fine job hammering the fundamentals, the man explained, principles like blocking and conditioning, which Paul Brown had won champion-ships with at Massillon Washington High two decades earlier. But the other finalist had blown the interviewers away with a highlight reel—in color and set to music—from games in which he'd coached. The other candidate had even enlisted cheerleaders to lead his players in calisthenics for the camera. Klausing's film, clips from a 14–0 Brad-dock victory that showcased his players' discipline and gamesmanship, fell flat by comparison. Off the field, glitz won out over substance. It was a lesson Klausing tried to keep in mind as he sculpted his Kutsher's talk.

Klausing's players didn't know a thing about glitz. They told sto-ries of their coach's drive, his immense expectations on the field, and his belief in the healing power of conditioning. None of his players, from the All-State superstars to the underclassmen warming the bench, had to think twice when asked how they managed to win so consis-tently. Training—hour after hour of excruciating work.

Big Bertha, a massive driving sled, haunted the Tigers dreams. It was rare for high school teams to use sleds, and even rarer to see any-thing larger than a two-man version. Big Bertha was ten yards wide and had spots for seven players. It was designed from memory by George Hays, the assistant who had played in the NFL. In the summer before Braddock's 1956 season, Hays mentioned to Klausing how much the drills on Big Bertha had helped his professional team-mates improve their blocking. Up until then, the Braddock coaches had been wearing football pants to practice, sacrificing their own bodies to teach the boys proper blocking technique. Klausing enlisted a manager at U.S. Steel to weld the sled together. His name was Harry Stuhldreher and he was particularly well suited to the task. A former Notre Dame quarterback and member of the legendary Four Horsemen backfield of 1924, Stuhldreher knew exactly the kind of sled Klausing had in mind. A latticework of scrap steel and thin padding, the finished product weighed a ton. Steelworkers borrowed a crane from the mill to hoist it off the truck and onto Braddock's practice field. When Klausing instructed the first group of players to hit it, they bounced off.

"Lower," he said, "and drive your feet."

On the next attempt, the sled budged a foot.

"Too high. Get lower and keep your feet moving. All together."

On the next try, they drove the sled a yard. By the end of the season, they were pushing Big Bertha up and down the field. Successive generations of Tigers had endured the same exhausting initiation.

Six games stood between the Braddock Tigers and Massillon Washington High School's record, and seven would put them over the top. Maybe, Klausing allowed, he was following Paul Brown's career trajectory after all. He had traveled to Cleveland two years earlier to hear Brown speak, and the experience strengthened his admiration for the man. Brown beamed confidence. The older coach had a reputation for discipline. Back in Massillon, he would make his high school students *stand* on the sideline during games, an uncommon practice for the time. What did they need to sit for, he'd ask, playing as poorly as they were? He conditioned his players mercilessly, emphasizing speed and endurance. He was known for blowing up without a moment's notice, and he had fired assistants for being a few minutes late. But he was also respected—above all, by his players.

Klausing had copied some of Brown's methods to the letter, especially his emphasis on the ABCs: agility, blocking, and contact. Braddock High players frequently ran a hellish drill straight from Brown's playbook—fifteen uninterrupted minutes of high knees, sled work, and tackling. But Klausing had a soft spot that Brown rarely showed, a way of joking with his players in quiet moments. Away from the field, you had to let boys be boys, he believed. He presented a hard face in practice, but he always tried to be a guardian and a well-rounded man the rest of the time. Perhaps that was the single most important idea he could offer an auditorium full of coaches who were eager for a leg up. He turned to the front of his notebook and scribbled two sentences in blue ink on the top of the first page:

"We don't coach football. We coach boys."

With Joann off at the pool, Klausing dressed in his workout clothes and tennis shoes and headed downstairs. He crossed the resort's freshly mowed lawn and walked toward the tennis courts. He was thrilled that he had been selected to give a talk at the clinic. He knew he had done something worthy of attention at Braddock High, but he also understood that his claim on gridiron glory was tenuous. Winning seven straight games would be a challenge, no matter how many times he'd done it before. Some of his previous games had been won on a prayer. The victory over North Braddock Scott in 1958 had come after an interception by Mark Rutkowksi and a thirty-seven-yard field goal by a 225-pound tackle-turned-placekicker. The ball had actually *hit the crossbar* before bouncing over on Roland Mudd's field goal. Klausing had spent hours contemplating the improbability of that play. If the ball had rolled the other way, a simple question of balance, their streak and their shot at history would have ended. He wouldn't be heading to the tennis courts at a resort in the Catskills, and people wouldn't be mentioning his name in the same sentence as Paul Brown's. A Catholic by conversion, Klausing believed in a higher plan. Though a world-class coach, he could in no other way account for the dozens of turns in his favor during the previous five years.

The coming season would be a battle. North Braddock Scott, a perennial competitor, would retain its best players. With new talent coming up, they'd be stronger than ever. Newspapers had been speculating that either Hopewell or Midland, two Class A teams on Braddock's schedule, would spoil the Tigers run. No matter whom they faced, Klausing's players would have targets on their backs.

At the same time, a host of new challenges loomed for Braddock—none bigger than the loss of starting quarterback Mark Rutkowski. In 1958, Rutkowski was named to *Scholastic* magazine's All-American team and won the Most Valuable Player award in the Western Pennsylvania Interscholastic Athletic League. He'd also been selected as starting quarterback for the vaunted Pennsylvania team in an annual interstate matchup with Ohio's best high school players. That game would take place in a few weeks, the final hurrah in Rutkowski's charmed high school career. Few teams could survive the loss of such a notable player.

Rutkowski's 1958 backup would take over as starting quarterback in '59. John Jacobs was talented, and maybe even more versatile than Rutkowski. Both players had incredible arms, but Jacobs could run the ball as well. He was lightning quick and scrappy as a hungry dog. But Jacobs had strained his back, a major concern heading into the season. From time to time, his lower back tightened and his lumbar region screamed with pain. He could hardly lift his arm when that happened, to say nothing of dodging tacklers. Doctors said vague things about an aggravated muscle. With a record on the line—and, for Jacobs, a shot at a college scholarship—the strength of that back was key.

In Western Pennsylvania, opposing fans liked to talk about Klausing's blind luck, especially when it came to attracting talented players. Anyone could win with the likes of Mark Rutkowski, they said, neglecting to see how Klausing and his dedicated assistants had formed Rutkowski as an elite player. Klausing and John Zuger, an assistant coach on the Tigers, had spent hours watching the quarterback lob balls downfield. Zuger had worked with Rutkowski in an alley each summer, positioning him against a wall to teach him not to twist his arm out at the end of his release. When things were bad at home for the boy, as they often were with an alcoholic father, the coaches taught him to channel his frustrations into perfecting the few things in life he could control—his step drops, his blitz reads, and his checkdowns. Klausing had a gift for spotting untapped potential. He often recruited from the track squad or the JV basketball team at Braddock High, cultivating seeds of ability in sophomore athletes that, with careful attention, would blossom into mature talent by senior year. He understood that nothing would silence his critics. One more perfect season, though—a new national record—would quiet them down some.

Klausing arrived at the tennis courts to find his dinner companion from the evening before already warming up. Playing tennis with Red Auerbach. Boy. Getting licked by him, more like. It became clear as soon as they started that the Celtics coach was a much better player. At forty-one, Auerbach retained all the agility of the basketball star he'd once been. He was a natural athlete, smooth and quick, and he was able to summon incredible power with no apparent effort.

On the other side of the court, Klausing sprinted from line to line. A former college football player, he was no slouch.

"Best one-hundred-fifty-pound center I ever had," his Penn State coach Bob Higgins had once kidded him.

Best and only. Most players weighed in at over two hundred pounds, and centers were typically among the heaviest on the field.

"I may be small, Coach, but I'm fast," Klausing had shot back.

It had helped that the war was going on. While Klausing was preparing to become an officer in the marines, putting in two years of college before Officer Candidate School, many would-be players had already shipped out. The pool of available athletes had thinned, and small fries back home got a once-in-a-lifetime opportunity. Klausing loved football and had grabbed that opportunity with both hands. He impressed a lot of people on the way. He may not have had a size advantage, but he had a kind of blind determination that made up for it.

Drawing on that determination now, he hurled himself at Auerbach's returns, somehow managing to keep a portion of them in play. But it wasn't enough. A laser shot down the line zipped past his outstretched racket. He was losing badly.

At the merciful end of two sets, the high school coach bade his opponent good game.

"If basketball doesn't work out for you," Klausing quipped at the net, "there's always the pro circuit."

Auerbach slapped him on the back and they retired to the bench to towel off. After they'd had a chance to rest, they headed to the club's restaurant for an early lunch. Still in their tennis clothes, the sweaty duo chose a clean square table in the light of a large window. Kutsher's was posh, the fanciest place Klausing had ever stayed. Success on the field was its own reward, but a high school coach could get used to amenities like these.

Auerbach, cheerful in victory, wanted a preview of Klausing's speech. What made him so damned successful? When Klausing first arrived at Braddock High, the football team had been mediocre.

"Chuck," the team's outgoing coach, Henry Furrie, had warned him in 1954, "you don't want this job. The kids are undisciplined. The administration isn't in it. It's an unwinnable situation."

In the nine previous seasons, the Tigers had gone 21–54–4, including one disastrous year when the team managed only twenty-five combined points. By contrast, the teams they faced routinely scored thirty points against them each game. Braddock shared a field with North Braddock Scott, its biggest rival. Scott Field had seats for close to ten thousand fans, but the Tigers were lucky to attract a measly thousand on Friday nights. To say that Klausing faced an uphill battle was putting it mildly.

Remarkably, in the five seasons since he took over, Klausing's Tigers hadn't lost a single game. Braddock had become a winning town by association. Friday-night home games always sold out, and with fans sneaking in, the spectators piled two or three deep in each aisle. Just as Paul Brown had done at Massillon High, Klausing took a hopeless group of individuals and turned it into an unstoppable force.

"It's no big secret," Klausing told Auerbach with characteristic understatement. "We work hard and we try to get the most out of our boys. There are maybe only a couple of things I'm doing differently."

In the first place, Klausing couldn't understand why more football coaches didn't drill their players on punt blocking. Most treated it like some uncontrollable part of the game, a matter of luck more than training. Klausing held three or four boys back every practice, lined them up, and didn't let them leave until he was satisfied they were exploding off the line fast enough, raising their hands high enough, and timing their leaps perfectly. His defensive line was one of the quickest and most specialized in the country. They averaged close to one blocked punt per game. Most teams were lucky to get a few in a season.

And then, Klausing admitted with a smile, there were his trick plays. With the immense talent on the Tigers in recent years, he hadn't needed to use trickery so often. Early on, though, his play calling had been downright devious. After a stint in the marines, and once he'd finished his last two years of college, Klausing accepted his first coaching job at a small high school in Pitcairn, Pennsylvania. Newly married and financially strapped, he also took a part-time job as a high school football referee calling games outside Pitcairn's division. To get his thirty dollars per game, he had to pass officiating tests throughout the season. In the course of studying rule books and running simulations, he had developed a robust repertoire of tricks.

At Pitcairn, he'd once won a game by dressing a kid in blue jeans and a faded practice jersey, hiding him on the far sideline, and having him jump onto the field, unguarded, at a crucial moment. When the opposing coach complained, the head referee took out his rule book to review the league's uniform policy. Jersey with numbers on back—*check*. Helmet—the player had slipped one on before taking the field. Cleats—sure enough. Looking doubtfully at the scrawny receiver, the referee asked if he was wearing the requisite kneepads. The underclassman, who was still gasping after his fifty-yard touchdown run, dutifully rolled up his blue jeans. Spotting the kneepads, the opposing coach threw his hands up in frustration. Everyone in high school used tricks. It's just that Klausing used them better. Coaches who played against him still kept a rule book close by.

Auerbach laughed. As a fellow coach who knew a thing or two about success, he understood Klausing was being modest. Blocked punts and trick plays didn't account for forty-six games without a loss. Discipline and tireless preparation won games, not gimmicks or easy angles. But you had to hand it to Klausing. At a sports clinic full of coaches eager to land a hot tip, the "hard work" shtick was a nonstarter. Better, in his talk, if the young coach avoided recapping the hours he spent each night studying film, the scouting trips, and the two weeks every summer of grueling three-a-day practices when he melted his boys like Monongahela Valley steel and forged them into football players. Klausing had learned his lesson from the Massillon interview: Off the field, glitz carried the day.

Attentive waiters shuffled by, swooping in to refill water, bus silverware, take their orders. When you were with Red Auerbach, Klausing noted, the service was exquisite. Auerbach was a staple at Kutsher's Country Club. The Celtics coach had moonlighted for years, heading the club's summer basketball team. In the early 1950s, as the NBA was just coming into its own, some of the best nonprofessional play in the country took place in the Borscht Belt, a string of Jewish-owned hotels that stretched from Sullivan to Ulster counties in Downstate New York. Amid the loud boasts and louder bets of management, the hotels fielded teams of summer bellhops—well-paid young men who happened to be the best college basketball talent in the country. Spectators, comprising both paying guests and professional bookies, piled courtside at each game on the summer circuit. Thousands of dollars changed hands as vacationing couples and greasy gamblers cheered on their home clubs. For patrons, it was especially exciting to root for the bellhop who'd carried their bags. In 1953, one of the bellhops on Auerbach's team had been a high schooler named Wilt Chamberlain. He was good enough at sixteen to be playing—and beating—college All-Americans. Auerbach had ridden the headstrong young player hard, demanding more than raw talent out of him. It was a frustrating experience. Still, the coach had never laid eyes on a more promising player. The first time he saw Chamberlain walk, all grace and glide, the man who was fast becoming the most successful coach in the NBA had stopped admiringly in his tracks to watch.

Auerbach no longer coached the Kutsher's team, but the service didn't suffer when he walked through the door. The country club was renowned for its kosher meals—beef brisket, matzo ball soup, and pastrami sandwiches—and the helpings were enormous. After his workout, Klausing was ravenous. What hair Auerbach had left hardly looked upset. Klausing apologized again for not giving him a better match. Auerbach brushed the apology aside, leaning back in his seat with a satisfied grin.

As they ate, the conversation veered easily between their respective sports. Like football, basketball was evolving, in large part thanks to a new generation of players. Auerbach had drafted the league's first black player, Chuck Cooper, nine years earlier. Jackie Robinson had already broken the color barrier in baseball when he joined the Brooklyn Dodgers in 1947, but circumstance had long kept minority players from advancing on the hard court.

The thing was, Auerbach explained, it had been awfully hard for black kids to learn how to play basketball. YMCAs, which had the best youth leagues in just about every city in the country, didn't end their national segregation policy until 1946. Even then, local chapters were slow to open their gyms. But in 1931, the Voit Rubber Company introduced the world's first rubber basketball. It was an accidental civil rights triumph. Where white players paying twenty dollars for a leather ball didn't dare play outdoors, black players with one-dollar balls started putting hoops up in their yards and driveways. Outdoor courts began showing up in alleyways and public parks, and black athletes began playing more basketball, merging traditional indoor styles with athletic street play. Now black players were redefining the game in the pros. Star Celtics center Bill Russell, who was perhaps the biggest talent the NBA had ever seen, had just led Auerbach's team to its recent championship.

Braddock High was an integrated school, but racism still burned hot in the steel towns of Western Pennsylvania. The mills created a caste system, with black workers stuck at the bottom. When he first arrived at Braddock High, Klausing had been forced to break up dozens of lopsided fights—gangs of white students picking on smaller groups of black students, or vice versa. Instead of punishing the offenders, he took them into the gym, passed out boxing gloves, and let two boys at a time have at it. Klausing boxed in high school, and he had seen the way a fair fight could change your opinion of an adversary. Exhausted, dripping sweat, the same boys who had been at each other's throats on the blacktop often finished those improvised bouts hugging. Sports could alter the way you looked at the world, Klausing believed. His father had often told him stories of Jim Thorpe, whom the elder Klausing had seen play football in the 1920s. Half white and half American Indian, Thorpe was the best athlete of his era. Loved by fans, he helped chip away at the bigotry of the age with success on the field.

The Tigers were starting to do the same thing in Braddock, where black players had flourished. Even so, Klausing lamented that his best white players got scholarships to big schools while scouts rarely took an interest in his black players. If the situation was changing, like everyone said, it seemed to be changing slowly. A look around the dining room suggested as much. A representative sample of the best coaching talent in two sports had started to trickle in for lunch. It was a monochrome group.

Klausing and Auerbach chatted into the early afternoon. For the Tigers coach, it was reassuring to talk with someone who understood the pressures of the limelight. Auerbach advised him to stick with what he knew—hard work and discipline, mixed with compassion off the field—and especially to not get distracted by the fanfare. That went double for his players. It would be easy for the 1959 Tigers to lose focus under the intoxicating influence of the inevitable press coverage.

After lunch, Klausing returned to his room. Breathless, he told Joann everything—the humiliating tennis match, the jovial lunch, Auerbach's eminent, rough-around-the-edges kindness. Joann was delighted. She reminded her husband that he deserved to be there, in the ranks of the great coaches. Klausing had accomplished something monumental in his five seasons at Braddock, and now was on the brink of making history.

But he couldn't rest on achievement. After checking the clinic program to see which of the day's speakers he wanted to hear—taking special care to look up Jim Owens—Klausing returned to his notes. Joann laughed. Her husband had been tinkering with the talk for weeks, had kept her up at night rehearsing. But there was no such thing as too much preparation, Klausing believed. Any one of his returning players could attest to that. In backyards across Braddock, the incoming Tigers had already started to fret about the season ahead. The torch of five undefeated teams   and the record, which had become a rallying cry in town as residents traded gossip about a looming steel strike— now fell to them.

Chapter Two

A RITE OF PASSAGE

SONNY BURRELLI, A WAVY-HAIRED Italian man in his mid-thirties, leaned heavier against the side of his bus, slouching into the shadow of the elephant-ear mirror. Morning light had crested the rim of the hill above. A lifetime in the Monongahela Valley had taught Burrelli that a blue sky meant trouble. Haze normally hovered over the region. Steel mills had been silent nearly a month. Soot had stopped falling in the night, dusting cars and porches, and the air had lost the old-egg smell of heavy industry.

Steelworkers across the country had walked off the job on July 15. Now mid-August, Mother Nature had made a comeback. Birds sunned themselves on telephone wires. Deep jungle hues dominated a slope on the far side of the Monongahela River. Only a few cigarette burns, hints of the coming fall, dotted the green canvas.

Braddock High School, a castle-shaped building of red brick, sat two-thirds of the way up the valley's steep bank on a small lookout at the intersection of Lillie Avenue and Moody Street. A line of the Pennsylvania Railroad ran above the high school. The tracks formed the political and psychological border separating the boroughs of Braddock and North Braddock. North Braddock was wealthier than

Braddock, whiter. Literally and figuratively, residents of the hilltop town looked down on their neighbors—they dropped below the tracks to shop and attend church, but always kept a halo of distinction around them. Their children attended North Braddock Scott High School, just one block up and two over from Braddock High.

From his perch on the street in front of Braddock High, Burrelli could see the flowing water of the Monongahela River. Braddock's main streets ran parallel to a straight section of the river, and its side streets jutted perpendicularly over the northern floodplain and up the valley's steep bank. There were no barges running. With the region's mills offline, there was no coal or coke to deliver. The water, normally a conveyer belt of rippled steel, shimmered in the light.

Braddock began to stir in the early morning. A few churchgoers ambled along the streets on their way to the day's first Mass. Most were older, without children, and white—black services wouldn't start until midmorning. Men wore felt hats and stiff dark suits, and women wore polka-dot dresses and heels. As they shuffled downhill to avoid turning an ankle, they resembled children's windup toys marching across tabletop battlefields.

Where the slope began to level out, Braddock Avenue cut the length of town, a ruler shot from one end to the other. No streetcars rattled in the early morning, and only a few automobiles grumbled along the rows of shuttered storefronts. On weekday afternoons, by contrast, the town would be choked with traffic. Shoppers normally overflowed the sidewalks. The avenue, at a length of just over a mile, could take an hour to walk from one end to the other. Growing up, children believed their town was much bigger than it really was. Alive with noise, jammed with shoppers from nearby boroughs, it seemed immense.

An enormous bridge marked the eastern terminus of Braddock Avenue, a five-hundred-foot span jutting over the Monongahela. It brought hundreds of cars daily, families from nearby Homestead,

Whitaker, and Duquesne, for afternoons full of errands and leisure. At the opposite end of town stood the pride of the Monongahela Valley: the Edgar Thomson Steel Works. Known to all in the valley as ET, the massive mill had been spewing raw steel since 1875. It had been industrialist and steel magnate Andrew Carnegie's first major plant, the linchpin to his empire and the catalyst to an industrial boom that made America the mightiest country on earth. The symbolism—Braddock as the nation's industrial town—did not go unnoticed by prideful residents or municipal boosters. Fidel Castro had taken Cuba in January, and fear over communist aggression reached levels not seen since Senator Joseph McCarthy's rise to prominence nine years earlier. For an entire region, Edgar Thomson epitomized endurance and American might.

Named after the president of the Pennsylvania Railroad, the mill had grown considerably since turning out its first molten heat more than eight decades earlier. A network of smokestacks and painted buildings as big as battleships spanned ten acres. Private railroad tracks crisscrossed the grounds like scabby sutures in the earth. Scrap iron sat in heaps beside enormous metal ladles, which flew through the air carrying charges of liquid steel during the mill's normal operations. Dozens of sheds and storage houses squatted between the larger buildings. From the hillside above the mill, the installations looked like a second town, a rough mirror of the first.

With the strike on, this other Braddock looked abandoned. Without the drone of normal operations, townspeople long conditioned to regulate life by the mill's vibrations and industrial pulses felt anxious. Half a million steelworkers had walked off the job, the largest industrial strike in the nation's history. Strikers drew no paychecks. Braddock, which relied on the mill for its survival, held its breath.

After a few minutes, Burrelli spotted a young man in a baseball cap and letterman jacket rounding the corner. The man carried a duffel bag in one hand. Head down in concentration, he looked like a student. When he came nearer, Burrelli recognized the initials on the man's hat: ND. It was a Notre Dame insignia, but everyone in town knew the letters stood for "No Defeat."

"Hi, Coach," Burrelli said, nodding as Klausing walked up.

"Sonny," Klausing said. "Good to see you."

The men were about the same age, though the Tigers coach looked younger. Newspaper men covering high school football in the region often used the word "boyish." At thirty-four, Klausing had a faintly doughy face, what might be called baby fat on an adolescent. He could look strict, leveling his eyes under his hat brim and arching his small frame forward. Just as often, he'd drop his lower lip like a good ol' boy to reveal rows of gleaming white teeth.

"Ready for another run?"

Klausing chuckled, shook his head. "Too soon to tell. Ask me on the drive back."

One of the Burrelli brothers had been driving Klausing's players for the past five seasons. Ralph, Richard, Robert, and Sonny were heirs to the throne of the Burrelli Transit Service, a private bus company serving the Mon Valley. Their father, Leonardo, had started the business in 1927 with two jitney cabs—unlicensed taxis that carried passengers along a preset route. The bus racket was cutthroat, with small outfits like Deere Brothers and Miller Bus Lines competing for the best routes. Sometimes rival companies aped one another's schedules to poach passengers. To the horror of motorists, it was often the fastest and most aggressive drivers who won out. The Burrelli brothers had served Braddock High well over the years. Klausing chose to overlook the fact that they had grown up in North Braddock, had gone to rival Scott High, and so had good reason to get lost ferrying the Tigers to the most important games.

Burrelli and Klausing waited by the bus for the others to show. Summer's heat hadn't broken, but the air felt cool in the early morning. Klausing lifted his face to the sun. The friendly sky was a strange token of the labor unrest that had engulfed the region. Embittered workers had been shouting slogans for a month, but the fecund valley just smiled back at them.

The nice weather was incongruous to Klausing's own roiling thoughts. The abstract anxiousness of the short summer had departed, replaced by something more visceral, urgent. He'd lost fifteen graduating seniors the previous spring, including his All-American quarterback, Mark Rutkowski. This year's players had trooped into the gym for physicals a week earlier. Some of the seniors had filled out nicely, but on average, his team looked small.

In addition to Rutkowski, Jim Hux, the Tigers star offensive end and the best receiver Klausing had ever coached, was now gone. Hux and Rutkowski had had the kind of special synchronicity that good coaches built offenses around. They had played together on Braddock's youth team, formed a close bond in junior high, and dominated throughout high school. Now they were gone. Hux's replacement, Ray Henderson, could block a bulldozer on either end of the line, but he had about the worst hands Klausing had ever seen. Football was primarily a running game, and Henderson would be a key addition blocking at right end. But the pass had served the Tigers well, and Klausing didn't want to abandon it completely. Opposite Henderson on the left side of the offensive line was Alvin "Elbow" Smith. One of these boys would have to step up if the Tigers were going to have any chance against strong defensive opponents.

Local media coverage had added to Klausing's preseason strain. An article in that week's Braddock *Free Press* titled CAN THE TIGERS GROW NEW CLAWS FOR KLAUS? scrutinized the team's chances and openly questioned whether the state-record forty-six-game streak could continue much longer. Klausing normally didn't worry about the press, but with the national record in his sights, he could do without aspersions from his team's hometown paper. Another *Free Press* article, this one aimed at Braddock's gambling contingent, stated that "the odds favor a Tiger loss sometime this year," and reminded readers that "quite a few rough games are on tap, any of which could be the 'Waterloo' for the locals." That made Klausing Napoléon, he surmised.

At a coaching clinic in Atlantic City the previous year, Klausing had heard Frank Broyles, the new head coach at the University of Arkansas, extol the tactical prowess of Field Marshal Erwin Rommel, Germany's "Desert Fox." Broyles said he'd gleaned plenty about football from reading the Nazi strategist's letters. The remark had intimidated the hell out of the auditorium full of coaches—all of whom wondered for the first time in their careers whether they were reading enough military correspondence. Football and war—the comparison was as old as the game.

Klausing had spent the summer preparing for this latest campaign. Coaches across the region were putting Tigers red and white on their tackling dummies, instructing their players to visualize the takedown, to dream of knocking off the champs. Gamblers had good reason to back the challengers. This year's field looked especially promising. The Tigers had scraped by Midland High 9–7 in 1958, Braddock's closest outcome in three years. Canonsburg High, traditionally a breather for Klausing's boys, had merged with a nearby school and would be flush with new talent. And the specter of North Braddock Scott, embittered after its 9–6 loss the previous season, hung over everything. A few days after what newspapers dubbed "the Game of the Century," Klausing was shocked to see players on Scott's practice field. The team's season had ended with the loss to Braddock, and its players wouldn't play another down of football for nine months. Klausing stopped the car to chat with Joe McCune, North Braddock's head coach.

"What's up, Joe?" Klausing asked. "Why do you have the kids out?"

"Chuck, it's like this: If we're going to beat you next year, we've got to start right now."

McCune was a tough son of a gun, an old-school gridiron man who'd played semi-pro football with the McKeesport Ironmen. Many considered his North Braddock Scott boys the second-best Class A team in the state. The coincidence of proximity—three blocks and a set of train tracks separated North Braddock Scott from Braddock High, home of the best Class A team in the state—spawned enough barroom theorizing to fill a library. The likeliest explanation was also the simplest: The towns hated each other, and in preparation for a yearly battle, their football teams had become superb.

Assistant Bob Teitt showed up in front of Burrelli's bus before long, followed by Harry Carr, the Tigers' advanced scout. At five-foot-four, 120 pounds, Carr had the distinction of being smaller than every Braddock player—a precarious position for a soft-spoken young coach who found it difficult to inspire discipline. Carr had studied to become a priest before returning home to take care of his mother. He was a Latin teacher now at Braddock Junior High. Though he possessed a religious man's demeanor, gentle and forgiving, he had a deep love of football.

In near-perfect contrast to Carr, John Zuger, the line coach, inspired the fear of God in Tigers players. Zuger arrived next, cutting an impressive figure as he glided toward his colleagues. Tall and angular—with a thick neck; large, powerful arms; and a crew cut—he was the perfect picture of a jock. He was twenty-nine years old, and he had played varsity football at Indiana University—first as quarterback and then, after injuring his hand on an opposing player's helmet, as an offensive lineman. He had grown up in nearby Homestead, where he returned after college to look for a job. When he went to interview with the superintendent of schools in Braddock, the administrator did a double take.

"You're an art teacher?" the superintendent asked.

"Yes, sir." Zuger grinned.

The brute football player was also a gifted painter. He got a job teaching at Braddock Junior High, and the art department got a new code of discipline. Once, after a student neglected to do an assignment for Zuger's class, the player-turned-teacher walked over, asked the boy to stand, and then shoved him to the ground with both hands. He was equally pitiless on the football field. Some of the players resented him for it, but many of the team's hardest cases responded to that style of quick justice. Zuger operated on a wavelength that sons of steelmen, rough-and-tumble Western Pennsylvania boys, understood. Phil Lucarelli, the boy who'd received the brutal lesson in art class, would be joining the Tigers as a sophomore in '59. He had nothing but respect for the hard-nosed coach, whom he hadn't dared cross again.

Bobby Williams, the trainer, showed up along with the student managers. Williams, who was in his early thirties, had been the janitor at Braddock High School before taking on his new role. When the previous Tigers trainer quit before the 1956 season, Klausing went to the school board for help. Ankles wouldn't tape themselves, and first aid supplies had to be set up and replenished. With five kids at home and a team to coach, Klausing already felt stretched thin. A board member recommended the school janitor as a temporary solution. Klausing wasn't sure—Williams was a legendary boozer—but he went along with the plan. To his delight, Williams threw himself into the job. Players who complained about Klausing's tourniquet-tight ankle wraps appreciated the new trainer's lighter touch. What started as a temporary solution became a permanent fix. Klausing, who had been trained in Red Cross first aid, took over whenever a serious injury occurred. Bones that couldn't be set on the field got sent straight to Braddock Hospital, where the team's on-call physician, Dr. Shapiro, got the boys back into playing shape in no time. Williams manned the small trainer's room at Braddock High. He dispensed folksy wisdom about cramps and sprains and taped dozens of ankles each week.

With the coaching staff assembled, the student managers arranged the coaches' luggage into the cargo compartments under the bus. Then they set to work organizing the cache of equipment the team would be bringing up to summer training camp. Fifty sets of shoulder pads took skill and spatial reasoning to fit together under a bus. On top of everything else, Klausing had brought along several boxes of sweat clothes, which he'd purchased in the off-season. In his six years with the Tigers, Klausing had sourced hundreds of jock straps, army surplus beanies, and T-shirts for his players to wear. For many of the boys with older brothers, these were the first new clothes they had ever owned.

Shuffling in and out of the locker room, the managers tackled their task with the same kind of proficiency that had made the Tigers so successful on the field. A heavy truck, owned by the Borough of Braddock and earmarked for government business, caught the overflow of equipment that wouldn't fit under the bus. If Klausing had asked for an airplane, he might have gotten that, too. For the winningest coach in town history, they might have built the runway on Braddock Avenue.

Players began arriving before the 8:45 deadline. Some of the veterans joked with the assistants. They asked Zuger what he thought of the new crop of sophomores and fended off accusations that they'd grown soft over the summer.

"I'm a brick," bragged junior running back John "Doughboy" Gay. "You never seen anybody in better shape, Coach Teitt."

If lax with the assistants, an air of quiet respect predominated around Klausing. He didn't encourage this, but the unspoken rules of varsity football dictated reverence.

Those players who lived closest to school had walked over, saying their good-byes to their families before setting out. Others got out of cars at the curb in front of the high school. A few mothers tagged along and made embarrassing displays, kissing their boys in public, sniffling loudly. Camp lasted two weeks and was the longest stretch most of the Tigers had ever spent away from home. If the good-byes were tough on the mothers, the prolonged absence always sneaked up on the players. Coaches distributed stationery and postage at camp. What would start as terse updates about food and weather usually turned, by the fourth or fifth day, into weepy meditations on home and family. Though the boys would never confess it to one another, homesickness abounded. Pillow-muffled sobs were a common sound at night, and even the most committed players thought about quitting at least once during the long two weeks.

Now, in front of the school, teenagers shrugged off their mothers' affections. They slung their duffels over their shoulders and crossed the tarmac like ace pilots. They joined their friends by the bus, back-slapping and roughhousing, and hardly turned to wave good-bye to their gloomy parents.

At nine o'clock, Klausing gave the order. The assistant coaches corralled the boys like cattle.

"C'mon now," Zuger yelled, "get up in there!"

Seniors got the first pick of seats, and juniors followed. Wide-eyed sophomores filled in the vacant spaces. No amount of mean-mugging could hide the anxiety on the faces of the team's newest members. Upperclassmen had been taunting them for months, hurling innuendo about the hell that lay ahead.

"I heard they don't let you sleep," said sophomore Jim Clark to a teammate as they climbed into the bus.

For consolation, younger players reminded themselves that the team would be practicing at a new location. The spartan conditions at the Tigers' usual facility, Camp Corbly, were legendary. Corbly was a primitive church retreat near Punxsutawney, an installation of rough wooden cabins in a clearing on a hillside. Boys who had never gone hiking, who had never seen a cow outside of a butcher's shop, suddenly found themselves in rural Pennsylvania, living in rustic cabins and fending off critters. Even in late August, while the rest of Western Pennsylvania slept comfortably without sheets, the temperature at night had dipped as low as forty degrees at camp. Before morning practice, teeth chattering, players had taken turns climbing a center bunk to hold their jock straps up to an exposed lightbulb. No shock in nature compared to a chilly jock strap first thing in the morning. Players slept in long underwear, which Klausing had purchased in bulk from an army surplus outlet. More than a few boys, unwilling to part with the extra layer of warmth, attempted to wear the long johns under their pads during morning practice. When the sun peeked over the trees, the cow pasture where the team worked out began to bake. The scent of old cow pies stung the players' nostrils and huge flies came out in droves. One boy, William Branch, lost so much sweat during a morning practice in 1957 that he almost passed out. The rough wool underwear had rubbed his skin raw in spots.

Worse than the cold nights at Corbly were the showers. The water was like ice. Most players chose to bathe in a nearby river. Fatigued after a hard day, they would float on their backs and half-hope to be swept away. Klausing had found that many of his black players couldn't swim. Few public pools were open to them. Black residents could check out books from Braddock's opulent Carnegie Library, but weren't permitted to use the facility's upstairs gym or swim in its gorgeous indoor pool. Carnegie had famously written that "neither rank, office, nor wealth receives the slightest consideration" at his libraries. But race did.

Klausing had performed dozens of dramatic rescues at Corbly. Doughboy had almost dragged his coach underwater two years earlier after he wandered too far out, got caught in the current, and began flailing for help. Klausing dived in, and Doughboy made a mad lunge for him. He outweighed Klausing by seventy pounds and would have taken him right to the bottom, but the coach dodged, swam underneath his panicked player, and put him in a choke hold. When they got to shore, and after coughing up a half gallon of water, Doughboy promised he would never break the rules again.

Over the years, a few aspiring players had crumbled after a few days of the grueling practices and primitive amenities at Corbly. In 1958, a coalition of five underclassmen sneaked out one evening and set off down the road on foot. It was a good eighty miles to Braddock, but the boys figured they could hitchhike. After a frustrating hour watching cars fly by, the deserters stopped in at a local bar. A sheriff who'd come by for a nightcap correctly surmised that they were football players. He drove out to Corbly and roused Klausing from his cabin.

"Coach, you better go pick up your players," he said. "I think there's going to be trouble."

A group of young black men stood out in rural Pennsylvania. When Klausing got to the bar, his boys were playing pinball. They told their coach they'd tried to hitchhike, but nobody gave them a second look. Klausing made them call their parents, and then waited until their rides showed up. He would dress any boy who wanted to play, but he had no room on his team for quitters.

To save money, Corbly's administrators had started scaling back on their food. What had once been full, healthful meals became bland rations. Klausing couldn't abide that. He would happily work his players to the brink of death, sequester them away from their homes and families in cabins with no heat or plumbing, but he also knew that boys needed something to look forward to at the end of each day. Morale had been low the previous summer. A fight almost broke out between the Tigers and another team sharing the facility. Klausing punished his team severely, running them until they dropped, but he knew they weren't entirely to blame. Conditions had become altogether too rough.

This year, with so much on the line, he couldn't afford to start off on the wrong foot. Klausing had cast about for a new camp. A teacher at Braddock High knew a man on the board of trustees at Waynesburg College, which was about an hour and a half outside Braddock. After a few phone calls, the Tigers got a new facility. Players would be staying in dorms replete with indoor plumbing.

"You're getting off easy," Roland Mudd, the senior tackle, told a passing sophomore on the bus.

Wisely, the new player didn't disagree.

With everyone settled, Klausing called roll. The coaches took their seats up front. Burrelli started the family bus, which shook and fired. He let it idle a few anxious moments, and then pressed down the throttle. Cruising down the steep slope away from Braddock High, they passed three barbershops in two blocks. Then Burrelli turned right onto Braddock Avenue. The old bus, which had carried previous Tigers teams to so many victories, rattled and swayed, tossing the players in their seats. Outside, the town was still mostly empty. The team lurched by Hamilton Elementary, and then sped past Braddock Hospital. Six blocks and two additional barbershops later, Burrelli turned the bus up a rise toward the Rankin Bridge. Soon they were out over the Monongahela River, which snaked eighty feet below. The sun, still low in the sky, bounced off the water and struck players' faces.

On the bus, senior John Jacobs could hardly sit still. He kept turning around in his seat, grinning ear to ear at John Plisco, the Tigers' chubby left tackle.

"What do you keep looking back for?" Plisco asked.

Jacobs—Jake, friends called him—just shrugged. He was bursting with enthusiasm. Starting quarterback—hell, the role suited him. He didn't mean to be cocky, but that's just the way things went. Mark Rutkowski had been a great quarterback and a real swell guy. Jacobs would miss him, even. But he was sure glad to be rid of him. After waiting in the wings, he was primed to be number one. He had been working with Coach Zuger all summer, spending long afternoons on the grassy field outside Talbot Towers, Braddock's enormous public housing project. He was throwing more accurately than ever. He felt ready.

The bus grew loud with chatter, and Klausing did nothing to tamp it down. There would be plenty of silence later on, after fatigue and soreness set in. Players caught up on summer news. Majorettes from North Braddock Scott had competed in a baton-twirling competition earlier that week, and some of the players gave their appraisals.

"The legs on them!" said Dan O'Shea, the Tigers center.

After discussing the matter, players agreed that North Braddock's majorettes were okay, even if they couldn't hold a candle to Braddock's girls. Anyone who thought otherwise would have been called out as a traitor.

Others talked about the car chase that had quickened the blood in town a few days earlier. The case was still unfolding, but new details had emerged. Thieves had smashed into a department store in nearby Wilmerding, making off with a portable TV set and hundreds of dollars' worth of transistor radios. A patrolman gave chase, and the criminals sped away in their car through East Pittsburgh and North Braddock, eventually careening down into Braddock at a hundred miles an hour. A wrong turn on a dead-end street forced the thieves to abandon their vehicle, and they fled on foot.

Players hypothesized about their likeliest escape route. A debate soon engulfed the middle section of the bus: Was it better to slip into the pandemonium of Braddock Avenue or stick to side streets? Ken Reaves, a wiry sophomore whose father was a police officer in Braddock, knew it would be a long shot either way. He and his older brothers had occasionally tried to break curfew over the years, only to find their father's patrolmen friends staking out every corner. Braddock, with one exit at each end of town, a river to the south, and a set of railroad tracks to the north, was the last place in the world you wanted to find yourself running from the law.

Doughboy, the halfback, had had more experience fleeing the cops than just about anyone else. He was frequently seen hurling his massive frame around corners and up alleyways, a frustrated beat cop in tow. It was a hell of a workout regimen for the junior, whose nickname derived from the hand-me-down army shirts he wore most days. Quick as he was, Doughboy had slipped up after his sophomore year. He ripped off a haberdashery, and the sweaters and prim slacks—a departure from his olive drab wardrobe—aroused suspicion. His story about a part-time job fell apart under scrutiny, and the cops yanked him out of class. He was sentenced to reform school, and when he got out, he had a ready-made reputation as the biggest, baddest bruiser on the team. Doughboy put the fear of God into younger players. As the bus raced forward, more than one sophomore fretted over how best to avoid him while confined together at camp.

Waynesburg College lay due south of Pittsburgh through the wooded countryside of Western Pennsylvania. The bus weaved between deep-hued hills and skirted farmland that had been cut from the edges of dense woods. With the boys anticipating what lay ahead, the ride seemed to take forever. Eventually, though, the bus pulled along a narrow street studded with oak and maple trees, which foregrounded brick buildings set away from the road.

Players didn't immediately realize they had reached the campus. Few of them had ever stepped foot near a college. A handful had seen the University of Pittsburgh football team play at Pitt Stadium, an experience that had forever branded in their minds the Platonic ideal of a big-time school. Waynesburg seemed sleepy by comparison. Fall classes had not yet begun, and the quiet grassy expanses on either side looked too big for the small brick buildings clustered here and there. The boys weren't used to open space. Penned in by the Mon Valley's steep geography, Braddock's shops, schools, and houses filled every patch of legally zoned earth. The broad sweep of Waynesburg's campus disoriented the boys, who looked out the windows like a safari group gazing at African plains.

Klausing stood at the front of the bus and called attention. "I don't want anyone to go tearing around. Remember that you're guests here."

Practice wouldn't begin until the following morning, but the rules went into effect immediately. In addition to the standing decrees—no fighting, no cussing—the boys were instructed to keep their voices low, get their gear quickly, and begin settling in. Klausing had a reputation for doling out punishment, and none of the players contemplated disobedience. At the first high school where he coached, Klausing had developed a reputation as a vicious paddler. One afternoon, a group of smoking students had frantically shoved their lit cigarettes into their pockets when they saw him coming. It was better to risk a fringed coat than a Klausing beating, they reasoned. At the bell, the boys went inside and hung up their winter gear. When a fire alarm brought everyone outside minutes later, Klausing asked a nearby teacher what had happened. Distraught, she said that her coatroom had burst into flames.

Klausing no longer used corporal punishment. Instead he relied on military-style discipline. At a previous summer camp, when a mouthy boy refused to stop telling jokes after lights out, Klausing ordered the comedian outside.

"You owe me ten bucketsful," he said, handing him the zinc pail that the Tigers used for water.

In the dead of night, the boy groped to find the river fifty yards away. He dipped the pail and then stumbled back. Every time his foot hit a rock, though, he spilled some of his water.

"This one doesn't count," Klausing said when the boy returned. "I want full buckets. Get me ten more, and I'm timing you."

The disobedient player made eighteen trips in all, sometimes losing a portion of his water with only yards to go. Muddy and freezing, he slinked back to his bunk. He had learned his lesson.

Klausing and the assistants climbed off the bus, and the players followed. The managers had arrived in the borough truck ahead of them. Now they set about undoing their careful packing, lining the pads and the extra balls in front of the bus. The boys claimed their equipment and then turned to the large double doors of the gym.

Built of brick and stanchioned with metal braces, the structure was enormous. Waynesburg College's athletics program had an excellent reputation. The football team had a history of upsetting Penn

State, a regional institution. In 1939, the Yellow Jackets took on Fordham University in the nation's first-ever televised football game. NBC announcer Bill Stern made the call as Waynesburg's Bobby Brooks went sixty-three yards to score the first touchdown witnessed live in living rooms across the country.

The school's basketball team didn't have the same clout—it hadn't broken .500 in nearly a decade—but the team's facilities were first-rate. As they walked into the gym, the Tigers glanced around approvingly.

"Look at all the seats," said Doughboy, peering up.

The building made their high school's aging gym seem comically small by comparison. An arched ceiling, lost to darkness, hung overhead. Banners from long-ago triumphs sagged in the rafters. With the main floor lights off, long shadows crisscrossed the bleachers. A number of small dorm rooms lined a balcony overlooking the basketball court, an unusual configuration designed to keep student athletes focused on their athletic commitments. When not keeling over from contact drills and wind sprints, this was where the Tigers would live.

Room assignments, like everything else, followed seniority. Each room was identical: a bunk bed and four cinder block walls. Seniors made their choices based on proximity to the bathrooms. In the middle of the night, disoriented and hobbled by aching muscles, an extra thirty yards could be excruciating. Black players bunked with black players, and white players with white players. Like much of the segregation in Western Pennsylvania, this was neither required nor addressed. It's just the way things went.

The coaches paired off. Klausing and Bob Teitt would bunk together. Klausing placed his bag at the foot of the bed and then sized up the room. A cold cinder block wall never failed to remind him of life on a marine base. He'd joined the marines to pay for college. Trained as an officer, he never saw any action; the first atomic bomb fell as he and his platoon were preparing to invade Japan. His memories from those years were happy, and he often fondly recalled the fraternity of serious men living together with a shared purpose. He viewed football camp as an extension of that ideal.

Klausing had once led a platoon of Mexican Americans from Texas. Like many of his players now, few of them could swim. This became evident as they practiced maneuvering from a transport ship to a landing craft in moderate weather. Klausing had had to dive in repeatedly to make rescues. Instead of berating his platoon, he decided to teach his boys to swim. One by one, he called them into the water. He showed them how to hold their breath and kick their legs. He instituted a buddy system so they could look after each other. Soon the entire platoon was doing laps, crisscrossing back and forth with strokes that were unstylish but confident. It looked like aquatics practice at the YMCA.

That successful afternoon impressed Klausing deeply. He had nurtured the dream of becoming a coach since he was a boy, a private variation on "astronaut" or "doctor." Out of his platoon's willingness to learn, to trust him in the face of near-crippling fear, he experienced the responsibility of being a coach for the first time. It was the moment when the job he'd always aspired to became tangible to him, and he loved it from the start.

Amenities at Waynesburg College, which included indoor toilets and hot water, were luxurious compared to those of Camp Corbly. Quarterback John Jacobs marveled at the line of sinks in the tiled bathroom, which were made of gleaming white porcelain.

"This isn't bad," Jacobs said to Mike Pratko, a backup halfback and Jacobs's best friend on the team. "Couldn't you see yourself someplace like this? For college, I mean?"

Jacobs had plans to get far away from Braddock after graduation. Maybe he'd even go to California. He imagined living in a dorm, walking to class and ogling coeds, playing ball against the biggest teams in the country: Notre Dame, Army, Oklahoma. Standing in the pristine dormitory, that dream felt closer than ever.

Pratko shrugged. He hadn't thought about college. If you couldn't run faster or throw farther than the next hundred boys, the mill or the military awaited you after high school.

"Hey," Jacobs said. "You think any of the college girls are back early?"

Pratko grinned. If anyone could woo an older girl, it would be Jacobs. On a team full of egos, the quarterback's confidence was unrivaled.

"Why don't we just stay in tonight," Pratko said, changing the subject before his friend could formulate a plan.

The last thing they needed before summer practice was a whole heap of trouble.

The first players puked around eight thirty the following morning. Half an hour's sprinting up a giant hill between the gym and the practice field had dislodged breakfast, and undigested eggs lay in piles on the ground. Between whistles, all but the fittest players doubled over, gasping for air. Center Dan O'Shea's face had turned crimson and looked ready to pop.

"Welcome to camp," Klausing announced, smiling.

At the whistle, players tore off up the hill again. A few stragglers didn't make it, their legs giving out before they reached the top.

"That one didn't count," Klausing said, repeating a familiar mantra. "If you don't do it as a team, you don't do it at all."

Coach used the term "intestinal fortitude" to describe a collection of traits he looked for in players. Kids with intestinal fortitude worked harder, practiced longer, and played with pain. During boot camp in the marines, Klausing's drill sergeant had once ordered the men in his platoon to fall flat on their faces. It was a cruel exercise, and one Klausing would never subject his players to—but it did succeed in separating the boys into two groups. Those who could do it, like Klausing, had intestinal fortitude. Those who couldn't weren't worth a damn on the battlefield.

Klausing used a similar strain of logic with his players. When outgoing senior Jim Hux took a direct blow and was diagnosed with a hip pointer—a contusion on the hip bone—at a crucial juncture the previous year, the coaches figured he'd be out for the remainder of the season. Hip pointers usually took three weeks to heal, and it was a painful recovery. Hux suited up the next game, though, played sparingly, and then started the following week against North Braddock Scott. He had intestinal fortitude.

After another gut-emptying sprint, a few linemen dropped to their knees. Coach Zuger, the art teacher, barked at them to stand. Klausing surveyed his team. Most players looked on the verge of keeling over. Running back Ben Powell stood upright, gasping for air but refusing to lean on his knees for support.

After sprints, Klausing sent the players to the practice field a few hundred yards away. Cleats clomped on a stretch of asphalt that lay in between. Players wore full pads, but no helmets. Klausing had seen heat illness in the marines, and he would do everything he could not to subject his high school boys to it. Fatalities from heatstroke, which occurred when the body's temperature rose above 104 degrees, were becoming more common around the country. Football had been receiving negative press nationwide as a result. In response, some stubborn coaches had doubled down, withholding water and intensifying their practices. Paul "Bear" Bryant, the second-year head coach at the University of Alabama, had famously put his 1954 Texas A&M team through its paces in a tumbleweed town called Junction. While working out in the summer heat, Bryant denied his players water and rest, nearly killing at least one boy in the process.

Klausing had a hunch that helmets, which concentrated heat in a bubble over the brain, were partly to blame for the high instance of heatstroke in football players. His boys wore helmets only during scrimmages and contact drills. He believed in keeping them hydrated and healthy, especially while putting them through hell.

On the field, players lined up for the Bandit drill. Boys started in a hitting position—they bent their knees, kept their feet shoulder width apart, and raised their heads. During the drill's first cycle, the instructions were simple enough: From a hitting stance, players were to move their feet up and down. On a hand signal, they had to make a quarter turn to the right or the left, or else drop down into push-up position and spring back up. Anyone who ever played youth league football had done something similar in practice.

But things quickly got more complex. The drill tested concentration in addition to physical endurance. After a few minutes, Klausing introduced a new hand signal. With a directional wave, players shuffled five yards in the indicated direction: left, right, forward, or backward. Players incorporated these new instructions without much trouble, though the lines began to waver as the gaps between each Tiger shrank and expanded unevenly. Thighs began to burn, and legs, already heavy from the hill sprints, threatened to quit.

That's when Klausing added another set of signals. A two-handed wave sent players careening thirty yards right or left, crossing their legs as they moved. Next came backward running, and then bear crawling. Shoulder rolling came after leapfrogging, which preceded monkey rolling and grass drilling. Each series of steps was as exotic as its name. Soon the drill devolved into bedlam. There were four rows of Tigers running in every direction, jumping over one another, shuffling and sprinting and diving across the field. At the head of this loony display stood Klausing, who was waving his arms madly in the air like an orchestra conductor. Players collided, stepped on one another's hands and feet, and collapsed from exhaustion. Bodies soon littered the field in front of Klausing, who eventually stopped the drill. He waited just a moment for the lines to re-form. Then he started in again. After a wrenching half hour, honed by repetition and compelled by the threat of a daylong Bandit workout, the players finally started to execute their steps in sync.

Summer camp was a kind of gestation—coaches took the boys from the most elemental stages of football development to the most complex. After the Bandit drill, the team moved on to blocking. Players pushed Waynesburg's two-man sled up and down the field. Whenever Coach Zuger spotted a boy using poor technique, he stepped in front of the player, dropped into a stance, and charged. These demonstrations always ended with a dazed Tiger lying on his back.

Tackling drills came next, and helmets went on. Players flew into each other, and the concussive pops of colliding pads filled the air. Noses and lips bled. The single-bar face masks were only partially effective at stopping impacts. Fingers got twisted or craned backwards. Metal cleats gauged skin, ripping it off arms and legs. Bobby Williams, the Tigers trainer, would be busy that afternoon.

When the brute drills had been run to Klausing's satisfaction, coaches broke the players out by their offensive positions. Klausing took the running backs, the heart of the Tigers' offense. Football revolved around the running game. The pass had helped Klausing out of some tight spots in previous seasons, and Rutkowski became a hot ticket with his arm. Nevertheless, the run accounted for the Tigers' consistency. In 1955, halfback Joe Reaves had led the state in scoring with twenty-one touchdowns, setting the tone for a ground-based offense that by 1957 would be averaging 33.9 points per game. John Jacobs was a gifted athlete and a promising quarterback—and hell on wheels when he kept the ball and scrambled. He didn't have the throwing accuracy that Rutkowski did, but his skillset would be a return to form for the Tigers.

Backfield drills resembled a ballet rehearsal. Everything in the backfield was a dance—the angle of an instep, the opening swivel of the hips, and even the way the eyes scanned the defensive line had to be perfect. Each running back's movements had to sync with the rest of the backfield, as well as with the line. In the intricate machine of the offense, the backs were the precision parts. Klausing and his assistants had a sharp eye for detail. A flat-footed halfback got a shove in the side, the football signal for "keep your balance." If a back crossed his feet, exposed the ball, or stuttered before hitting a gap, he heard about it immediately.

This year's running backs seemed heaven-sent. Ben Powell—a slender halfback with remarkably long legs—ran like a deer. He bounded down the field with long, graceful strides, which he guided with his superb field vision and impeccable reactions. Powell was able to sense opposing players before they got close enough to bring him down. Deerlike to the core, he could be magnificently timid off the field. Former teachers spent months trying to coax just a few words out of him in class. Powell expressed himself through his speed, and in that language, breaking up the seam, he was an orator. He had a legitimate claim on being the best flat-out runner in the state. In eighth grade, he broke the regional junior high school record in the 100-yard dash. He grew up in North Versailles, a small town just outside Braddock, where football talent flowed like tap water.

Doughboy was the second halfback in Klausing's Wing T offense. A power runner and a devastating blocker—to say nothing of an irrepressible braggart—Doughboy pushed through defenders like a bowling ball moved through pins. His brush with the law had only made him tougher. Coach Klausing had once visited the wayward player at reform school. The coach had a soft spot for Doughboy. He knew the gruff player didn't do well with discipline, and he expected the worst. But Klausing got a happy surprise in the reform school's administrative offices.

"Chuck, he's the best kid we've ever had," the principal informed him. "There hasn't been a single successful escape since he got here. He keeps everyone else in line!"

Doughboy had become the reform school's de facto enforcer,

manhandling delinquents into adhering to a strict code of conduct. When kids flew the coup, the principal asked Doughboy to come along in his truck. Without fail, escapees always made their way toward the entrance to a nearby interstate. The principal trolled the road between the school and the interstate for his wayward charges. When he spotted them, he pulled over and set Doughboy loose.

The halfback had put on thirty pounds of muscle in the clink. When he got out as a sophomore, he looked twenty years old. He prowled the halls at Braddock High like a junkyard dog walking his beat. He crowed about his football prowess, and he challenged students to contests of strength in the gym. "Come here!" he yelled at older boys. "Let's see what you got!" He ran down the boys who were too afraid to face him.

During the 1958 season, he had put up an impressive 542 yards rushing, including eight touchdowns. On any other team, he'd be the offensive centerpiece. On a Tigers team with Ben Powell—who also scored eight touchdowns in 1958, despite being sidelined with injuries for three games—he was just a role-player.

Unfortunately for Doughboy, another rising star had diluted the talent pool even further. Curtis "Willy" Vick came out of nearby North Versailles a year after Powell. Vick had power and speed in equal measure. Though only a junior, he had earned the coveted starting fullback position. The previous year, his first on the Tigers, he'd proved dangerous inside and a threat to break for long yards. Klausing never thought he'd see a running back as gifted as Powell on a high school team. Watching Vick as a sophomore changed his mind. During one memorable play, the running back busted his way between two unblocked linemen, dropped his shoulder to down a safety in the open field, and then tore down the sideline in a gear no one had seen him use before then. The hometown crowd, getting a preview of the next generation of Tigers greatness, exploded in the stands when he crossed the goal line for a fifty-five-yard touchdown.

Here was the future, an assurance that the streak might continue indefinitely.

Doughboy, not surprisingly, found Vick insufferable. Handsome and good natured, the fullback charmed people wherever he went. He dated frequently and even went out with white girls now and then. If not unheard of at Braddock High, where school dances were still segregated, mixed race couples were still a rarity.

Klausing loved the boy. Filling in on defense during practice the previous year, Vick had read a fake perfectly, leaping forward to make a tackle. But his defensive teammate fell for the misdirection, and the two collided head-on. The impact dislocated Vick's jaw, which was splayed visibly to one side. Groaning in agony, the running back quick-stepped over to Klausing and pointed to his mangled face. Fortunately, the Red Cross first aid book Klausing carried with him contained an illustrative picture to suit the occasion. Bobby Williams, the trainer, didn't want anything to do with resetting the jaw, so Vick waited on the field as Klausing rehearsed the procedure a few times in the air. Facing his sophomore running back, he wrenched the jaw back into place. Vick suited up the following game, and Klausing added him to his list of players with intestinal fortitude.

"Curt," Doughboy said when the morning's running drills began, "let me show you how it's done."

Vick smiled, characteristically easygoing. Lining up for the next drill, Doughboy led with the wrong foot.

"Hellfire!" Klausing yelled. "John, would you pay attention?"

Gritting his teeth, the halfback jogged back to the line.

Practice broke at the hottest part of the day, and players dragged their shocked bodies back to the gym to change their clothes. Bleary eyed from the previous night's half sleep and hobbled by deep bruises, they filed into the mess for lunch. Some players, their stomachs up-side down from the impact drills, could hardly look at food. Others ate as if they hadn't seen a morsel in weeks.

Sophomores lined up last. Doughboy, at a table with the other running backs, studied the new players' faces for the slightest sign of discontent. He hoped one of them would complain. When none did, he hollered anyway.

"What's wrong? Not as good as your mama's cooking?"

The sophomores avoided eye contact, and ripples of laughter passed through the cafeteria. For protection, the youngest players sat to-gether.

Not all the older players gave the newbies a hard time. Junior Dan O'Shea, the Tigers' starting center, had spent much of the morning's position practice working with Jim Clark, his sophomore backup. Clark had painful blisters on his feet, which were weeping into his shoes. Nevertheless, he worked his butt off to impress Klausing. John Jacobs gave Ken Reaves, the backup to the backup quarterback, a fair shake. Ben Powell, the star halfback, never said an unkind word to his legion of backups, and seniors like offensive end Ray Hender-son and offensive guard Vernon Stanfield kept their heads down most of the time, focusing on the work of camp and on keeping their starting positions.

A few loud voices drowned out the rest, was all, chiding the soph-omores and reminding them of their place on the totem pole. It was the price of becoming a Braddock High Tiger, a dream that all pres-ent had nurtured since grade school.

The Tigers had been undefeated for five straight seasons; every boy in Braddock coveted a spot on the team. The sophomores had been in the stands the previous year when Mark Rutkowski inter-cepted Tom Fantaski's pass and closed the curtain on "the Game of the Century." They had lived and died on each play and cast them-selves as their favorite players afterwards. The Baltimore Colts had beaten the New York Giants in sudden death overtime in the 1958

NFL Championship Game. That heart-stopping victory, which pro-pelled Johnny Unitas to national stardom overnight, paled in com-parison to the Braddock–North Braddock game for anyone lucky enough to have witnessed it. The sophomores took the older players' ribbing stoically, without complaint. To a man, they were willing to spill blood to earn their stripes.

Some of the sophomores, like Ken Reaves, came to the team under the long shadows of their older brothers. A Reaves boy had been on the Tigers every year since Klausing started at Braddock High. In 1954 and 1955, bruiser Joe Reaves helped lead the Tigers to their first undefeated seasons ever. Blocking two defenders at a run, throwing them to the side like mud off his jersey, he opened holes that a freight train could have passed through untouched. His little brother Larry was only a freshman when Klausing took over, but had inherited enough of his older brother's talent to practice with the varsity team. A big brute of a tackle, Larry started his sophomore year. After his senior season in 1957, he received twenty-one feelers from college teams across the country. He chose to attend Arizona State, lured by the desert sun and the school's new head coach, Frank Kush.

Now Ken Reaves, the baby, had a chance to pick up the torch. Unlike his brothers, the young Reaves hadn't filled out as a sopho-more. Ken was scrawny, with a pair of toothpick legs that hardly seemed capable of holding up under the blunt force of a tackle. But Reaves blood flowed in his veins, and for that reason alone the coaches expected great things.

Sitting with his assistants, Klausing evaluated the scene in front of him. All the players had their food, and those who could stomach it after the hard practice were eating heartily. Some families in Brad-dock didn't eat three square meals on a regular basis. Even decent jobs often didn't fully support large households—and Braddock had many large households.

Ken Reaves's father, a policeman, took home three thousand dol-lars per year. It was a respectable sum, but Ken had five brothers and three sisters. To make ends meet, the entire Reaves clan pitched in, working a few nights each week cleaning the Paramount Theater. The Reaves brothers pushed brooms down the wide center aisles while their sisters picked up between the seats. Phil Lucarelli, the boy Coach Zuger had shoved in junior high art class, had seven brothers and two sisters. His father, a supervisor at Edgar Thomson, took contracting work on the side to put food on the table. John Jacobs's father, the chief of police in North Versailles, drank and gambled. A few years earlier, on a school trip, Jacobs went through the Heinz factory tour twice just so he could have a second helping of the free snacks they gave out. Offensive end Ray Henderson had lost his father when he was just a boy. Henderson worked at a barrel factory in middle school, and then got a job setting pins at a bowling alley. He gave the money he made to his mother to help pay bills. Klausing knew these boys' stories and knew that a wholesome meal meant the world to them. Though he was a dictator on the field, it made him happy to see them enjoying their food.

The coaches got together after lunch to talk. John Jacobs had looked strong at morning practice. His work with Coach Zuger over the summer had paid off. Jacobs had a pesky tendency to let his wrist fall outward on his follow-through, a surefire recipe for a knuckleball. Zuger helped reprogram the boy's motion in the off-season, and Jacobs had been throwing tight spirals ever since.

The senior quarterback looked even better running the quarterback option. With Rutkowski's accuracy, Klausing's team had passed more than most high school squads in the previous three seasons. But Jacobs was a nimble quarterback with a decent arm and excellent foot speed. The senior had a nose for the option and no fear when he tucked the ball. He could pick up big yards for the Tigers on the ground. The only knock against him was his back. The mysterious ailment struck without warning, sometimes completely incapacitating the boy. It was enough to keep Klausing up at night.

Players returned to their dorm rooms after lunch and collapsed. It was one thirty in the afternoon on the first full day of camp, though it felt like they hadn't slept in days. Guard Ray Grudowski had put on bulk over the summer and had trouble hefting himself onto the top bunk. As he climbed, both he and the bed emitted a pained trill. Tackle John Plisco didn't notice. He had already fallen asleep in the lower bunk. Players had only half an hour before the next practice began, and there wasn't a minute to waste on idle chatter.

Before settling into bed, John Jacobs heard a commotion in the bathrooms and got up to investigate. Coaches Klausing and Zuger were busy administering some camp justice. Any player caught cussing had to put half a bar of soap in his mouth.

"You want Ivory or Lifebuoy?" Zuger asked Joel Peoples.

It was a rhetorical question. Zuger broke the bar in half, and Klausing looked at his watch to keep time. Peoples would have to endure a full two minutes for the word he had used.

Klausing hated cussing. As a boy, he'd had his own problem with loose lips. In grade school, he had taught a Bulgarian classmate to say, "Son of a *beech*." When Klausing's teacher found out, she whacked him in the face hard enough to leave a mark. A few years later, working as a lifeguard at a local lake one summer, Klausing let a string of expletives fly with children present. His supervisor—who happened to be Frankie Sinkwich, the starting tailback at the University of Georgia—chased him onto a dock, picked up an oar, and smacked him across the midsection. Sinkwich went on to win the Heisman Trophy, and when he hit you with an oar, you remembered. What finally cured Klausing, though, was his conversion to Catholicism. Though he had first flirted with Catholicism to get close to his future wife, he followed through with all his heart. His players had been paying for it ever since.

The boys woke from their deep sleep to the sound of Zuger's twangy, insistent voice.

"Rise and shine! Let's play some football!"

Players were dressed and jogging to the field before the veil of sleep had lifted fully. The afternoon sun scorched their temples. A dreary line formed at the base of the large hill—then the whistle, the stampede, and the players were taking the mountain exactly as they had that morning. Life had become a sweaty repetition.

Waynesburg's soft grass cradled exhausted players who fell down. The entire team admired the plush practice field, a welcome departure from the misshapen stretch of dirt and cinders they practiced on back in Braddock. After every season, scabs that covered players' elbows and legs contained artifacts of soot and black rock. Falling on Waynesburg's grass was a treat, even if Coach Zuger barked that they were staying down too long.

After defensive position workouts, the players put on their helmets for live drills. A suicide squad, which consisted of second- and third-string players, took the field on defense. Phil Lucarelli strapped on his helmet and prepared for his first hit on varsity.

Coach Zuger called the backup defense around him. "If you have a direct line on the ball carrier," he ordered, "you ring his bell."

Senior Mike Pratko stood in the center of the huddle. A veteran on the suicide squad, Pratko played every position. He'd even worked out as quarterback, though he didn't have the athleticism of Jacobs, his roommate and best friend. On defense now, Pratko peered over at the first-string players. They had just broken their huddle. Offensive guards Vernon Stanfield and Ray Grudowski took their places on the line. In pads, they looked like gargantuan pillars flanking the center.

Geez, Pratko thought. *Those guys must have put on twenty pounds of muscle over the summer!*

When Zuger finished talking to the defense, the players jogged to the line. The scrawny-looking second- and third-stringers looked into the snarling faces of their teammates. Jacobs worked through his count, and center Dan O'Shea snapped the ball. In a flash, it was over. Ray Grudowski, the guard, had lifted a sophomore off his feet and was lying on top of him. Curtis Vick had taken the handoff, but Lucarelli put a surprising hit on him as he squeezed through the line. Throwing his hands in the air, Zuger ran high-kneed onto the field.

"Yes, Lucarelli! That's exactly right! That's it!"

Lucarelli dusted himself off, and Vick gave him a sideways glance. The sophomore had made a statement, though Vick sure as hell wouldn't let it happen again. They jogged back to the line, where players readjusted their pads, leveled their single-bar face masks, and prepared to do it all over again.

Afternoon practice ended at four thirty. The day's work wasn't done, however. One final practice remained. Dinner passed solemnly. The weight of the many days that lay ahead had set in. Everyone ate ravenously now. Doughboy didn't even look at the sophomores, and they didn't skirt his table as they passed. It was a truce born of fatigue.

Coaches also ate quietly. Weary from the long day in the sun, voices raspy from yelling, they retreated into themselves. Klausing already missed his wife and children. He depended on Joann, who was his confidante, his cheerleader, and it was difficult to spend even a short time away. He loved his family and he loved his team. Caught between those loves, he often felt an impossible tension, the one pulling harder at times and forcing the other to yield.

Summer two-a-days were common for football teams across the country, but three-a-days were rare, the unique purview of a coach who demanded something more. Players wore no pads for the third practice, which was called a "skull session," but it was no less intense than the two that had come before. This was the most cerebral part of the Tigers' preparations. Every play, every situation they might encounter, had to be analyzed and rehearsed.

Players filed into a crammed classroom in the gymnasium building. Each player brought a playbook and a pencil, and Klausing expected them to take copious notes. Diagrams soon filled the chalkboard, a chess game of *X*s and *O*s.

"If a linebacker shoots the gap on a fifty series, who picks him up?"

"How can a safety read a reverse?"

The meetings sometimes had the pace of rapid question-and-answer sessions. When responses required nuance, sessions took the air of a Socratic seminar. Coaches led players down twisting paths of false logic to highlight pitfalls and flawed assumptions.

After the skull session, the team went back to the field. In the last light of the afternoon they walked through the diagramed plays. New players committed weak side reads and defensive coverages to memory. Football was a game of execution. Talent and luck had their place, but the team that executed better usually won.

When the third practice ended, and as darkness set over Waynesburg's campus, the players filed back to their dorm rooms. In days to come, when stamina returned, the evening's free time would be pleasant—a chance to relax, to explore the cavernous gym, and to write letters home. This evening, though, after torpid showers, the players dragged their exhausted bodies to bed. Klausing strolled down the hallway, the last to turn in. All the lights were out. An hour after practice, to a player, the Tigers slept.

Chapter Three

NO WORK

SONNY BURRELLI ARRIVED EARLY on Sunday morning to drive the team home. One look at Klausing's boys told the story. Doughboy stood quietly beside Curtis Vick and a group of sophomore players. Not a boast or threat passed the senior running back's lips. Johnny Jacobs wore a stolid, tight-mouthed expression in place of his usual grin. Tackle John Plisco and center Dan O'Shea seemed hardened, their summer pudge transformed to muscle. After two weeks, the Tigers had lost all the brashness and nervous energy they displayed on the trip up.

A few players chatted softly with one another while waiting for the coaches. Without being asked, others helped the managers pack equipment. Sweat-soaked pads testified to hundreds of drills, miles of sprints. So did the screaming muscles and pained expressions on the players' faces as they climbed gingerly up the bus's tall steps.

"How'd they do, Coach?"

"Fine, Sonny. It was a good camp."

The driver had spent enough time with the Tigers coach to know that he was pleased. The boys collapsed into the bus's vinyl seats. Assistant John Zuger strained and grimaced just like the players. Camp had been as full contact for him as it was for them. When Klausing coached at Pitcairn, he had often dispatched one of his assistants, Pete Antimarino, to round up local drunks for full-contact scrimmages. Even the meanest of those barflies couldn't compare to Coach Zuger, who didn't know the meaning of "walk-through." He played so hard during practices that he had knocked one of his junior high school players' front teeth out a few years earlier. Klausing, who had had his own front teeth knocked out during his first year at Penn State, made all his high school players wear mouthpieces while they practiced, but the rule was loosely enforced in junior high. Now, on the bus, Zuger's face tightened with each step. He eased himself into a seat at the front of the bus, hunched his shoulders, and exhaled in relief.

After Klausing climbed aboard, he and one of the student managers passed out sandwiches for the ride home. The Waynesburg College cafeteria had prepared the sandwiches at Klausing's request. It was a parting gift of nourishment from a coach whose team had made him proud. The players, their bodies accustomed to an intense daily regimen, removed the wax paper and ate the sandwiches right away. Then, luxuriating in the almost unbelievable knowledge that they were on their way home, they fell asleep. Klausing took his seat and Burrelli fired up the bus and pulled out.

At a certain point during the two-week camp, each Tiger had arrived at a liberating truth: There was no profit in fear. Punishing drills were a fact of life in the intense days preceding the regular season, and self-pity only made things worse. Klausing always recognized the change. When players lost their fear, they no longer hesitated. Without hesitation, the team began executing plays with precision. By the middle of the second week of camp, coaches made small adjustments, like piano tuners dialing in a massive instrument. Beyond that, interference became unnecessary. To an observer who hadn't seen this process from beginning to end, the Tigers' offense looked almost too simplistic to be effective. Opposing coaches often couldn't understand how the Tigers beat them with a basic Wing T set. When necessary, Klausing's play calling could be creative. More often, though, he stuck to a handful of running plays and a straight-forward option. He beat the majority of his opponents up at summer camp, long before they met on Friday night.

Klausing was eager to get back. He wanted to see Joann and the children. He had used the two weeks away to take stock of his professional future, and it was time to talk it over with Joann. At night, in his bunk, he had replayed the advice of his mentor, Neil Brown. Brown, a football institution in Western Pennsylvania (and no relation to Paul Brown, former coach of Massillon Washington High, whose record Klausing was chasing), coached at Clairton, one of the largest schools in Allegheny County. He was something of a sage in coaching circles in the region.

"You never want to stay in one place more than six years," he told Klausing one afternoon at a high school all-star game the two coached in a decade earlier. "If you can't accomplish your goals with a team in six years, it's time to move on. If you have accomplished what you set out to do, what possible reason could you have for sticking around? That's a mistake too many coaches make," he warned.

New blood kept the sport interesting, and Brown believed that coaches, like sharks, had to keep moving.

Klausing had followed his mentor's advice at Pitcairn, staying ex-actly six years. Now, on the eve of his sixth season with the Tigers, and with his biggest goal, a national record, in sight, it was time to start thinking about the future. Klausing had considered moving to another high school. If he had landed the Massillon job two years earlier, he would have enjoyed building on his success as a prep coach. But he also had five children at home. He knew that a college salary would take some of the financial burden away, and that a col-lege town, an academic environment, would give his children a leg up. He loved Western Pennsylvania, but he had no illusions about a child's prospects growing up in a steel town. The kids he grew up with had gone to the steel mill or the Westinghouse Air Brake plant. It was only by the grace of God—and the United States Marines— that he had attended college. When he joined the marines, they sent him to Penn State for two years before Officer Candidate School. When he got out of the service, he finished school at Slippery Rock University on the G.I. Bill. He wanted better for his children, a straight path to college. If he broke the record and could leave on top, Klausing decided he would pursue a university coaching job. He wasn't eager to leave Braddock, a town that had bestowed dozens of awards on him and frequently gave banquets in his honor. But, like his mentor, Klausing loved football. He wanted new challenges.

In the meantime, there was important business to attend to when the team returned to Braddock. The Western Pennsylvania Inter-scholastic Athletic League was set to rule on the eligibility of three of Klausing's new players: John Backa, Willie Thomas, and Leon Page. The transfers were coming into the Braddock School District from North Versailles. Players from the nearby town were free to go to any high school in the region, but the WPIAL had to ensure that atten-dance decisions were not materially motivated. A ride to school each morning was fine, but any promise of cash or special treatment would have been improper. The transfers had dutifully practiced with the Tigers at Waynesburg, and Klausing wanted to make sure they'd get to wear the red and white.

Eligibility rules were strictly enforced in Western Pennsylvania. Without exception, eligibility ran out when a student turned nine-teen years old. Investigations often turned up discrepancies, and en-tire seasons sometimes had to be forfeited. This had happened to Braddock High back in 1924, when an ineligible player cost the team all nine wins of what would have been its first perfect season. Craf-ton High School's disqualification from the WPIAL Class A finals in 1958 had worked out in Braddock's favor, positioning Klausing's boys to take their fifth straight WPIAL Class A title. Entry into the championship game was based on a points system that accounted for margin of victory, among other things, and Braddock had ranked third among undefeated teams in the WPIAL.

"You fall in the shit and come out smelling like a rose!" John Zuger had said to Klausing when news of Crafton's disqualification came down, amazed at his boss's unfaltering good luck.

Eligibility issues often did come down to strokes of luck. Dishonest coaches occasionally dressed players they knew to be ineligible, risking the balance of a season on a standout athlete. The majority of eligibility cases, though, involved innocent oversights. High schools didn't have resources to verify the housing and athletic histories of every student, and complex rules often created gray areas.

Klausing had been accused of using ineligible players, though he'd always been cleared of any wrongdoing. Toward the end of his first season at Braddock, in 1954, a late addition to the team nearly cost him his first championship. Before practice one day, with only a few weeks left in the season, the new coach had spotted the biggest kid he'd ever seen in the office at Braddock High. Klausing asked the boy, Ted Vawters, if he'd ever played football.

"I played for the Steubenville Big Red, Coach," Vawters said.

Klausing was speechless. The Big Red was known countrywide as one of Massillon Washington High School's venerable rivals, a team that had almost stymied Paul Brown several times during his record-breaking run.

Vawters explained that his mother had found a job in Braddock, where she had family, which prompted the move from Ohio. He was in the process of registering to attend Braddock High at that very moment. After some background questions, Klausing instructed Vawters to report to the equipment manager after school. Since the new student was transferring from another state, he would be eligible right away. But Klausing's lucky break almost backfired. Vawters suited up and played for Braddock in the WPIAL title game. After tying Midland High for the Class A championship—the only tie, to date, of Klausing's career at Braddock—the coach received an anonymous letter.

"Ted Vawters is nineteen years old," the note read, "and his birth certificate proves it."

Klausing's heart sank. Vawters had assured him he was only seventeen. Fortunately for the Tigers, he hadn't been lying—at least, not about his age. Vawters's legal name was David Austin. When Austin was four years old, his mother had swapped his birth certificate with a phony. She was starting a new job and couldn't afford to put her son in child care. She needed somewhere for him to go during the day, but he was too young to start kindergarten. So David Austin became Ted Vawters, and his mother enrolled him. Klausing's head was spinning when the smoke finally cleared on the WPIAL investigation. He never found out who'd sent the anonymous note. Vawters—Austin—came back the following year and played brilliantly. Klausing hoped that his three transfer students would be declared eligible for the coming 1959 season, but he wouldn't be taking any chances by putting them in a game until he was sure. His heart couldn't handle another eligibility mix-up.

The bus retraced its path through Waynesburg's campus and then hit open road. The team was silent, asleep, and the engine's moan filled the cabin. It felt safe in the bus, cloaked in a camaraderie wrought over two weeks of toil. There was a new season to look forward to, a new school year, and for those sleepy passengers rocking gently along the curves of the serene valley country, a sense of immutability, as though all of life would be a chauffeured ride toward greatness. They were Braddock High Tigers. They were invincible. They had no reason to believe that would ever change.

Klausing knew different. He was anxious to check on Mark Rutkowski. The former Tigers quarterback had injured himself while practicing for a regional all-star game. Rutkowski was the picture of an all-American: a square-jawed kid with a sharp mind and an iron resolve. Despite a rough upbringing with an abusive father, he seemed to have the best possible future laid out before him. He had scholarship offers from every part of the country. But all of that had come into jeopardy two weeks earlier.

The game, which took place August 1, was meant to be a last hurrah, a summer blowout between the best high school players from Pennsylvania and Ohio. During a preparatory scrimmage, Rutkowski had been tackled at an odd angle. He'd wrenched his knee painfully, and the damage looked serious. Bad knee injuries often ended careers, and any kind of cartilage tear would probably require invasive surgery. Rutkowski was a role model to the younger players on the Tigers, emblematic of the bright road available to them if they worked hard and performed on the field. The quarterback had put off choosing a college until the last possible minute. With scholarship offers still pending, Klausing worried what the injury might mean.

Western Pennsylvania—green, dark, and impenetrable—pressed against the highway. Where it had been cleared back at all, green waves rallied in the distance. Gullies had been dug along the road, trenches against the advancing plant life. Telephone lines dipped above the gullies and shale rock sat in blast piles off the road.

The region was wild, undeveloped. Its dense forests and complex geography, along with its legions of Eastern European immigrants, had given rise to a culture of myth and superstition. Omens like Rutkowski's injury were a thing to pay attention to. Mysterious things happened in the area. Recently, a man with no face had been haunting the back roads of Allegheny County. Teenagers reported seeing him at night, a ghoulish flash in their headlights. Many believed he was the disfigured ghost of some poor industrial worker killed in an accident. The faceless man really did exist. His name was Ray Robinson. As a child in Beaver Falls, Robinson had touched a high-tension electrical line on a bridge over the Beaver River. The intense shock cost him part of his left arm, and a fabric of featureless mottled skin grew where his face had been. Robinson walked at night to avoid gawkers, feeling his way along the paths by memory since he had no eyes. Interpreted through the veil of Western Pennsylvania superstition, he had become a ghost.

The bloody days of the French and Indian War colored much of the region's folklore. The conflict, an outgrowth of the Seven Years' War, started in Western Pennsylvania—then part of the Ohio Country—when French and British troops clashed over control of the interior of the North American continent. The protracted fighting infused the area's collective psyche with barbarism and bloodshed. Scores of gravestones dotted hillsides across the region, each with its own tale of fallen soldiers or scorned Indian warriors. Local celebrations marked the anniversaries of gruesome battles, and every third grader west of Harrisburg could recite the facts of General Edward Braddock's ill-fated march.

Commander-in-chief of the thirteen British colonies, General Braddock led a large column of soldiers across the Monongahela in 1755. He hoped to drive the French from Fort Duquesne, a strategic outpost at the convergence of the Monongahela and the Allegheny rivers, where Pittsburgh would later grow. His forces vastly outnumbered the French and Canadian regulars and their Indian allies, and the commander expected an easy victory. After crossing the river, British and colonial soldiers ran into a French and Indian party hurrying along a narrow path to set up an ambush. Chaos broke out, with General Braddock charging up from behind while his forward troops fell back. The French and Indians were better versed in wilderness combat than the British. They took to the trees and fired from protected positions. Braddock, accustomed to the open-field fighting of European skirmishes, kept his men out in the open. More than 450 of them were slaughtered. The general was shot through the lung and died four days later from his injuries. Two towns bearing his name rose on the site of the battle, a long slope at the edge of the Monongahela. Residents of the towns had been warring with each other ever since, and some wondered if the blood from those

450 soldiers could have seeped into the groundwater, a bitter season-
ing spurring a decades-old feud.

The team bus skirted the Mon Valley and continued toward the
river. As they neared Braddock, sensing their proximity to home, the
players began to wake. For two weeks they had been jolted to con-
sciousness by shouts and piercing whistles. Now, even without those
brutal alarms, they snapped to attention. Peering out the windows at
the passing scenery, they saw stillness. The steel strike had stretched
to a month and a half. It seemed strange to the Tigers, who had just
finished two weeks of grueling work, that steelmen in the area had
been idle all that time. Boys whose fathers worked in the mill felt the
weight of the silence differently than their teammates. Senior Mike
Pratko had a sense of the economic constraints the strike was putting
on his family. His father drove a small train, called a dink, at Edgar
Thomson, ferrying supplies and equipment to all corners of the massive yard. With the strike on, Pratko had been giving his father the
money he made selling papers and washing cars. It was a strange
thing for a boy to see his family's need, to know that his contribution
could be the difference between a decent meal and survival rations.

Skirting the town of Homestead, where nine thousand workers
had walked out on strike, the bus took the bridge across the river.
Eyes lingered on the Homestead mill, which sat unused and so not
entirely explainable, like a pagan monument devoid of context. Descending toward Braddock, the blue siding of the Edgar Thomson
Steel Works loomed at the far end of town. Braddock lived in the
shadow of its famous steel mill, which also sat silent and grave. Four
thousand five hundred workers were on strike at the plant. The entire
town of Braddock was idle.

No one in Braddock was surprised when talks between the United
Steelworkers of America (USWA), which represented half a million

steelworkers across the nation, and negotiators for the major steel companies fell apart. Work stoppages in the American steel industry were commonplace. There had been four other major steel strikes since World War II, one every three or four years. The last strike occurred in 1956, and so the walkout of July 1959 seemed right on schedule.

The strikes of the past decade and a half had followed a similar pattern: A general union contract, which governed everything from wages and working conditions to how much say the USWA had in settling worker grievances, would be on the verge of expiring. Before that happened, the president of the USWA and the industry's lead negotiator would get together to hammer out new terms, and the two would mostly see eye to eye. There would be disagreement on the finer points, usually relating to wage hikes, and the union would order its workers to strike. The popular conception, reinforced by dueling newspaper editorials and daily news coverage, as well as by the bombastic speeches of union reps and industry bigwigs, was that the two sides were locked in a bitter game of chicken, that no less than the future of the country's steel manufacturing sector was at stake.

In reality, no one at the bargaining table would seem particularly concerned. Strikes had practical benefits for both the companies and the union. For the union, strikes almost always resulted in an increase in wages or benefits. Negotiated concessions by the industry to raise wages appeased the union's members, who in turn filled the union coffers. The steel companies, on the other hand, got a free pass to raise the price of their product, justifying the increase to their customers as the only way to accommodate the union's demands and end a work stoppage that threatened the vitality of the American economy. Price hikes often more than offset cost increases, so profits rose. Steel strikes, in other words, had in large part been pieces of stagecraft following the war, the most public step in an otherwise private negotiating process. Even if the emotions of the steelworkers and plant managers were real, the outcomes of the strikes were largely preordained. In 1952, something changed.

As founder and president of the USWA, Philip Murray had overseen a dramatic expansion of collective bargaining in the American steel industry. A Scottish immigrant—a fact that lent his biography a nice symmetry with that of the architect of the country's steel boom, Andrew Carnegie—Murray got his start as a rabble-rouser while working in a Pennsylvania coal mine. When he found out that his boss had been cheating him out of wages, he punched the man and was promptly fired. Murray joined the United Mine Workers of America, an institution he believed could balance the unchecked power of the large mining companies. He educated himself through correspondence courses and allied himself with rising stars in the union, including John L. Lewis, the man who would soon found the Congress of Industrial Organizations (CIO).

Lewis's CIO, a strategic alliance of several unions representing workers across a number of industries, ushered in a new phase in the history of organized labor. Unlike the American Federation of Labor (AFL), which tended to represent the interests of craftsmen in the skilled trades, the CIO focused on the rights of industrial workers, such as those in the steel mills. Lewis appointed Murray head of the CIO's Steelworkers Organizing Committee (SWOC) in 1936. Under Murray's leadership, the SWOC quickly grew in influence, organizing workers and winning strategic victories at several U.S. Steel plants. As the largest steel manufacturer in the country, U.S. Steel was an important prize for labor. The SWOC voted to disband in 1942 in order to create a full-fledged union: the United Steelworkers of America. Murray was the union's first president. Compassionate and friendly, he inspired loyalty in the union's executive leadership. He was also popular with rank-and-file members. Along with Ben Fairless, CEO of U.S. Steel, he orchestrated the give-and-take routine that came to define steel negotiations through the mid-1950s. Steelworkers began to expect wage increases and improvements in working conditions with each round of contract renegotiations, and the steel companies, if not wild about making concessions, benefited from having a predictable opponent and an easy scapegoat for their price hikes.

In 1952, Murray died of a heart attack. The man who replaced him was a contrast in every way. David McDonald was an opportunist. A dapper man with expensive tastes, he had served as the union's secretary-treasurer under Murray. But the two had fallen out. Murray went so far as to denounce McDonald in a speech at a union convention in 1952, proclaiming: "There are going to be no little dictatorships in this union, no connivances, no bribery." He believed McDonald had been using the union's purse strings to buy loyalty. Following the speech, he limited the powers granted to the position of secretary-treasurer in an attempt to render McDonald irrelevant. But Murray died before he could freeze McDonald out completely. Facing their first change of leadership since the union's founding, and with Dwight Eisenhower, a Republican and no friend to organized labor, heading to the White House, union members didn't want a protracted internal struggle. McDonald positioned himself as Murray's successor and won an easy election.

Soon union members began to have the same doubts about McDonald that Murray had had. The new president enjoyed a large expense account. People took to calling him Dapper Dave, a reference to his fancy clothes and to the large tabs he ran at Pittsburgh's swankiest restaurants. These seemed like odd choices for the public face of the steelworkers, a group that proudly associated itself with Joe Magarac, the hardscrabble folk hero who labored over vats of molten metal without a shirt. McDonald elevated his cronies to key positions in the union leadership. When a candidate came forward to oppose McDonald's choice for vice president of the union, thugs beat up the challenger's supporters and set fire to an empty campaign van. McDonald spearheaded an effort to give himself and other members of the executive council a ten-thousand-dollar raise while simultaneously calling for a vote to raise union dues from three dollars to five dollars per month, a nearly 70 percent bump. A sizable faction of the union's membership was livid, and many rank-and-file steelmen wondered whether McDonald had their interests at heart.

All of this had played out in the years leading up to April 1959. The major steel companies, which bargained as a group, had hired a new lead negotiator. R. Conrad Cooper, a former University of Minnesota football star and a serious-minded man, intended to change the way the industry did business with the powerful steel union. Cooper invited McDonald to a private meeting. The union's general contract was set to expire in July and McDonald assumed the meeting would be nothing more than an informal chat to open negotiations—a handshake before the big game. His relationship with the industry's previous negotiator, John Stephens, had been friendly, and he had no reason to suspect that would change with Cooper. But when McDonald walked into the room, the new adversary handed him a letter.

McDonald read it, and his eyes widened. "That's a hell of a way to start out," he barked. "These terms are ridiculous and you know it. They're a provocation, not a serious bargaining proposal, and I reject them out of hand."

Cooper was pressing for a wage freeze. He also called for an end to a cost-of-living program the union had won in 1956, one of the few feathers in McDonald's cap during his otherwise uneventful presidency. The industry's opening play, and Cooper's first move as lead negotiator, was a proposed rollback of the most significant benefits that the steelworkers had won since McDonald took over. The days of amicable backroom dealings were over.

The union's weak leadership was just one factor in the industry's decision to take a hard line. A year earlier, in 1958, a worldwide recession had rattled the nation. The U.S. economy soared after World War II. With Europe's industrial capabilities vastly diminished, the United States drove world manufacturing. At the same time, the Korean War, which boiled overseas from 1950 to 1953, kept the government in a war-spending mode that helped accelerate the economy. The good times seemed like they would go on forever, and steelworkers' wages, which rose from $0.66 per hour in 1940 to $2.24 per hour in 1959, reflected that belief.

By the mid-1950s, though, growth in the steel industry had begun to slow. New competition came from overseas as Europe rebuilt its factories and modernized its industrial manufacturing capabilities. Labor costs continued to rise. The economy in general was stagnant, and consumers of steel weren't buying so rapidly as they had during the boom years. The continued profitability of America's marquee industry now looked uncertain.

The economic slowdown presented the big steel companies with an opportunity. An imperiled economy could be an important lever in negotiations with labor. With the country paying close attention to economic news by the late 1950s, steel executives believed they could win a public relations battle against the union. Labor negotiations weren't immune from public pressure, especially when that pressure spurred government officials to action. President Truman had famously intervened in a labor dispute in 1952, taking the extraordinary measure of nationalizing the steel industry to prevent a strike that he believed would jeopardize the country's ability to fight the Korean War. The Supreme Court struck down Truman's move and the strike went forward as planned, but the incident underscored how deep a sitting president was willing to wade into industry disputes if public pressure gave him a reason. With wounds from the 1958 recession still fresh, and with the economy struggling to get back on track, the industry believed it could make the case that steelworkers—already the highest paid industrial workers in the country—ought to tighten their belts for the greater good. The straightforward logic, coupled with David McDonald's image as an extravagant playboy—Dapper Dave—would play well in newspapers. Negotiators began fashioning a strategy to roll back benefits *and* look patriotic.

After Cooper's ambush, McDonald convened the union's negotiating team. In early May, the Steel Coordinating Committee and the union negotiators, about 150 people in all, met at the Roosevelt Hotel in New York City. McDonald pleaded with his adversaries to keep negotiations out of the press. In response, industry representatives held a press conference later that day. Their intention to win over the public was clear.

McDonald, perhaps not fully appreciating the strength of management's resolve, complained about the sober mood clouding the next few days of meetings. He had enjoyed joking around at previous contract negotiations and saw no reason why these latest discussions had to be any different. At one point, R. Conrad Cooper read a statement that ridiculed all collective bargaining in the steel industry since World War II. McDonald asked Cooper if he thought Ben Fairless, former CEO of U.S. Steel, had been wrong when he negotiated with Philip Murray.

"Yes," he responded flatly.

McDonald deadpanned that it was the only time in the meeting that Cooper used the word.

Talks were deadlocked. If the union went on strike, the industry planned to bury it in the press. McDonald couldn't find any leverage, which boded poorly for the union's prospects during a protracted stoppage. Capitulation of some kind seemed increasingly likely. Then, out of the blue, Cooper and the industry negotiating team handed McDonald an issue. On June 10, just a few weeks before the general contract was set to expire, Cooper gave McDonald another letter.

The new set of industry demands took aim at one of the main pillars of union power. Section 2(b) of the general union contract regulated the industry's ability to reduce the number of workers assigned to specific tasks. The industry had an interest in mechanizing parts of the steelmaking process in order to reduce labor costs, but section 2(b), which the union considered critical to its cause of ensuring job stability for workers, made many of these changes difficult. Now the industry wanted to scrap some of these provisions. McDonald couldn't believe his good fortune. The union's own membership had been lethargic to that point, unconvinced that modest wage hikes were worth a long dreary fight. But the industry's new demands, with the threat they carried of a reduced workforce, would set the troops on fire. McDonald issued a press release:

"[The steel companies] are determined to destroy the individual rights so carefully and painstakingly developed over the years. . . . Our answer to this proposal is that the United Steelworkers of America is not a company union."

Word of the strike went out on July 14, 1959, and the mills were quiet the following day. Like all strikes, the stoppage seemed to change the flow of time in towns like Braddock. More than 500,000 steelworkers walked off the job, the largest mobilization of striking workers in U.S. history. America's economic momentum ground to a halt. With 90 percent of the country's steel production offline, industries like auto manufacturing, municipal construction, and the railroads— all massive consumers of steel—limped along. Many large manufacturers had stockpiled steel in anticipation of a disruption. The longer the stoppage wore on, though, the worse the country's economic outlook became.

As usual, the opening hours of the strike were thrilling. Steelmen around the country crowed over their headlines:

STEELWORKERS WIN STRIKE.

THOUSANDS OF GUARDS AT PLANTS BEING ARMED.

Workers waited for U.S. Steel's quick surrender, for the other companies to follow suit. That's how it had always gone in the past, and the union saw no reason why things would change. Days wore on, though, and good news didn't arrive. The mills sat quiet. The workers waited, and without salaries they began to grow uneasy. Summer's momentum stopped right along with the slab rollers and blast furnaces, as if the cycles of nature were linked inextricably with American production. With fall approaching, the stoppage already seemed years old. Families ate donated food out of cans. The union helped where it could, but there were only enough resources to intervene in the direst circumstances. Negotiators on both sides dug in their heels. Full-page ads in newspapers across the country took the fight to the public.

In Braddock, steelmen received their last paycheck on July 21. Every morning, unfinished newspapers tucked underarm, workers descended the long slope toward Braddock Avenue. Most of the men in the outlying neighborhoods—few women worked the mills—were middle-tiered workers. They were the sons of immigrants and had spent their lives earning their hillside perches. Their one- and two-story houses, brick and aluminum-faced, were well maintained. The homes were not big, but they were dignified, exuding a sense of achievement. In almost every case, the people who owned them had grown up in conditions less favorable. American flags luffed in the breeze. Banners and homemade signs, tokens of solidarity, hung in windows and on railings.

BACK YOUR UNION!

AMERICAN WORKERS UNITE!

STEEL STRIKE IS ON!

The bite of those words, which only weeks before had made men bristle, seemed diminished.

During the day, many striking workers slipped into bars to slowly sip whatever money they had left. Bartenders stopped extending credit after two weeks. Hunger was a serious concern, and so the Allegheny County Surplus Food Bureau began giving food to the strikers after thirty days. On the picket line, workers walked according to a carefully regulated schedule and everyone wore brave faces. Elsewhere in town, residents avoided looking at the broad blue siding of Edgar

Thomson. The mill had rarely been silent. It usually rumbled day and night, rumbled through the ground as workers started their shifts and rumbled in the air after quitting time. The din had become part of life, as familiar as any landmark. It was a constant, audible record of the town's past and a soothing assurance of its future. The mill's silence made Braddock feel strange, foreign even to those who had never lived elsewhere.

To boost morale, the Greater Braddock Chamber of Commerce undertook a campaign to beautify the town. The central corridor had become grimy. Half a century of soot had accumulated on many of the storefronts, caking the mortar between bricks and giving bright stonework a dusky unshaven look. A hodgepodge of neglected neon signs competed with old painted murals—whiskey, talc, shaving products—some of which were flaking badly enough to reveal older advertisements underneath. Shopkeepers had grown complacent. The town had a reputation as the region's premier shopping district, so why fight to lure customers? In some cases, even basic upkeep fell by the wayside.

The chamber named its initiative the "Battle for Braddock," a tired play on a bloody history. Harry Kipple, a local painter, became a visible victim of the campaign and an object of gentle ribbing in town. In accordance with the Chamber's master plan, the painter was hard at work slathering silver paint over every inch of every light post on Braddock Avenue. Silver now coated his coveralls and hands, and he'd drizzled large splotches of it onto his work boots. A big man with broad shoulders and a strong jaw, he looked cast out of steel. Impressionable children gawked up, believing him a TV villain.

The chamber's efforts attracted local business owners, who saw profit in town unity during the strike. Ladders went up all along Braddock Avenue as stores made Battle for Braddock improvements. An army of handymen and general laborers worked at the steel mills, and with the strike on, skilled labor was easy to find. Brick layers, responsible for lining the steel furnaces with heat-resistant masonry during steelmaking, repointed storefronts. Painters refreshed older work and unlicensed contractors made money doing odd jobs. The Paramount Theater, a Braddock Avenue icon, closed temporarily while workers refurbished the interior. Foot-tall letters on the marquee assured passersby that it would reopen promptly. But if the Battle for Braddock brought some lucky men an odd job or two, it was a temporary salve. The campaign did little or nothing for the vast majority of strikers, save offer them a chance to chuckle at poor Harry Kipple.

A new wooden sign on the edge of town, another project of the officious chamber, welcomed the team bus home. WELCOME TO BRADDOCK, VALLEY'S GREATEST SHOPPING CENTER. Tacked to the bottom of the sign, like a footnote authenticating Braddock's greatness, a strip of wood boasted: HOME OF THE FIVE YEAR W.P.I.A.L. CLASS A FOOTBALL CHAMPIONS. The strike had dampened spirits across town, but football season was just around the corner.

Chapter Four

OPENER

Braddock High, at a glance, looked like a modest castle. It wasn't big or opulent, but it had a medieval air. Perched on a concrete pedestal on a residential street halfway up Braddock's steep slope, built of regal brick, the school commanded respect. Its tall central tower stood poised between two squat, squarish flanks. Broad windows ran in precise lines over its face, and through some of these portals flitted nervous teachers preparing their classrooms. In lieu of a moat, the school's heavy front doors were framed in a thick concrete arch. Freshmen, dewy and vibrant, bunched near the narrow steps leading to the doors. Upperclassmen pooled on the gently graded street farther off, chatting and gazing interestedly at passing cars.

It was autumn, the first day of school. Students wore freshly ironed outfits—pleated skirts and tucked-in blouses for girls, collared shirts over slacks for boys. Few had new clothes to show off. The strike had put a halt to the sacred ritual of back-to-school shopping on Braddock Avenue. For younger siblings, the market for hand-me-downs was slim this year. Styles from the previous seasons were making their second and third debuts.

At least pomade was cheap; the strike had done nothing to diminish the care that students gave their hair. Except for some of the shop kids, whose greasy locks fell forward in a twirl down their foreheads, the boys wore their cuts short, shellacked, and tufted up in front like pristine hedgerows. A few of the black students wore their manicured waves in an "Ivy League"—a mound of undulating hair cresting in the forward third of the scalp and then tapering smoothly back. There was more variety among the girls, whose fragrant hairdos found corollaries in the styles of the brightest starlets: Elizabeth Taylor in *Cat on a Hot Tin Roof,* Kim Novak in *Vertigo,* Lana Turner in *Imitation of Life.* The most common cut featured short, forked bangs fronting an auburn waterfall that landed just above the neck and finished in a buoyant up-curl.

Joe Stukus, Braddock's principal, took his position at the top of the steps. He stood bolt upright like a military officer. He spoke softly, properly, addressing students by their last names. He wore delicate wire-framed glasses and had short, fair hair, which he had combed back exactingly. From his position, Stukus could survey the Mon Valley and the powerful river below. It was a lovely clear day. For Stukus, it was all the more lovely because classes were starting. He adored Braddock High, which over the years had become inextricable from his identity. Above his head, a new American flag listed in the gentle breeze. Hawaii had joined the union two and a half weeks earlier. Alaska had become a state only nine months before that.

At the bell, Stukus opened the main doors and students thronged up the steps. The principal greeted them as a host inviting guests for a tour. When boys began to shove or elbow, he metamorphosed back into a principal, barking orders to fall in line. He was a good principal, respected by the faculty and considered strict but fair by students. He gave no quarter to Klausing's football players, and if they slackened academically, which many of them invariably did, they risked not playing on Friday nights. He was no enemy of the team— Coach Klausing thought highly of him—but neither was he an unquestioning confederate.

Many of the students at Braddock High, and most of the football players, spent the balance of their school day away from the main building. While the ritual of new beginnings was playing out in front of the brick castle, similar proceedings were taking place far below at an auxiliary campus. Students at Braddock High elected one of three tracks: science, general academics, or vocational tech. The vocational track, which was designed to give students an education in skilled labor, such as auto repair, carpentry, or electrical engineering, accounted for the largest number of young men in town. Steel mills needed workers, not philosophers. Most sons followed their fathers to Edgar Thomson after graduation. The foremen gave young men with advanced manual skills the best jobs, and it was never too early to start training.

Braddock Junior High, located in the flat part of town south of Braddock Avenue, doubled as the vocational tech school. From the high school building, where students attended core academic classes, vocational tech students walked down the hill, across a set of train tracks and a trolley line, to the other side of Braddock Avenue. There they started the real work of the day. The junior high building was enormous, an angular brick hulk large enough to house all of Braddock's sixth, seventh, and eighth graders, as well as close to two hundred vocational students from the senior high. It took up half a city block, and vocational tech classes made up the entire first floor.

The closest corollary to Joe Stukus in vocational tech was Al Burton. A popular teacher, Burton taught woodshop, mechanical drawing, and mathematics. He was an ex-navy man and had served as a gunner's mate first class in World War II. Every student in vocational tech knew of his navy background, and they all respected it. During the Normandy invasion, Burton's unit made four successful trips in their landing craft to deliver troops and equipment to the beachhead. On the fifth trip, they ran afoul of an acoustic mine. The explosion tore through the back end of the vessel. Twenty-seven soldiers and ten sailors were killed, but the LST stayed afloat. It had been built in the Dravo Shipyard in Pittsburgh from Western Pennsylvania steel.

Burton was a great friend to the football team, and a great resource. A few seasons earlier, Klausing and Zuger turned to Burton to solve a problem that had nagged football coaches since fans first started watching the game from bleachers. On Friday nights, Zuger sat up in the press box—the extravagant name given to the top row of bleachers at most schools. He kept careful track of opponents' sets, looking for areas of weakness. During the game he communicated with Klausing through a series of hand signals. But the information he could pass on was extremely limited. The two spoke at halftime, poring over Zuger's notes so they could exploit weaknesses in the opposing team's offensive and defensive sets. But rival coaches had lookouts in the stands, too, and usually managed to fix the most obvious problems. If Klausing and Zuger could work out some way to communicate during the game, the Tigers could gain a tremendous advantage.

Zuger brought the idea of a phone system to Klausing, but the head coach was skeptical. College and professional teams had phones, but it was unheard of in high school; premade systems were prohibitively expensive. So Zuger went to Al Burton with a challenge. Burton drew out plans for the coils and connections on drafting paper. Then he scoured for parts. He borrowed two handsets from rotary telephones and rigged a length of wire in a large spool. He designed a crank to supply the power needed to send the signal through about a hundred yards of line.

When Burton finished the contraption, Zuger took it to Klausing. They set it up between two classrooms and Zuger called out a formation in a normal speaking voice. Across the hall, Klausing's head shot up. "John, I hear you loud and clear!" he exclaimed, his own voice zipping back to his assistant. Not since Thomas Edison telephoned Watson had anyone been so impressed with a simple phone call.

While functional, the system was unwieldy at first. Burton worked to streamline his design. He constructed an eighteen-inch wooden box to hold all the components. Before every game, home or away, Zuger unspooled the telephone line in a long path from the sideline to the top of the bleachers, taping the wire to the ground as he went so it wouldn't come loose. The coaches spoke regularly during the games, comparing observations and adjusting sets to take advantage of their opponents' soft spots. Zuger often told Klausing when defenders were lax in their coverage, backpedaling prematurely or standing flatfooted. Klausing would signal a pass play, and a moment later Zuger would watch a surprised defender sprinting to recover. It was football orchestrated with scientific precision.

Braddock fans got a particular kick out of watching their coach talk on the phone. A joke began to circulate: Klausing was so thorough in preparing his team that he used Friday evenings to catch up with old friends. Players liked to joke about the phone system, too. Once, when an opposing player asked Roland Mudd what the phone was all about, the 220-pound Tigers tackle responded, "Coach is on the line with Knute Rockne. They're laughing their butts off about how weak the competition is this year!"

The Tigers had a rare bye the first week of the season. They would play Homestead High in week two, which gave them extra time to prepare. It also gave Klausing an extra week to fret over substitutions and game planning. In his basement office, under a bare lightbulb, he scanned the notes he'd made on his roster sheet. The starting offensive lineup was locked. Dan O'Shea would start at center. It was the position Klausing had played in college, and the one he scrutinized more closely than any other, except for quarterback. O'Shea was a junior but already a leader and a mentor to sophomores like

Jim Clark, his backup. If Jacobs, the quarterback, was a team's flash, its public face, Klausing believed that the center was its soul. O'Shea, quiet, determined, fit the bill.

Vernon Stanfield and Ray Grudowski were the Tigers' lean, mean guards. Grudowski was the senior class president, a sharp white boy with a stiff forearm, which he often rammed into opposing players' jugulars. Stanfield was tall and sinewy, with slender piano-player's fingers. His mother almost hadn't let him play football for fear that he'd ruin his music career. Fortunately for the Tigers, she'd relented. They weren't the biggest guards, but Grudowski and Stanfield played like bears on the line.

Chubby John Plisco would anchor the offensive front as right tackle, with Roland Mudd, a shit-talker second only to Doughboy, on the opposite side. Ray Henderson, the brute blocker who set bowling pins to help his family make ends meet, would start on the right end. Klausing knew Henderson wanted to catch the ball this year. He'd have to prove himself, though, and he'd have plenty of competition from Alvin "Elbow" Smith, the sure-handed left end.

Klausing had the best backfield playing high school Wing T football in the nation. Gay and Powell would start as halfbacks, with Curtis Vick at fullback.

Defense largely mirrored the offense, though it was subject to week-to-week substitutions to match the strengths of the opposing team's offense. The front four never changed, though; the offensive guards and tackles also formed the defensive line. Klausing worried about their size. Averaging just 190 pounds, they'd be vulnerable to the running game of a larger opponent. The linemen would be working Big Bertha, the seven-man driving sled, during every practice to prepare. There wasn't a team on the Tigers schedule whose line they could outmatch on paper.

Klausing was happy with his starting lineup, but he still felt uneasy. He was usually nervous in the days before an opener, but this year was worse. His mind darted uncomfortably to the record. That wasn't his style. He taught his players to focus on the minutiae of each play, on their footwork, on executing the precise motions and subtle feints he drew up. If they could do the little things perfectly, everything else—the scoring, the winning—would take care of itself. It was dangerous to focus on the big picture. It cost you discipline.

At the bell for the next period, clasping a driver's-training manual, Klausing left his subterranean office and set out for the small alleyway beside the school. He had started out teaching vocational math at Braddock High when he first arrived in 1954. He'd always been good with figures and didn't mind the material, but the course required plenty of pre-class planning. He would sit at his kitchen table writing up lessons at night, copying exercises out of books. He did this diligently, working each problem until he came up with at least two ways to explain the answer. It was a great help to his students, but his nightly preparation, combined with the time it took him to grade and solicitously comment on papers, took precious time from football.

Neil Brown, Klausing's mentor, had once told him that driver's training was the ideal course for a football coach. It required no forethought and little administrative work outside of class. And the job came with a perk: unconditional use of the school car, which could be used during prep periods to run tape to the lab or pick up equipment. Klausing had used the car to take his assistant coaches out to watch local football games. Coach Zuger had even gotten a speeding ticket in it after Klausing let him drive back from a University of Pittsburgh football a season earlier.

A politically connected teacher had been teaching driver's training when Klausing came to Braddock. Coveted faculty positions were usually granted on the basis of favoritism, rather than merit or teaching talent. Fortunately for Klausing, coaching a winning football team gave him a trump card over any political lackey. After the Tigers' first-ever undefeated season in Klausing's first year, he went to Mike Sullivan, the president of the school board, and asked for the driver's-training job. Sullivan, elated after the school's first WPIAL title, sent the other man down to vocational tech. When he asked just what in the hell he'd done wrong, Sullivan narrowed his eye and told him that Braddock High needed his prodigious talents elsewhere. Wisely, the man didn't protest further.

Klausing walked over to the driver's-training car to wait for his first group. He taught four students every hour. He enjoyed teaching the course, even if it didn't have the same scholastic weight as math or science. The kids were always enthusiastic, often nervous, and he liked helping them find confidence behind the wheel. Former students frequently came by to show off new licenses, and they often mentioned how breezy the driving test had been, as though they'd done it all before. In fact, they had.

In Braddock, a state policeman administered the driving test. When Klausing landed the driver's-training job, the first thing he did was buy a box of cigars for the officer, whom he also invited out to lunch. Klausing didn't drink—he'd tried a glass of whiskey when he was sixteen and it turned his stomach—but he didn't mind buying a few rounds for a new friend, either. He set the policeman up with one whiskey on top of another, which the man downed casually, despite being in uniform. After the lawman was good and loose, Klausing confessed that he didn't know much about driver's training. He wanted to give his kids the best possible instruction, of course, but he worried he wouldn't teach the proper skills.

Rosy-cheeked and glowing, the policeman slapped him on the back. "Don't worry, I'll show you everything!" he said.

They made a plan to meet at the school the following day. The policeman took Klausing through every stage of the driving test, from parallel parking to unprotected left-hand turns. He even showed him the exact route he used through town. Klausing based his lesson plan on the demonstration. Not a single student who took his driver's-training class had ever failed the test. A few, when they mentioned who their teacher was, had been given second and third chances.

"Your teacher is a helluva nice guy," the policeman would say, his evaluation notebook closed on his lap.

Klausing liked watching young people growing up and finding themselves. Sometimes he ran into old students in unexpected places, and it was always a treat to see how they were making out. This had happened once in 1956, on an outing to Forbes Field to see the Pittsburgh Pirates baseball team play. Klausing had stopped by the team's administrative offices to pick up a pair of complimentary tickets that a Braddock fan had arranged for him. When he got to the front desk, he was delighted to find a young woman from Braddock High working as a secretary.

"Milene, you're the luckiest person in the world," Klausing said when he saw his old student. "You're going to marry one of these baseball players."

"Fat chance," Milene said. "There are twenty-three players. Twenty-one of them are married, and two are Roberto Clemente and Román Mejías!"

Clemente was from Puerto Rico and Mejías was from Cuba, and neither man spoke great English. A few months later, a young player named Bill Mazeroski got called up from the minors. Milene and Bill began flirting, and before long they were wed. "You're the guy who predicted this," the Pirates' second baseman told Klausing whenever they ran into each other. If he wasn't already getting more free tickets than he could use from well-connected Tigers fans, Klausing would have been set for life after befriending Maz.

The first day of school meant a new crop of driver's-training students. When they arrived, all nerves and eagerness, Klausing introduced himself. The students knew who he was. Between the newspaper articles and the frequent banquets in his honor, he had become the most recognizable man in Braddock. But the coach didn't seem capable of playing the celebrity.

"My name is Mr. Klausing," he said with no trace of a wink, "and this is driver's training."

He led the group of would-be drivers around the car, pointing out relevant safety features. He joked with them about being able to go on dates at drive-ins soon, and then answered questions about the football team's outlook for the season, which seemed to interest everyone far more than the high beams on the high school's Plymouth.

"The boys are looking good," Klausing said in response. "It'll be a tough season, but I think we'll do okay."

It was the same thing he always said. He used the line a hundred times every day during football season, and twice that before matchups with North Braddock Scott.

At lunch, Klausing walked down to meet with his assistants, Bob Teitt, Harry Carr, and John Zuger, who all taught at the junior high building. The coaches met in John Zuger's art room. It was the most interesting classroom in Braddock, full of clay sculptures, still life paintings, and rough sketches of the human form. Loose squares of tile sat in a box to one side of Zuger's desk, the raw ingredients for a mosaic he planned to install in the high school gymnasium. He was a born artist, though he had the body and disposition of a football player.

Zuger had discovered art in first grade when his teacher, a nun at St. Mary's Magdalene primary school in Homestead, gave her class a sculpting assignment. While his classmates were fashioning trains careening off the tracks, Zuger loved Native American lore and sculpted an Indian on a horse. His teacher gushed over it. She displayed it in the window and pointed it out whenever visitors came to the classroom. Though the threshold for impressing the nun was admittedly low, the boy's talent was undeniable.

While his teachers encouraged his budding artistic side, Zuger's family wasn't nearly so supportive. Soon after sculpting the Indian on the horse, he made a model biplane using broom handles and scraps of wood.

When he finished, his uncle offered a gentle critique: "It looks like a piece of shit. What is that, a telegraph pole?"

That's when he learned that artists needed thick hides in Western Pennsylvania.

Zuger grew up in Homestead, which lent the Tigers' opening matchup added significance. His younger brother, Joe, had graduated from Homestead High only a year earlier. Joe had been recruited by Arizona State University's Frank Kush, a McKeesport native who often returned to Western Pennsylvania to find gridiron talent. Now the younger Zuger was starting at Arizona State alongside former Braddock star Larry Reaves. Zuger had enjoyed watching the Tigers crush his little brother's team in years past. In the spirit of brotherly love, he'd always said the same thing to his Braddock players in the locker room before the game: "Find number nine. His name is Zuger. I want you to flatten his ass."

This year, with Joe off at college, Zuger hadn't felt fired up in the same way—that is until he walked into a restaurant in Homestead earlier that week and had come across a group of locals who recognized him.

"Hey, Zuger!" one of them yelled. "You know why you're still undefeated? Because you recruit boys from other schools and you got all them niggers playing for you!"

Red faced, Zuger walked out. Now he had new motivation to beat the snot out of his old high school squad. He'd get his revenge on the field.

Braddock's four coaches sat around a table in the middle of the art room and opened their sack lunches. Joann had packed Klausing a tuna salad sandwich, which he unwrapped carefully and laid out on the crumpled wax paper. Food served at the high school cafeteria was reliably inedible. Workers there seemed to be in league against the better tastes of the students, who had grown up with hearty home cooking. The cafeteria served gray meat a dozen ways, soggy potatoes, and baked beans that seemed incapable of retaining a degree of warmth.

With the strike on, a greater number of students were relying on that slop, which was cheap. The odd boy who came to school with a chipped ham sandwich, a regional delicacy made from thin pieces of moist pork piled on a fat roll, could extract a healthy profit in books carried and homework completed.

The coaches ate and talked between mouthfuls of food. Over the years, assistants who served under Klausing had grown accustomed to his Socratic approach. On the field, in front of the players, the assistants never questioned anything their boss said or did. In private, to the uninitiated, it would be difficult during the course of a typical exchange to figure out who the head coach was. At summer camp a few years earlier, in the free period after lunch, Klausing and his backfield coaches had spent the better part of an hour debating the angle a halfback should take on a particular backfield block.

"Chuck!" Zuger had practically yelled across the table, forgetting himself in the heat of the exchange. "The first principle of blocking is to stay between the man and the ball! Well, this new angle doesn't hurt a thing, and look at the flexibility it gives us! We can keep him in the play!"

Most head coaches wouldn't permit that kind of open resistance, but Klausing encouraged it. With this latitude to think and speak freely, Klausing's assistants solved problems that may otherwise have gone unaddressed. Early in the 1958 season, the coaches had fretted over Melvin Coburn, a skilled athlete who just didn't seem capable of grasping the Tigers' system. When he went in at running back, Coburn rarely hit the right gaps. Blocking schemes didn't work unless the runner got to his mark at precisely the right moment. As often as not, Coburn ran to the wrong side entirely.

To indicate where a ball carrier should run on a given play, the Tigers numbered the gaps using a simple convention. Starting with the center and working right, the gaps were numbered 2, 4, 6, and 8—with 8 indicating a run to the outside of the offensive end. On the opposite side, starting to the left of the center, the gaps were numbered 1, 3, 5, and 7. Running backs also got a number. If a left halfback was a "20-back," then a play call of "26" would be a left half-back run off the right tackle. But Coburn had trouble with numbers, which assistant Bob Teitt soon realized. He noticed that the boy had to count slowly from both directions before each play.

So Teitt came up with a new play calling convention that used letters instead of numbers. He and Zuger presented the idea to Klausing, who had just about given up on Coburn. The head coach gave them the go-ahead to try the new system, and to everyone's amazement, the boy understood the letter structure like he'd been using it for years.

In the art room, Klausing began with a simple question: "What are Homestead's strengths?"

It would have been a good time for a joke, but none of the coaches dared make one. No one wanted to risk taking a team lightly—even a team like Homestead—only to see the magical streak come to an unexpected end. Success hadn't made the Tigers coaches overconfident. If anything, the streak had the opposite effect.

The Tigers had clobbered Homestead 31–7 the previous season, in spite of the fact that Jim Hux, the outstanding senior offensive end, had been out with a painful hip pointer. Ray "Butch" Henderson, then a junior, had filled in for Hux, and it was largely on the strength of that performance that Klausing had confidence in the tough-as-nails kid in the coming season. Butch had played strong on the line and even managed to catch a long pass for a touchdown, a rarity—he was notorious for dropping the ball. The Tigers' ground game had picked apart Homestead's defense, with Ben Powell earning 115 yards on eleven attempts. By the final quarter, leading 31–0, Klausing had put in the reserves. Homestead's lone touchdown came on a plodding ten-yard run from a boy named Pudgy Dent. Braddock's home crowd considered the score a fair trade-off. It was a treat to hear the player's odd name broadcast over the PA system.

The coaches traded all the information they had about Homestead's players. With a bye the first week, Klausing planned to attend

Homestead's opener on Friday. For the Tigers, the biggest concern was still Jacobs's back. Ron Davis, the backup quarterback, was a standout pitcher on the Braddock High baseball team, but he wasn't a natural football player and hadn't been at all comfortable in the pocket at summer camp. Baseball pitchers were like Zen monks, Klausing believed. They meditated on the mound, maintained a single-minded focus. Quarterbacks were more like cavalry soldiers, splitting their attention a dozen ways while keeping their eyes downfield. Davis got sacked in scrimmages as often as he managed to complete passes. He was so focused on the throw that he missed the blitz man diving at his knees.

Mark Rutkowski had been an exception to Klausing's belief that baseball pitchers didn't make natural quarterbacks. Rutkowski had been a standout pitcher and an All-State passer. He'd been a tremendous student on top of it, a gifted young man with enormous promise. The former Tigers quarterback had left town on a bus a few days earlier. Dartmouth was honoring its offer, Klausing had been relieved to find out. Rutkwoski's knee was still a mess, but at least he'd be on scholarship while he tried to recover.

The rest of the school day unfolded quickly. Curtis Vick and Doughboy had study hall with Miss Rita McGinley, an ever-smiling forty-year-old teacher who'd made a specialty of tutoring football players. Her family owned 42 percent of the Pittsburgh Steelers, which made the task easier for her. In exchange for a solid twenty minutes of English composition, McGinley would feed players a few tidbits of franchise gossip. In 1956, after a beloved Steelers rookie named Lowell Perry suffered a career-ending injury in a game, McGinley was able to give her Braddock High pupils a piece of encouraging news: The Steelers would be hiring Perry as an ends coach, making him the first black assistant in the NFL. With Principal Stukus checking grades for every athlete, McGinley's contribution to the team was enormous. She had helped keep the roster full, and had been a stalwart supporter of the Tigers at booster events and fund-raising functions.

When school let out, the Tigers trooped to the locker room. They dressed in pads and practice jerseys, but wore street shoes and carried their spikes out of the basement. They walked down the front steps of Braddock High, where a hundred or so students still milled out front, comparing summer stories and first impressions of new teachers. The Tigers traveled in a loose formation, and as they approached, all swagger and silence, the other students stepped aside. For sophomores like backup defensive end Phil Lucarelli, backup center Jim Clark, and Kenny Reaves, the third string quarterback, the moment was unforgettable. It was the first time the sophomores had worn varsity red in front of their peers. Even as they nodded to lifelong friends, they felt special, handpicked.

The Tigers walked to Library Street, which intersected with Braddock Avenue farther down the hill to form the de facto center of town. Library Street was home to the elaborate Carnegie Library, the first of more than 1,600 libraries that Andrew Carnegie built in the United States. Replete with a swimming pool, a steam room, and a full gymnasium, it was Braddock's crown jewel, as much a recreation center as a place to check out books.

The Tigers turned left on Library Street, higher up the steep bank. At the northern edge of town, the players walked under the train tracks of the Pennsylvania Railroad. Grime and car exhaust had turned the inside of the damp overpass coal black. It was an unbreakable rule for the Tigers that players could never cross above the tracks. Trains zipped through at all hours, and every few years someone in the region died from a careless accident. Klausing threatened to bench any player he caught scampering up the bank near school instead of walking the few blocks to the cut-through. That hadn't stopped players from sneaking up on warm summer nights to stud the tracks with pennies, which would be flattened like pancakes by passing trains, but someone always kept a vigilant eye for Braddock coaches.

The team emerged from the short tunnel in North Braddock. Here Library Street became Jones Avenue. North Braddock didn't have a Carnegie Library, which was one more reason the town hated its southern neighbor. Edgar Thomson Field lay a block up on the left. The players groaned inwardly when they came within sight of it. Its dusty, cinder-strewn surface would soon exfoliate all the pleasant grass stains they had accumulated at Waynesburg College. Scott Field sat off to the right, a sunken field that looked like the excavated footprint of a huge building. The Tigers could see the North Braddock Scott players filing down from their own school to their first regular-season practice. The players on each team gazed at each other. At a distance of a few hundred yards, the Tigers couldn't see their rivals' expressions. They suspected, though, that the North Braddock players were scowling. The previous year's 9–6 loss still stung.

Dan Rice, Braddock's faculty manager, fell into step beside Klausing, who was trailing his team up the hill. "How they looking this year, Chuck?" Rice asked.

Klausing picked up notes of alcohol on the man's breath. Rice had a reputation as a drinker. He sometimes took long, wet lunches before afternoon classes.

"Looking good," Klausing said in his trademark way. "It'll be a tough season, but I think we'll do okay."

Dan Rice was a legend among Braddock High students. He was an easy grader and a spot in one of his gym classes was highly coveted. Once, when John Zuger complained about all the administrative work that went into teaching—the grading, the attendance—Rice had demonstrated his tried-and-true method for handling annoying paperwork. He took the grade sheet, penciled *A* at the top, and drew a line down the column beside his students' names.

Rice was an immaculate dresser. He and his wife owned a dry cleaning business on Braddock Avenue. People joked that Rice liked to help himself to the finest clothes. When he taught gym, Rice never put on a school athletic uniform. He stretched himself out on the bleachers in a double-breasted suit, crossed his legs, and called out drills to his students. Sometimes he didn't even do that much, and instead sat back reading the paper, his eyelids growing heavy from his liquid lunch.

During WWII, when male teachers were in short supply, Rice had stepped in as Braddock's football coach. His career win–loss record was an unimpressive 14–22, but his drunken shenanigans—and he *always* seemed to be drunk—had given the fans something to talk about.

In 1944, Rice's Tigers had played an away game in the town of Altoona, due east of Pittsburgh. When they arrived in the town, Rice picked up a six-hundred-dollar guarantee check from Altoona High. Visiting teams typically received financial reimbursement from home teams—a guarantee—which represented some portion of the ticket sales. Dan cashed the check and gave his players a few dollars for lunch before the game. Then he went to a bar and got smashed. Soon he was bragging all over town that his Tigers were unstoppable, a claim the team's record at the time didn't exactly bear out. A few loyal Altoona fans took up a collection. They raised five hundred dollars and staked it all on the outcome of the afternoon's matchup. Rice, his pockets bulging with the guarantee money, accepted the bet on the spot. Altoona's police chief held on to the dough in case the tipsy coach came to his senses.

When he realized what he'd done, Rice panicked. So he ran into a bar and drank some more. Back at the field, the Tigers warmed up without their coach. When game time came, the head referee told the players he couldn't wait any longer. Braddock's captain, a boy named Stan Zajdel, called the coin toss and lost. Altoona received the opening kickoff and returned it for a touchdown. Amid the crowd's loud cheering, a drunken Dan Rice appeared out of nowhere and sprinted onto the field. He claimed the touchdown didn't count, insisting that each team had to have its coach present before a game could begin. The referee, who had never heard of any such rule, told him to take his seat. Rice went nuts, running around like a banshee. His players had to restrain him physically, with a few of the bigger linemen sitting on top of him until he cooled off. Fortunately, fullback Bob Sandidge came through with a pair of touchdowns to save the day. The Tigers won 19–7, and the coach got to keep his job—and the five hundred bucks.

Rice walked into North Braddock beside Klausing. "How's Jacobs looking?" he asked.

"Fine," Klausing said. "He'll be ready."

"I think I'll just watch a bit of practice, if that's all right."

Though he had administrative responsibilities pertaining to the entire Braddock High faculty, Rice had confined the scope of his duties as faculty manager to the athletic department. He was the school's self-appointed athletic director and a staunch booster for the Tigers. As far as Klausing was concerned, this important ally was welcome at practice anytime he liked.

The Tigers worked hard during the bye week. The practices felt more like an extension of summer workouts than the first week of the regular season. Players pushed the sleds up and down the field, driving Big Bertha hundreds of yards over the cinders and clumps of dried grass. During water breaks they slurped from a ladle that they dipped in a zinc bucket, crowding around and gasping for air. Klausing always left enough time for the sophomores, who drank last, to quench their thirst. The weather was turning, but the afternoons were still hot. Unlike many coaches across the country, who believed frequent water breaks made their players soft, Klausing insisted on keeping his boys hydrated.

On Friday afternoon, the four Braddock coaches drove out to Homestead to scout their opponent. They arrived to the game late, just before the opening kickoff. Homestead's stadium was completely full. Fans were standing two- and three-deep in the bleachers, exhilarated at the start of the season. More than five thousand were in attendance, and it was a sure bet that no one in the crowd would be eager to help the Braddock coaches find seats. The matchup against the Tigers the following week was the most important on Homestead's schedule. The same was true for every team the Tigers played. Wherever Klausing and the other coaches went, they were marked men.

"Should we call it a night?" Bob Teitt asked.

Harry Carr, the diminutive assistant who had trained to be a priest, specialized in scouting Braddock's opponents. He knew every inch of every stadium in Western Pennsylvania.

"I know what to do," Carr said.

He led the coaches to the far side of the bleachers, where the band had set up. One row had been left empty directly in front of the horn section. The band would certainly blow the eardrums off anyone foolish enough to sit there.

"It never fails," Carr said.

The coaches took their seats and Klausing looked back just in time to meet the eyes of the bandleader, who was shocked to see the four of them settling in. Klausing raised his hands, almost apologetically, and the band exploded into action for the opening kickoff. The four coaches covered their ears. It was a noisy game, but they had a perfect view of the field.

Over the following week of practice, the Tigers prepared for Homestead's run-based offense. Braddock's line was considerably smaller than it had been in years past, and they'd be playing bigger opponents all season. That meant they'd need exacting technique, superhuman tenacity, for sixty minutes every week. On offense, Klausing planned to utilize the quarterback option more than he had in the past. With Jacobs's foot speed, the option play was now a potent weapon in Braddock's arsenal. Jacobs's back seemed to hold up, which was a relief. The stretching exercises Klausing and Zuger had come up with in consultation with the team's physician, Dr. Shapiro, seemed to have helped.

Ray Henderson, the offensive end replacing Jim Hux, still couldn't catch a pass reliably. He made up for it by being a beast on the line. Big Bertha had been veering to one side whenever Henderson was part of the hitting group. Eventually the coaches put him in the middle spot to keep the sled on course. The boy was mean and muscular, and he played like he had something to prove. Klausing liked that.

Curtis Vick, the standout junior fullback, was getting better with every snap, much to Doughboy's consternation. The reform school parolee could be unexpectedly sensitive when he felt underappreciated. The previous season, trailing Midland 7–2 with just a few minutes to play, the Tigers got the ball on their own 20. Doughboy had run brilliantly all game, though the Tigers hadn't been able to capitalize with a touchdown. With one shot left, Doughboy went to work. Play after play, the powerful back drove off tackle. For seventy-eight yards, he was the Tigers' sole offensive gainer. Then, from the 2-yard line, with the end zone under his nose, he went three downs without moving the ball an inch. Klausing called the fourth down play to Ben Powell, who danced in for an easy touchdown. Doughboy threw off his helmet, his eyes filling with tears. It was a telling display of vulnerability from a troubled kid with a criminal past.

This season, he had wasted no time targeting Vick, whom he saw as a threat to his offensive production. "Coach got you running against the soft defense. He's trying to build your confidence. You know I'm getting the calls this season, right?"

The coaches had done their job and the team was as prepared for the start of the season as they'd ever be. In the pep rally in the school gym on Friday afternoon, Klausing thanked the student body for their support and loyalty. Then he introduced the 1959 Tigers football team. The cheerleaders flashed their pompoms and the band let loose a loud brass exclamation. It was game day in Western Pennsylvania.

The bus ride to Homestead took less than ten minutes. A caravan of cars trailed the team across the river in the late afternoon. There was at least one advantage to the strike: You didn't have to bribe someone to cover your shift on game day.

The area outside the Homestead Stadium was clogged with fans. If the bleachers had been full during Homestead's opener a week earlier, they'd be standing in the aisles tonight. All Braddock's dignitaries were well dressed. Larry Reardon, the superintendent of schools at Braddock, chatted with Bill Campbell, his counterpart from Homestead. The two were close friends, and the matchup gave them an opportunity to prod and chide one another. Reardon had been doing his fair share of the chiding lately—five straight undefeated seasons made it easy—though that still didn't temper the brashness with which Campbell predicted an easy victory for Homestead.

Mike Sullivan, the president of the Braddock School Board, and Dan Rice showed up with their wives. The elegant, tipsy foursome cut a swath through the fans mingling before the game. Braddock High games were tailor-made for schmoozing and politics. When they finally took their seats in the bleachers, Sullivan left his wife to glad-hand supporters. He was careful to mention that he was the one who had brought Chuck Klausing to Braddock. Hiring the coach was the best political maneuver Sullivan had ever made, and his grip on power grew stronger with each game the Tigers won.

The Braddock players followed their coach into the visiting team's locker room. They had done a massive review the day before, outlining in chalk every play they expected to see on defense, every set that Homestead might run on offense. The first plays of the game had been carefully scripted, rehearsed in the gym at Braddock High to avoid spying eyes, and committed to memory.

Players sat on the benches in the locker room. The pregame meal, which they'd eaten at the Elks Lodge in Braddock earlier that afternoon, sat unsteadily in their nervous stomachs. Doughboy stood from the bench and walked the length of the locker room, and then took his seat, only to stand again and repeat the trip. He looked like a junkyard dog on patrol. John Jacobs tapped the heels of his cleats in a quick jitter step.

Klausing had never been one for grand speeches. Standing before his players, he reminded them that they had one job to do: Execute what they'd practiced. When he finished, the assistants said a few words about position assignments. Then Klausing told the players to take a knee. Out loud they prayed for a safe game. Privately, each Tiger prayed for victory. When the prayer was over, Klausing ordered his boys out of the locker room. The players smacked the cinder block wall on their way out.

The din of the pregame crowd grew as the boys rounded the bleachers and took the field. Because of the proximity of the two towns, the crowd was evenly split between Homestead fans and Braddock fans. Klausing walked out behind his boys. As he stepped across the field, he spotted his father in the stands. Joann was seated just below with her brother. When they locked eyes, Klausing gave a small nod to his wife. This was his private cheering section.

Homestead came out to a roaring home crowd. The noise didn't abate as both teams warmed up. It was football season in Western Pennsylvania, and for Homestead, this game against Braddock may as well have been the championship. Whoever felled the mighty Tigers could lose every other game of the season and still hold their heads high. After warm-ups, both teams took their positions on the sidelines. Klausing could feel his players' anxiousness as the captains walked out to midfield. He was anxious, too, even if he hid it well beneath his Notre Dame cap. The referee flipped the coin and Jacobs called heads. The Tigers won the toss and elected to receive the kickoff. Klausing called for his starters. The game was on.

Homestead's band opened up with the same horns that had rocked the Braddock coaches a week earlier. The kickoff was low, a short knuckle ball that rolled across the grass. Vick ran up and fell on the ball at the Tigers' 45-yard line. As John Jacobs took the field, the Braddock faithful in the stands screamed unrestrainedly. The Homestead cheerleaders responded with a loud cheer that brought Homestead's fans to their feet.

Mark Rutkowski had always looked methodical appraising the defense—efficient, with no wasted movement or drawn-out counts. Jacobs was a stark contrast. He took his time, making wide sweeps with his head, soaking up the moment. Long-limbed, bouncing lightly, as if unable to contain his pent-up eagerness, he gave the impression of smirking behind the single bar of his face mask.

O'Shea snapped the ball and Jacobs spun out to the left. It was an option, with Ben Powell trailing. A Homestead lineman met Jacobs near scrimmage. The quarterback juked but changed his mind at the last second. He turned to flick the ball to Powell, but the Homestead defender was too quick. Jacobs went down for a gain of just one yard.

On the next play, Jacobs dropped back and looked downfield. Ray Henderson, the Tigers offensive end, sprinted up the left seam and Jacobs unloaded. The ball was well thrown, an arcing spiral that met Henderson in stride. It would have been a touchdown if he'd hauled it in, but the ball thudded off the blocking end's clumsy hands and landed incomplete.

Klausing didn't want Henderson to get discouraged. The end had inconsistent enough hands on his best day, and if he lost confidence, he'd be utterly useless in the passing game. Uncharacteristically, the coach called another pass play, overriding the opening series his players had rehearsed. O'Shea snapped the ball to Jacobs after another slow count, and Henderson ran a buttonhook, an eight-yard sprint capped with a quick curl. Jacobs, tracking him the whole way, delivered the ball at the turn. Henderson held on, catching the pass just beyond the 50-yard line. Two defenders had angles on him and

heaved themselves at his waist. But Henderson, a tree trunk of muscle and solid thighs, absorbed the hits and managed to free his legs
from a tangle of arms and shoulder pads. It was an open field after
that. With Homestead's defenders on his tail, Henderson sprinted
to the end zone for a fifty-four-yard touchdown. It was exactly the
opening drive Klausing had wanted.

But Braddock couldn't relax for long. Homestead's backs looked
strong on the next series, bursting through the Tigers defensive line.
Klausing had been nervous about the size of his front line, which
averaged just 190 pounds, and now they were getting pushed around
by Homestead's blockers. On the opening three plays of Homestead's
series, three separate running backs ran for long yards, advancing the
ball all the way to the Tigers' 10. On the next play, Vernon Stanfield,
the senior lineman, shot through the line and pounced on Homestead's quarterback, Spencer Rice, for a loss. Backed up to the 21,
Homestead couldn't gain any more traction. They lost yards on the
next two plays. Field goal attempts were sufficiently rare—and sufficiently low-percentage—that Homestead opted to go for it on fourth
down. They came up empty and turned the ball over on downs.

Both teams were quiet for the remainder of the first quarter, but
it was all Jacobs in the second. The senior quarterback had phenomenal speed and ran end run options to perfection. With a dump-off
man trailing, he juked and jived for easy five- and ten-yard gains. On
the second series of the quarter, he broke through for eleven yards
before lateraling to Ben Powell, who ran for twelve more. Two plays
later, Doughboy caught a short pass and went twenty-three yards for
a touchdown to cap a seventy-nine-yard drive. Roland Mudd made
up for his missed extra point after the first touchdown, and Braddock
led 13–0.

It was a massacre from then on. Jacobs leapt over the goal line on
a quarterback keeper to end the first Tigers' drive of the second half.
Powell scored on a forty-yard run soon after, and Klausing, content
with the 27–0 lead, took most of his starters out. Backup Ronnie

Davis took over at quarterback. Baseball player or no, he promptly led the Tigers downfield fifty-one yards on eight plays for another score. Homestead fumbled the kickoff, and Braddock scored again three plays later off a forty-yard draw play to backup Tony Thompson.

The Tigers won 47–0. It was their forty-seventh game without a loss. Even as they were walking out of the stadium, conspiracy-minded Homestead fans charged Klausing with orchestrating the coincidental result, running up the score for the simple symmetry of it. It was a preposterous accusation—Klausing had taken his starters out in the third quarter—but Homestead fans needed a salve to take the sting out of their awful defeat.

In all, the Tigers accrued 283 yards rushing and 191 yards passing, extravagant totals for a high school game. Jacobs completed six out of seven passes during his quick evening's work, and would have been perfect if not for Henderson's jittery fingers. One newspaperman who'd speculated that the Tigers streak couldn't last in 1959 placed a redemptive headline at the front of his sports column: BRADDOCK'S YEAR TO LOSE? ASK HOMESTEAD (47–0).

Chapter Five

FORGING PERFECTION

THE TIGERS' GREATNESS had not always been so. It was winter 1954 when Dr. Tom Kelly—principal of Pitcairn High, a small school in a sleepy town tucked in a crevice in the Mon Valley—knocked on the door of Chuck Klausing's office. Klausing was twenty-eight years old. Pitcairn's football season had just ended, and the young coach was counting the days until summer practice started again.

"Chuck," the principal said, "there are some people who want to talk with you."

"What's it about?" Klausing asked.

"They're from Braddock. I think they're going to offer you a job."

Klausing had spent the past six seasons at Pitcairn developing and refining his coaching philosophy. He had figured out the *X*s and *O*s as well as any coach in the region, though that's not what set him apart. Klausing had developed an unusually holistic approach to coaching high schoolers. A coach's job had as much to do with shaping young men as with diagraming plays, he believed. His first season at Pitcairn, he instituted a cooldown period at the end of each practice. For fifteen minutes he sat his boys down and gave a small lecture on a life skill. The skills ranged from the practical—how to wash thoroughly, how to behave on a date—to the abstract—the value of becoming a leader. If players wondered why they were getting a survey in health, civics, philosophy, and psychology, they soon came to appreciate the short break at the end of practice when they had the chance to absorb the wisdom of a magnetic man who wasn't much older than they were. The young coach didn't believe that personal integrity and on-field performance were separate concerns, and it wasn't long before he'd transferred that belief to his boys.

Early on, the life lessons saved Klausing's job. His team went 3–5 his first year at Pitcairn, and managed only 1–7 his second.

"Well, men, we won all but seven," he joked after the last game of that awful season.

Local fathers wanted to run the coach out of town. But Pitcairn's mothers rallied around Klausing, whose positive influence had rubbed off on their sons. Any man who could get a teenager to wash before supper and express gratitude afterwards could certainly get a town's football problems sorted out. The next season, Klausing's third, his team went 7–1. He wouldn't post another losing season with the school. He had figured out how to take a small team with no real athletic gift and turn it into a competitor. It required an unerring mix of preparation and discipline, along with the know-how to show each player that he was ultimately responsible for the team's success.

"We're not teaching them to win football games," Klausing would tell his ragtag group of assistants, a few of whom were local characters with no official position at the school. "We're teaching leadership skills. Everything follows from that."

By the end of the 1953 season, Klausing had made a name for himself in local football circles. Though Pitcairn wasn't a top-flight school, coaches throughout the region had noticed the team's sudden turnaround. Officials in Braddock caught wind, and the two men waiting in the Pitcairn office were excited to meet the man they hoped would lead the Tigers out of the wilderness.

At best, Braddock High had been uneven in its first half century on the gridiron. The school fielded its first football squad in 1903, when the game itself was still young. Touchdowns were worth five points and the proposed forward pass was a topic of heated debate. The same year, a film crew sponsored by Thomas Edison attended the Princeton–Yale matchup and captured the first known moving film of the American sport. Jerky and off-speed, the resulting footage showed leatherheads in burlap pants playing scrum-style ball similar to rugby. The pace of the game was fast and the positions loosely defined. Just about every matchup brought broken noses and left players mud-caked and spent. It was the perfect spectacle for Western Pennsylvania's hard-living steelmen.

Braddock High dropped its 1903 opener to Homestead, a 23–0 shutout. Competition was scarce, so Braddock, which negotiated its own matchups with nearby teams, played Homestead a second time. They won that game 5–0 but then lost their next two contests with Wilkinsburg. Braddock's coach, whose name is lost to history, would have been the first man to incur the ire of a rough crowd of budding football fans in the fast-growing steel town that Andrew Carnegie built. Booze flowed as readily then as it did in the 1950s, and steelmen could be relied on to wager over anything with an outcome.

Mill workers in Braddock, which had sixteen thousand residents at the turn of the century, took a particular interest in football. The sport offered a compelling distraction from the woes of steelwork. Before the eight-hour day and the living wage, to say nothing of the safety protocols later won by organized labor, life in the mills was harrowing. In March 1903, six men died and fourteen others were disfigured in an explosion at the Edgar Thomson Works. The men had been working to repair an enormous blast furnace when a pocket of gas trapped inside the furnace ignited. Lime and molten metal rained down and covered the workers head to toe. Larger debris—"downcomer," in the parlance of the workers—burned through skin and bone like hot coals through butter. With the specter of violent death hanging over each shift, workers relished the opportunity to sit back and watch the local boys fight it out on the field.

Football evolved quickly in the early twentieth century. In 1905, twenty players on college and semi-pro teams around the country died from injuries sustained playing football. Calls went out to terminate the sport on high school and college campuses nationwide. President Theodore Roosevelt quelled the uprising by advocating safer play instead. A rules committee emerged out of a meeting of the major college teams. To avoid the scrum play that often resulted in players being trampled, the committee instituted the forward pass. Reformers believed the pass would spread players over the field and encourage speed and finesse over brute power. By 1910, the rules committee had decided that seven players must be on the line of scrimmage at the snap and instituted penalties for blockers who held or pulled opposing players. Over the following decade, touchdowns came to be worth six points, and new pass eligibility rules helped create the receiving positions. Football came to resemble the sport that Chuck Klausing grew up playing on the sandlots and grass fields of Wilmerding, Pennsylvania.

Braddock High adapted to the changes, and despite the team's lackluster performance during this time, thousands of fans turned out for games. A new coach, Bill Evans, took over in 1914 and dropped all seven contests, managing only one touchdown in the balance. The following season, Braddock played neighboring North Braddock Scott for the first time. The Purple Raiders bested the Tigers 3–0. Evans's disgrace was mitigated by a win over North Braddock the next season. It was the first Tigers victory in a series that would become astonishingly contentious. Attendance at the Braddock–North Braddock game was far higher than at any other game, and fans got rowdier. Hundreds of dollars changed hands, and bookies took special care handicapping the matchup, hounding coaches for tips about injuries and promising to pay players who performed well.

After three seasons at Braddock, Evans decided he'd rather take his chances with the Germans than spend another season answering to drunken steelworkers. He enlisted in the army, leaving behind a career record of three wins, fifteen losses, and four ties.

World War I rolled into Western Pennsylvania like a freight train. Demand for equipment and munitions forced local mills to peak capacity. Workers soon bucked the heavy load. In May 1916, men and women employed at the Edgar Thomson Works went on strike for an eight-hour workday. Joining ranks with workers from nearby towns, they marched through the streets behind a local band. Steel companies had made money hand over fist in the early years of the war, and workers thought the windfall might help usher long-hoped-for labor reforms. They thought wrong. Private guards amassed at the edge of the mill. Tensions rose and strikers surged toward the gates. Guards fired into the crowd, and three Braddock residents were killed. The governor of Pennsylvania declared martial law. Rather than arresting the guards, police rounded up dozens of strikers. For the workers, it was a heartbreaking testament to the steel industry's power and political importance.

Throughout the war, local men enlisted in droves. Others were drafted under the new Selective Service Act of 1917. With few male teachers to serve as coaches and little chance of selling out games, Braddock High suspended its football program between 1917 and 1919. Contention in the steel industry, however, took no breaks. In September 1919, with football still on hiatus, Braddock's steelworkers struck again, this time as part of a nationwide effort. The strike, which was organized by the Amalgamated Association, a labor organization representing the interests of skilled iron- and steelworkers, included 350,000 workers across the country and succeeded in bringing half the nation's steel production to a standstill.

To cull public favor, the industry used the media to spread rumors about communist incursion into the union's leadership. Russia's 1917 revolution had brought the menace of communism front and center, and steel companies masterfully played on national fears. It was a tactic that would prove effective for decades to come. Suspicion that Reds had infiltrated organized labor abounded, causing many in the press and in public office to advocate crackdowns on union activity. Law enforcement responded accordingly. Police made frequent sweeps during the 1919 stoppage, looking for communist agitators. Out of these busts, local heroes emerged. In Braddock, a priest named Adalbert Kazinsky stood defiantly atop the steps of St. Michael's Church and refused entry to police. In services he preached the rights of man and the inhumanity of exploitation, and he became a source of guidance and inspiration for Braddock's labor effort.

Plant managers, meanwhile, hired tens of thousands of temporary workers to fill in for strikers. Many of the scabs were black men who had migrated from the South in search of better lives. Strikers hurled insults—and sometimes hurled rocks—as the new workers crossed the picket lines. Racial tensions would hang over steel towns for decades to come. Eventually, amid a tide of negative public opinion, the strike collapsed. Dispirited workers returned to the mills. Organized labor, weakened by its failure, would struggle to regain its footing for another two decades.

After the war, Braddock began to rebuild its football program. The first great season of Braddock High football arrived in 1924. The Tigers won each of their nine games that season. The feather in the cap was an uncanny 58–0 drubbing of North Braddock Scott, prompting a town-wide party that ran late into the chilly fall night. New coach Johnny Reed became a hero in Braddock, which was now at the height of its population boom, with more than twenty thousand residents. But success was illusory. An investigation at the end of the season revealed that the Tigers had used an ineligible player, a boy who had grown up in Braddock but whose family had moved out of town before the start of the season. The team forfeited all its wins. Worse, Johnny Reed jumped ship in 1927, taking a job as head coach of rival North Braddock Scott. It was a slight not soon forgotten in Braddock. Reed would stay at Scott for nearly three decades, amassing an impressive streak of his own in the process.

In 1931, with the Great Depression in full swing, the annual Braddock–North Braddock Scott matchup turned ugly. Braddock lost 13–6 in a game interrupted by frequent fistfights in the stands and on the field. Fans were bloodied and players and coaches could barely stop brawling long enough to get through four consecutive downs. Administrators decided that the enmity between the teams had become unsafe. The annual game wasn't rescheduled the following year, and wouldn't be played again for a decade and a half.

The Depression battered Braddock Avenue. Orders for steel dried up nationwide, slowing production. Steelworkers found their hours and their paychecks cut to a minimum. Shops had no customers as result, and the Borough of Braddock had trouble collecting property taxes. It was a lesson too soon forgotten: When steelworkers were out of a job, the whole region faced catastrophe.

For a time, the bad luck extended to football. The Tigers had losing seasons between 1932 and 1936, including a disastrous 0–10 campaign in 1935. The team finally won eight games in 1937, the first winning season in over a decade, and over the next nine seasons, the Tigers went on a tear. Braddock posted twenty straight victories at ET Field, where it played its home games during the 1930s and '40s. Fans came to expect success, but a resumed rivalry with North Braddock Scott augured disappointment. In 1947, with the country still exuberant after the end of World War II, the two teams met for the first time since the bloody contest of '31. Braddock lost the first game of the new series 17–13, and lost its good luck. The Tigers finished the season a dismal 1–7–1.

In 1950, Henry Furrie took over as Braddock's head coach. He described the team to friends as a sinking ship, and after the 1953 season, his fourth at the helm, he'd had enough. His overall record was 12–20–2. He had dropped the second-to-last game of the season to North Braddock Scott, which rolled over the Tigers 20–6. It was the third loss to Scott in four years. Furrie finished out his career at Braddock with an uneven victory over Rankin High. Then he walked over to Dan Rice, the school's athletic director, and gave his notice.

"Sorry to see you go," Rice said without conviction.

Furrie had no idea that his final win against Rankin would be his most lasting contribution to Braddock—the first win in a streak that would grip the nation.

Two men were waiting for Chuck Klausing when he reached the Pitcairn office.

"Chuck, this is Mr. Sullivan and Mr. Bell from the Braddock School Board," Dr. Kelly said. "You gentlemen can use my office to talk."

For a man whose star coach was about to get taken out from under him, the principal was more than accommodating. In fact, Dr. Kelly had recommended Klausing for the position. He liked the young man, whose ambition had outgrown the two-hundred-student high school. After leaving the men in his office to talk, Dr. Kelly walked out to find his athletic director. He had to break the bad news.

Klausing knew all about the Braddock Tigers. He'd grown up two miles away in the small town of Wilmerding. Klausing's dad had taken him to Braddock High football games in the 1930s, and his wife, Joann, was a former Braddock High cheerleader. Klausing had seen Furrie's team play the previous season, and he'd taken special note of Joe Reaves, the powerful Tigers running back. With a couple kids like Reaves, he thought, he could forge a real powerhouse.

"Chuck, you've had quite a run here at Pitcairn. How have you kept it up?"

Mike Sullivan, president of the Braddock School Board, was

wearing an expensive tweed suit. Braddock's school board was a powerful political body. The borough had its own mayor and town council, its own taxes and tax collectors, its own supervisors, chief of police, and school board. A few hundred yards away, the Borough of North Braddock had an identical apparatus. The system bred a culture of concentrated local power, a collection of mini-fiefdoms. Mike Sullivan had spent a career cultivating his political base, and he'd chosen the school board as the perch from which to wield his influence. He led a coalition of four board members, the majority on the seven-man body. This *was* the hiring committee, Klausing understood.

"Well," Klausing said, taking a deep breath, "I think it comes down to coaching boys, not football."

He let that phrase hang in the air for just a moment. At twenty-eight, Klausing had already figured out how to work a room.

"You have to teach your players to be leaders on and off the field," he continued. "You have to make every boy accountable for his own success. The rest is just hard work, discipline, and preparation."

It was a good speech, though not entirely necessary. The men from Braddock had done their homework. Western Pennsylvania was a small place in many ways, and Klausing had made friends in the right circles. In addition to Dr. Kelly, the region's football intelligentsia had already given him a sterling recommendation. Even if they hadn't, there wasn't exactly a lot of competition for the job. Braddock's outgoing coach, Henry Furrie, hadn't been subtle about his dissatisfaction. He believed the players, rough sons of steelmen, were too undisciplined to fall in line behind even the strongest-willed coach. He also believed the administration was uncommitted to maintaining a top-notch program. The team languished with broken equipment, soiled jerseys, and underpaid assistants—conditions that rarely bred championships. Klausing was acquainted with Furrie; he had heard the knocks against Braddock High firsthand.

"Chuck," the board president said, anticipating any hesitation, "we want you to come to Braddock. We'll give you six hundred dollars a year to coach, on top of your teaching salary. We'll also give you a commitment. We want a winning program, and I guarantee you'll have the full support of the school board. If it's in our power to give, you'll get it."

Klausing thought for a moment. Then, looking Sullivan right in the eye, he made his first request. "If I come to Braddock, I'll want a film system."

College teams had been using film to great effect over the last decade, homing in on missed opportunities and individual mistakes, the kind that could be difficult to spot in real time. Klausing had experimented with film at Pitcairn, enlisting an assistant to film practices and games from the bed of a truck with borrowed equipment, and he recognized the possibilities. If he was going to build a team around a roster full of undisciplined talent at Braddock High, he'd need every tool he could get.

Sullivan was impressed with Klausing's directness. He looked briefly at his colleague on the board, Mr. Bell, and smiled. "Yes, I think that's something we can arrange."

If he'd wanted them, Klausing probably could have gotten the keys to Sullivan's car. The board president hated that his beloved town was losing football games to the nearby boroughs like Homestead and Rankin, and especially to neighboring North Braddock. Many of the region's power brokers met in card rooms and pool halls up and down the Monongahela River. "This is your year, Sully!" rival school administrators kidded him. A powerful football team was a mark of honor in Western Pennsylvania, and he had grown tired of the boasts, the lost bets, and the humiliation. The Tigers had never been a professional priority for Sullivan, who was too busy hiring teachers and handing out favors to give the losing squad his full attention. But now he saw a political opportunity. Others in Braddock—his constituents, for example—were as fed up as he was with the awful Tigers. If he could build up the football program and turn

Braddock High into a winner, he would be a hero in town. Nothing united a population behind its elected officials like a Cinderella story, and the Tigers were it. Braddock, with its well-paid steelworkers and thriving shops, had a stable tax base. Sullivan vowed to divert a portion of the school board's sizable purse to the athletic department.

After ironing out a few more details, Klausing accepted the job on the spot. He was placated by Sullivan's commitment to bring victory to Braddock, no matter the cost. The men ended the meeting with a round of handshakes, a gentlemen's agreement that the coach would wear Tigers red and white the following year. On his way home, Klausing thought back to his rocky first seasons at Pitcairn. Back then, the administration had given him a few purchase orders for equipment and a pat on the back. The new coach had used the orders to buy two balls and a can of ball cleaner. Throughout the 1948 season, Pitcairn had used one of the balls for home games and one for practice. Now Klausing was off to Braddock, a town that got real attention in the regional press, one that could be a stepping-stone to a college coaching position. Sullivan had promised him all the equipment he'd need.

Klausing arrived home in Pitcairn. Joann was making supper in the kitchen. She let out a loud "Yippee!" which made the kids laugh. Joann, a Braddock native, thought the world of her hometown. She considered it the crown jewel of the Mon Valley. She knew, too, that Braddock people were a special breed, intense in life and sport. Her husband would soon become one of the most scrutinized men around. She tightened her arms around his neck and kissed him. She would have to be a calming influence through coming storms.

Before Klausing could sign a contract, Mike Sullivan was unexpectedly tempted to go back on his agreement. A powerful local family, the McGinleys, put forth their own candidate for the Braddock job. Barney McGinley owned a minority stake in the Pittsburgh Steelers, which he'd acquired in a deal with his longtime friend Art

Rooney Sr., the Steelers' founding owner. A former Pittsburgh defensive end named George Hays had decided he wanted to get into coaching, and the McGinley family made it known that they wanted their man to step in at Braddock. As Klausing had long since realized, a major high school job was a great place to launch a coaching career. The McGinleys weren't bullies—Rita, Barney's daughter, was a popular teacher at Braddock High—but the family had influence. They were a gridiron dynasty in a region obsessed with football.

Sullivan mulled it over. He wanted Klausing at the helm of his reinvented Tigers, but the McGinleys would be a good family to do a favor for. In the end, Sullivan stuck to his guns and offered Klausing the contract. He wanted a winning team even more than he wanted a political ace in the hole—which, for a man who rarely missed the chance to play an angle, was saying something. As a conciliatory gesture, the politically minded board president hired Hays as an assistant coach. The McGinleys relented, and Braddock High football entered a new era.

Furrie may have been disgruntled, but he had a point. Braddock's facilities were second-rate. Klausing's new basement office at Braddock High was dank, an unventilated room at the bottom corner of a building that had been built in the 1890s. It smelled like the team's sweat-soiled pads had been sitting in the nearby lockers just as long.

Incredibly, the practice field was even worse. Every free inch of space in Braddock was crammed tight with houses and shops. Most homes didn't have yards, and those that did boasted little more than a patch of grass bordering a driveway. The Tigers practiced on Edgar Thomson Field, an odd-shaped park in North Braddock that lay just across the railroad tracks from Braddock High. In its day, ET Field had been first-rate. It once hosted semi-professional baseball teams like the Homestead Grays and the Zulu Cannibals. Over the years, developers had carved into its sides, scraping away precious real estate and shrinking its playing surface. Chalking anything that resembled a full-sized football field was impossible. Cinders from the nearby railroad and soot from the region's gritty, polluted air blanketed the grass, which the groundskeeper had long since grown tired of reseeding. The sod went to dirt, which turned to mud whenever it rained. In the sun, the mud became a shell as hard as concrete.

Klausing met with George Hays, his new assistant, before the first summer practice. Hays harbored no ill feelings about the hiring decision. He was a quiet man with a massive jaw and a professional football player's physique. After hanging up his spikes, he was just happy to be part of a team again. The former player had a deep understanding of the game. He seemed especially passionate about blocking and tackling, skills that had brought him success in the NFL. Klausing had been apprehensive about not handpicking his assistants, but he saw that the man the McGinleys had backed would be an asset.

Hays wasn't the only staff member Klausing inherited. Cronyism abounded in a town ruled by a one-party political machine. Democrats controlled every elected office in Braddock, and Election Day effectively took place in May, not November, since the primaries decided the whole caboodle. Political appointments accounted for an overwhelming number of local jobs. Mike Sullivan had crammed the school full of teachers, janitors, supervisors, and coaches, most of whom happened to be the brothers, cousins, in-laws, and sons of his benefactors. Klausing had to take a political appointee on his coaching staff, in addition to Hays. The man didn't seem to know a damn thing about football.

If Klausing had a mind to complain to Sullivan about dirty politics, he didn't have much leverage in the matter. Football coaches were required to teach a minimum number of hours each day. Klausing had been certified to teach math and physical education at Pitcairn, but vocational math, which required a separate credential, was the only subject open at Braddock High when he was hired. Sullivan assured him that the problem would be taken care of, but on the eve of the team's opening practice, Klausing still hadn't received his certification.

"You're kidding!" Sullivan said when Klausing came to his office to complain.

The board president grabbed the phone and dialed the office of David Lawrence, the mayor of Pittsburgh. Lawrence was an old friend of Sullivan's. He was equally befuddled. He'd asked his assistant to get the credential problem sorted out weeks earlier, he explained, promising to put a stern boot to his aide.

The boot did the trick. Klausing's certification came through a few days later. When he opened the official letter, he discovered he'd been cleared to teach every subject in every grade from kindergarten through high school, including several foreign languages. Overnight he had become the most qualified teacher in Allegheny County. He posted the letter on the refrigerator and smiled as Joann read through it.

"Say something to me in French," she teased.

It was an object lesson in how things got done in Western Pennsylvania.

Klausing, Hays, and Sullivan's man met at the high school early on a warm morning in late August 1954. Klausing wore a new Notre Dame hat and all three men wore athletic shorts, though the political appointee, soft in body and plump in the legs, looked uncomfortable in his.

"Gentlemen," Klausing told his coaches, "this is a new start for Braddock High. I'd like to win a championship this season, and I'll need your help."

No one doubted his seriousness, though privately they questioned his grasp on reality. The men spent twenty minutes reviewing Klausing's plan for practice. Then they walked up to ET Field. As they passed under the railroad tracks and rounded the corner, Klausing took a few deep, bracing breaths. He couldn't explain why, but he felt very palpably that he had an opportunity with the Tigers to do something great. He knew that he would be measured as a coach by the seasons that lay ahead, and he felt ready. Unfortunately, Braddock's facilities were not. Drawing to the edge of ET Field, all four coaches stopped dead in their tracks.

Klausing put his hands on his hips. "Looks like we'll need a new place to practice."

A weeklong church carnival had pulled up stakes the night before. Workers had used heavy trucks to haul away the rides and booths, leaving deep tracks in the rain-soaked earth. The ground looked swollen in places, like a tidal surge on a stormy sea. Fist-sized rocks floated in the mud. Klausing tried to walk out, but the soft muck swallowed his shoes.

The first players would arrive within the hour. Braddock didn't have another level field large enough to practice on. Given the situation, no idea would have seemed too inane. One of Sullivan's men suggested roping off a flat street near the river for practice. They were discussing the idea when Klausing remembered Frick Park in Pittsburgh, which was about five miles away. It was a beautiful open space, well maintained, and there was a stretch of grass big enough to play on. A streetcar originating in Braddock would take them right there. The cost was seventeen cents per person, round-trip. Klausing asked his assistants to throw all the money they had into a pile. They began counting in earnest, hoping they had enough to cover the fare.

When the nineteen players on the incoming varsity team arrived, Klausing sized them up slowly.

"We're taking a trip," he said finally. "Go get your gear."

The players retrieved their pads from the equipment room and then walked down to catch the streetcar. When it stopped along Braddock Avenue, the players climbed aboard, holding their breath to protect against the dizzying fumes that seeped up from the idling engine. Half an hour later, they arrived at Frick Park for their first practice.

Klausing used fire hoses, which he borrowed from a nearby fire department, to mark the lines on the field. Braddock High didn't have any tackling dummies, so Klausing and Hays had worn thigh pads and trotted onto the field with the boys. They started the team off with calisthenics, and then it was straight into a blocking drill. The players lined up, dropped into their stances two at a time, and tried to wrestle Klausing and Hays off the line. The new coach wanted to measure his team's fight. A few of the players held back, refraining from hitting the coaches—especially Hays, a recently re-tired NFL player—full speed. Others threw their bodies ahead with complete abandon. Joe Reaves was every bit the brute Klausing had hoped. The junior exploded out of his stance and shoved Klausing backwards. The new Tigers coach tumbled onto his backside, caus-ing Reaves to stop dead in his tracks. The whole team waited to see what would happen.

"Did you all see that?" the coach said, picking up his Notre Dame hat and whacking it against his leg. "If you don't do that every time, you're doing it wrong."

As the morning wore on, senior halfback Jimmy Gilliam caught Klausing's eye. Gilliam was a big Southern boy who charged defend-ers like a bull. He and his mother had moved to Braddock from Ala-bama recently, and Klausing found out the reason: Gilliam's father had been murdered by the Ku Klux Klan. Klausing searched hard for signs of psychological distress in his player. A young man who'd been through that kind of trauma had every right to develop a car-sized chip on his shoulder. But Gilliam never showed anything but compassion and good humor on the field. His mother had taught him never to hate anyone for what happened to his father, and espe-cially implored him not to confuse all white men with a few men in white sheets.

At one point in the long workout, the coaches had the players push Coach Hays's Buick up and down the field. Klausing realized with surprise that his new players were performing beautifully, act-ing both respectful and compliant. After what Furrie told him, he'd half-expected a pack of stray dogs at practice. Joe Reaves, in particu-lar, had a reputation as a troublemaker. The principal of Braddock

High, Joe Stukus, had once gotten so fed up with Reaves's truancy that he tracked the boy to the Paramount Theater on Braddock Avenue and ordered the man in the projection booth to turn up the houselights in the middle of a Western. Reaves gawked back to find his principal glaring at him. Klausing had heard the story, and he came prepared to deal with insubordination. But the players, Reaves included, all followed his orders without hesitation. Klausing started piecing together why that might have been. By removing them from Braddock, he had inadvertently skirted the worst behavior problems that plagued Furrie during his tenure. Players couldn't go running off for a bite to eat—it was just too far—and without the gaggle of local spectators that always amassed to size up the newest Tigers, there was less temptation for the boys to clown it up. In the end, the mud at ET Field had been a stroke of good luck.

Klausing sat his team down when the morning practice drew to an end. He asked the players how they thought the day had gone. Everyone agreed the workout had been first-rate. The boys especially liked that Klausing and Hays had been on the field taking snaps, getting dirty and dinged up right alongside them.

"Well," Klausing said flatly. "I haven't made up my mind if we'll have a team this year. There aren't enough of you yet. If I go into the season with nineteen players, I'll have to play most of you men both ways. You'll get worn out and banged up, and then where will we be?"

Klausing had a hunch he knew why there were so few players. The older boys had a habit of hazing any sophomores brave enough to come out for the team. They roughed them up, made them run, and took their pocket money. The hazing was so brutal that most players put in a year on Braddock's freshman team and then skipped an entire year of playing just to avoid it, joining varsity as juniors and losing a critical year of development in the offing. The hazing was especially bad for black players, who caught the worst beatings. Of the nineteen Tigers who'd traveled to Frick Park that morning, only three were black. They were the three biggest kids on the team and so had managed to avoid the worst of it.

"Who are the seniors here?" Klausing asked.

Ten players raised their hands.

"You're my captains. I'll only say this once, so listen up: The hazing is going to stop. I want you to show me that you've got character. We need a set of team rules, a code that every player who wears a Braddock jersey can follow, and you're going to write them."

Klausing tore a clean page out of the notepad he'd carried to practice and handed it to Joe DeNone, the Tigers' handsome senior quarterback. While the nine juniors tossed balls back and forth, the seniors huddled in private and tried to come up with a set of rules that would prove to their coach that they wanted to play. When they finished, the seniors presented their list. It was a page long and covered everything from drinking and swearing to staying out past dark on school nights. Players weren't to disrespect their parents, teachers, girls at school, or each other. The first rule on the list: "No hazing."

"We still need more players," Klausing said when they were finished. "Since you scared them away, you're going to find me some new ones. Tomorrow I'll decide if we have enough to field a team."

The Tigers forewent the planned second practice that afternoon. Coaches distributed the remaining streetcar fare. Then they left. The boys were on their own, with the season hanging in the balance.

Led by the seniors, the team formed a plan. They divided Braddock into a loose grid. All afternoon and into the evening, Tigers players fanned out. They knocked on doors and visited popular haunts where teenagers were busy squeezing the last moments out of their summer vacation. Joe Reaves went to Lumberger's Pool Hall, a popular hangout for black high schoolers. White players made stops at Isaly's, an ice-cream shop on Braddock Avenue, and the United Candy store.

Early the next day, Klausing drove apprehensively to meet his team at Braddock High. He'd made a high-stakes gambit. If the players struck out, he may have bluffed himself right out of any last-ing credibility with them. He'd signed a contract, made a commit-ment to Mike Sullivan, and he didn't have it in mind to cancel the season.

As soon as he pulled up to the school, he knew his career was safe. Several players had already arrived and more were walking to the front of the school from all sides. It looked like his team had doubled overnight. In all, the ranks had swollen to thirty-three, including ten black players. That morning, the newly fortified Tigers took the streetcar back to Frick Park. The seniors presented their list of team rules to the recent recruits, making them swear to follow them. Klausing was pleased. He was turning his players into leaders, just as he'd told Sullivan he would. He had also planted the seeds of team unity. Most important of all, it looked like the Braddock boys wanted to play football.

The Tigers practiced for a week at Frick Park. The players were rough around the edges and lacking in fundamentals, but they were tough. Klausing had never seen high schoolers hit as hard as some of his new players. Many of the boys worked all summer long, hoisting sacks of concrete on construction sites or heavy wooden barrels in local factories for a few pennies of spending money. They were strong, inured to pain, and unafraid of hard work. With the rules in place and the senior captains patrolling for trouble, they were also well disciplined. After a week of practice, there hadn't been a single haz-ing incident.

The day before the last summer workout, Klausing knocked on Mike Sullivan's office door. There was one important piece of busi-ness to attend to.

"What can I do for you, Chuck?" Sullivan asked.

"We need new uniforms. We can't play in what we've got."

After the last game of the previous season, the Tigers' muddy jerseys had been stuffed back into the lockers and forgotten. No one even bothered to wash them. The mud had hardened into a chalky crud, and the funk of the dismal 1953 season still clung to their fibers. To bolster his case, Klausing had brought one of the jerseys with him, which he removed from a paper bag. The red coloring had faded to an unappealing maroon, and the numbers on the back were cracked and corroding. The jersey filled the office with a rank odor, like unwashed feet.

"I see what you mean," Sullivan said, flipping open a notebook on his desk. "Okay, that's easy. We'll get new ones."

Klausing was pleased to find that his new boss was sticking to his pledge of support. After practice the following day, Klausing told the players to follow him into the small locker room. Space was so cramped that they could hardly all stand inside.

"Grab all the jerseys," he said.

The players complied, holding the cruddy uniforms at arm's length. Klausing led them to the furnace room.

"The Tigers were a losing team last year, but that's in the past. We aren't respected, but we will be. We're starting over this season, and we're going to win."

With that, he stepped forward and opened the heavy iron door.

"Toss 'em in," he said.

As the jerseys ignited, curls of black smoke billowed through the chimney and out into the dusky sky above the high school. Players told their friends about the exorcism, and news of Klausing's promise of a new era of Braddock High football spread.

The Tigers played their first game of the season away on a rain-soaked field in front of five thousand fans. Their opponent, Wilkinsburg High, was heavily favored. Joe DeNone, the quarterback, played defense in the first quarter and intercepted a pass to set up the first touchdown of the Klausing era. Wilkinsburg fans assumed it was a fluke. Their coach had scheduled Braddock High to give the Wilkinsburg players a soft opening opponent, a warm-up game. But when the second quarter came to a close and the score was still 7–0, people in the stands began to get restless. The Tigers held through the third quarter, stopping an offense that was rumored to be among the best in the region. Rain poured down and players' cleats sank into the field. Wilkinsburg scored late in the fourth, giving the home crowd hope, but the ball got stuck in the damp ground on the extra point attempt and the kicker booted it well off target. The remaining seconds ticked off the clock. The Tigers won 7–6. About a thousand Braddock fans had traveled for the game, and a large contingent rushed onto the field at the closing whistle. Even with the hype around Klausing, it was one of the most unexpected wins in Braddock's football history.

Klausing's boys never looked back. The escalating verbs in the newspaper headlines told the story: BRADDOCK IN 14–0 WIN OVER HOMESTEAD, TIGERS DOWN MCKEES ROCKS 20–7, ELIZABETH RAPPED 39–6, BRADDOCK BLANKS BRENTWOOD 27–0. In practice, Klausing and Hays hammered the fundamentals: footwork, blocking, getting off the line. DeNone, the senior quarterback, fed the ball to Joe Reaves and Jim Gilliam, and the bruisers perfected a power game that yielded five hard-won yards at a time. The Tigers posted seven straight victories, including three shutouts. Fan attendance increased with every contest, and townspeople began whispering what would have seemed like a ridiculous question a few months earlier: Could Klausing bring Braddock its first undefeated season since Johnny Reed's 1924 team was disqualified?

The Friday of the Braddock–North Braddock matchup turned into an unofficial holiday in town. Pedestrians took to the streets, bringing traffic on Braddock Avenue to a crawl. Though the weather had turned sour, a mass of people followed the team from Braddock High to North Braddock Scott Field, most of them walking the three blocks on foot. The spectacle would become commonplace, a joyous tradition in the bright seasons to come.

A reporter named John Smonski stood on the sidelines during the game that evening. He wore a sopping-wet overcoat, which he used to shield his notepad from the rain. Smonski covered sports all over the region for the Braddock *Free Press,* but the Tigers were his favorite beat. He'd been covering Braddock High games for two decades, starting with the high school paper when he was a student there. In all that time, he had never seen anything like the spectacle before him. The stadium was bulging at the sides with people. In their black slickers, the crowd looked like some kind of frenzied cult army. Even as the rain lashed down, Smonski managed to reach under his coat to scribble every play. He would stay up late that night to write his article:

> *The victory came the hard way as Coach Chuck Klausing's lads were trailing 12–7 with but six and a half minutes left in the final quarter and in possession on their own 11 yard line. In covering the 89 yards the Tigers moved for five first downs and with 2 minutes showing on the clock, Jim Gilliam tore loose for a 35 yard run up the middle for the winning points.*

The Tigers won 13–12. They were undefeated, and just like that, Klausing had led Braddock High to its best regular season ever. Car horns blared up and down Braddock Avenue long after the stadium had cleared out. By morning, the results of the region's other contests had come in. The undefeated Tigers would be playing Midland for the Western Pennsylvania Interscholastic Athletic League Class A title.

The Midland matchup drew 6,300 spectators. The Tigers took the field with confidence, and under the guiding eyes of Klausing, who wore his by-then-famous Notre Dame hat, they played like champions. In the second quarter, Jim Gilliam returned a punt to midfield. Joe Reaves took the handoff and faked the run, but then dropped back and threw to receiver Mark Oliver, who outraced a Midland defender for a touchdown. Braddock looked like it was heading for another win.

But penalties and bad luck plagued the Tigers for the rest of the game. Jim Gilliam and Joe Reaves assaulted the Midland line, but several runs were called back for holding. Braddock's strong-as-steel defense didn't give up a first down in the second half, but a fluke play gave Midland a window of opportunity. On third and ten, with time ticking down, the Midland quarterback hurled the ball from his own 27-yard line. The Midland receiver dropped the pass, but the referee didn't blow the whistle. Another Midland player picked up the loose ball and bolted to the end zone. Klausing came running onto the field, which Braddock fans already knew was uncharacteristic. The referee closest to the dropped ball looked like a kid who just got caught playing hooky; he knew he'd made a mistake. After conferring for an excruciating five minutes, the head referee signaled that the touchdown would stand. Midland kicked the extra point, tying the game. There wouldn't be another score.

With no overtime, the teams were crowned co-champions. It wasn't the win Klausing wanted, but it was the Tigers' first WPIAL title. When the team bus rolled into town, Kenny Bashioum, the driver, cursed through the windshield. It seemed like the entire town had taken to the streets, and a great many of them appeared drunk. When they spotted the bus, the townspeople flocked around it on all sides. Hollering for them to get out of the way, Bashioum inched forward, slowly parting the revelers on his way to Braddock High.

Chapter Six

NATIVE SONS

JOHN JACOBS WOKE EARLY on Monday and sat on the edge of his bed. He threw his head back and let out a quick, dry cough. His throat felt itchy. After slurping some water from the bathroom sink, he returned to his small room and pulled open his dresser drawer. He dressed, and then quietly gathered his books and left the house. His ride wasn't due for another twenty minutes, but the dark-haired quarterback liked to disappear in the mornings. His old man was often hungover, and it was easier to avoid him than risk an unpleasant breakfast. Jacobs eased the door closed behind him, walked out to the road, and waited.

John Jacobs Sr. was the chief of police in North Versailles, a quaint hilltop borough four miles east of Braddock. He was popular in town, and his friends called him Big Jake. Father and son were Big Jake and Little Jake, respectively, though lately no appreciable size difference remained between them.

When he was sober, Big Jake was a good man. He was respected by the boys at the station and generally admired in the community. He had a fine set of hands, which he used to help neighbors build walls and jump-start cars. He tackled roofing jobs to help his younger brother, a carpenter with a debilitating fear of heights. Good, strong hands ran in the family.

When he was sober, Big Jake was a good father. He took his son to Steelers games and bouts of pickup baseball in town. The old man was a catcher from way back who punished any runner that challenged the plate. Athleticism, like good hands, ran in the family. Big Jake taught his son to throw a football and advised him when to tuck the ball and run. When Jake was younger, the two played catch for hours in front of the house. Big Jake hung a tire from a tree and the two spent long afternoons drilling passes through it.

But Big Jake wasn't sober often. Steelers games often ended in embarrassment after the old man drank so much Iron City beer that he passed out in the parking lot. For a period he was ousted from his job, suspended pending an investigation. He had shot someone on duty, and details were murky. He disappeared for weeks-long stretches during his suspension, and though he eventually reassumed his position as chief, the mental strain of the affair was substantial.

Big Jake could be abusive, which was nothing unusual in Western Pennsylvania. Little Jake ran away when he was a boy, taking shelter in a shoddy tree house. He fell out of the tree in the middle of the night, but it was still better than what was waiting for him at home. When the younger Jake filled out, added muscle, the abuse turned psychological. Big Jake had a sharp eye for his boy's vulnerabilities. Whenever the budding quarterback came off the bench during his first year at Braddock High, his father homed in on his every mistake. How could any son of his throw back-to-back incomplete passes? Miss an open man down the sideline? Get tackled by the slowest defender on the field?

The family sometimes went to Vince's Pizza after the games. The proprietor smoked cigarettes while tossing the dough. He once guaranteed Little Jake free pizza for as long as the Tigers remained undefeated. It was a sucker's guarantee, and old Vince rued the day he made it. As often as not, the evenings at Vince's went well. Little Jake and his mom joked back and forth and laughed about her complete ignorance of all things related to football. Big Jake glad-handed everyone in the place, and his big belly laugh put the whole world at ease. When he was sober, he was loved by all. Other times, the outings to Vince's were almost unbearable. Little Jake and his mother would sit quietly through dinner as Big Jake swilled beer and picked apart each play.

By senior year it was better for Jacobs to avoid the old man altogether. He left the house early and came back late. Sometimes he didn't eat all day, electing to starve rather than go home. Summers were hard, all free time and dreary afternoons. Most kids dreaded the end of summer vacation, but Jacobs welcomed it. Football practices ran late during the school year, and by the time he got home, his dad would be at work or at the bar. If things went well this season, Jacobs had college to look forward to. He didn't plan to spend another year in Braddock. Football was his ticket out.

Jacobs waited, his book bag at his feet. Before long, a familiar station wagon crested the hill and the quarterback stepped out to meet it.

"Hi, Coach," Jacobs said, sliding into the middle bench seat. Then, craning behind him: "Girls."

Two of Klausing's daughters—Patti, nine, and Mary-Lou, seven—had come along for the ride. They attended a Catholic school in Pitcairn, where Klausing would drop them off after taking a group of his players to school. Jake flashed a goofy smile and the girls laughed. Klausing pulled away from the shoulder and aimed the goliath station wagon higher into the hills of North Versailles. Jacobs's mood eased with each passing block. His throat tickled and ached a little, as it had that morning, but he kept from coughing in front of Coach. Mostly he thought of cheerleaders and majorettes. He had long ago realized what a beautiful gift high school was.

North Versailles, the breeding ground for so much Tigers talent, was defined by its hills. Braddock shot away from the Monongahela like one side of a pyramid, but North Versailles looked more like a mountain range on a postcard from Peru. A dozen tree-dotted hill-ocks had created geographically distinct communities within the town. Klausing believed the steep inclines made the local boys better athletes because of all the climbing and descending they grew up doing.

In the station wagon, Klausing's daughters gazed at the back of John Jacobs's head, which rocked forward now and then as he dis-creetly cleared his throat. The station wagon dipped into a small val-ley and then climbed farther into Crestas Terrace, a predominantly black section of North Versailles. There were none of the wide paved streets here that they had in Braddock. Neighborhood kids grew up playing football and softball on whatever scraggly patch of earth they could find, and boys learned to keep their footing and show their speed on the most uneven surfaces. Boys who came out of North Versailles were the fastest and best balanced in Allegheny County, and they just seemed to get faster in pads.

Klausing stopped low on the hill where backup running back Bill King was waiting.

"Good morning," Klausing said, greeting King as he climbed into the station wagon.

"Good morning, Coach, Jake," King said.

Klausing's father, the mayor of nearby Wilmerding and a lay preacher, had baptized King sixteen years earlier. He would come at a moment's notice, day or night, to accommodate the redemptive im-pulses of a guilty conscience. Klausing suspected that several of his players would become preachers after graduation. Few callings drew more respect in steel communities than the pulpit. For boys with a verbal flair, it was an enticing alternative to the mill or the military.

King turned and winked playfully at Klausing's girls as the station wagon lurched away. They shot big toothy grins back at him. Klaus-ing's kids were unofficial mascots for the Tigers. Patti and Mary-Lou, along with Tommy, the coach's five-year-old son, were regulars at ban-quets and team meetings. The two youngest daughters, one-year-old

Kathy and two-year-old Nancy, were familiar bundles in Joann's arms. Players teased and joked with the older children as they did with their own little siblings. The family joke was that the little ones had so many older brothers they had trouble remembering all their names.

Klausing drove on. Curtis Vick lived higher on the hill. When the station wagon pulled over in front of his house, the graceful fullback glided into the open seat next to Jacobs.

"Coach, are we ready for Hopewell this week?" Vick asked.

"I imagine we are," Klausing said. "We'll have to find out in practice."

"Are you kidding?" Jacobs responded. "We're going to cream them!"

Vick wore his hair wavy, like the black doo-wop singers in the Del-Vikings. A sharp dresser, he was wearing a crisp, collared shirt tucked into slacks that he hoisted high on his waist. He was smooth, smart, and agreeable. He even dated white girls, which made him a rarity in Braddock—in the country as a whole.

Klausing picked up underclassmen Leon Page and Willie Thomas, and then drove to the last stop on his route. Ben Powell was the first player Klausing had recruited out of North Versailles. Braddock's underclassmen had looked anemic heading into the 1957 season, Klausing's fourth with the Tigers. The team especially needed young backfield talent to replace graduating seniors. The strength of a high school team's roster ebbed and flowed as older players finished school and younger players made their way up through the system. Only through equal parts luck and ingenious calculation could a coach hope that rising stars would peak at just the right time. Klausing could do more than most with a shallow roster, but he had also wanted to seed his program with all the young talent he could. No one was talking about the record back in 1957, but the coach knew that consistency would keep his boys in the *W* column.

There had been breathless talk among area coaches before the

1957–58 school year about Ben Powell, a North Versailles boy who broke the WPIAL junior high record in the 100-yard dash a year earlier. With no high school of its own, kids who lived in North Versailles could attend any senior high in the area. Coaches recruited Powell aggressively, and McKeesport High even offered to send a taxi to take him to school each morning. Shy and withdrawn, Powell recoiled from the hard-sell tactics. Klausing seemed different. He didn't promise any unearned playing time. He simply offered Powell a chance to prove himself on what was already being called one of the best squads in the state. For good measure, and to match McKeesport's offer, he threw in a guaranteed ride to school each day. He'd pick Powell up himself and take him home in the afternoon.

Klausing's softer pitch worked. When he drove out to North Versailles on the first day of the school year to pick up his new recruit, he found four other sophomores waiting for him. Powell had told his friends about the man in the Notre Dame hat. The group didn't look like much, a handful of scrawny black kids and one white boy named John Jacobs, but Klausing gladly gave them a lift. He had no idea that those sophomores would soon develop into some of the best football talents in the state.

Three years later, Powell looked sheepish waiting by the side of the road as the nearly full station wagon pulled over. His baggy, ill-fitting clothes concealed a runner's body that had grown longer and more muscular in the last few years. The clothes made him look smaller than he really was. Powell got into the station wagon and mumbled a greeting. No one could get him to say more than a few words at a time. Doughboy delighted in harassing his backfield rivals, and after Vick, Powell was his favorite target. The star back never had the confidence to stand up to the barbs off the field, which made his transformation on the gridiron seem all the more miraculous.

"All set?" Klausing asked as he turned the car down a steep street. Loaded with passengers, the station wagon listed like an ocean liner. No matter how slowly he drove, Klausing and his leaf-spring suspension lost the eternal battle with the potholes in the road. Klausing winced whenever the axles let out a particularly bone jarring *clunk*.

"There it goes," he said, shaking his head.

Black players had thrived on the Tigers in the previous five seasons. Klausing had no interest in being a crusader, and he didn't consider himself one. He wanted to win and he knew he'd need the best talent available to him to do that. If that meant doing the right thing, treating everyone equally, so much the better.

After abolished hazing on the team in 1954, Klausing instituted a challenge-system to make sure he got the best players in the lineup on Friday nights. Challenges worked differently for different positions, but always included head-to-head contests. Surrounded by cheering teammates, two linemen faced off in a circle. The boy who could push his adversary out of bounds was declared the winner. It was painful and ritualistic, but it was fair. Ability was rewarded over skin color—a revolutionary concept when it was first introduced to the Tigers.

Klausing's personal feelings about race had been cemented long before he took up the whistle. He'd been raised by Lutheran parents to approach people humbly and without judgment. In high school, he also had the good fortune to make a friend who would forever imprint upon him just how foolish it was to pigeonhole a person based on race. One afternoon, while agonizing over a Latin assignment in study hall, he had looked up to see the sympathetic face of the new boy in school.

"Can I help you with that?" Tom Casey asked.

"If you can, it'll be a miracle," Klausing replied.

Casey was an outlier from the start. He could read Latin like a Vatican cardinal and spoke the dead language like it was his native tongue. He was also the only black student that Wilmerding High had ever had when he transferred in as a junior in 1940. Casey's family had just moved to town, and it didn't take long for the new kid to establish himself as the top scholar in his class.

Klausing's admiration began over a Latin primer but was forged on the field. Casey was a gifted football player, a phenomenal sprinter who seemed capable of playing every position. During practice early in the year, he showed just how versatile he could be. Klausing was long-snapping to Wilmerding's starting punter, Ralph Pici, and Casey began shagging balls for the pair. Each time Pici punted, Casey punted back. Only Casey's punts sailed ten yards over Pici's head.

After a handful of beautiful booming kicks, Klausing turned to the starting punter with a grim expression. "Your days are numbered," he said.

Wilmerding High had a tremendous season in 1940. To no one's surprise, Casey was a standout on both sides of the ball, changing his position to best exploit opponents' weaknesses. After graduating, Casey enrolled at Hampton University, a black college in Virginia. But with World War II raging and boys joining up in droves, he decided to enlist in the Marine Corps. He had perfect grades and read Latin fluently, but in the service he became a cook. Klausing had mediocre grades, but the marines sent him to Penn State for two years of college classes before Officer Candidate School.

After the war, Casey continued his studies at Hampton University, where he was a standout on the football team. After graduating, he signed with the New York Yankees, a football team in the All-America Football Conference (AAFC), a short-lived but well respected challenger to the NFL. Klausing was sitting in a movie theater one afternoon in 1948 when a Fox Movietone newsreel came on. Suddenly he saw his old friend up on the screen. The twenty-four-year-old Casey had just set the record for the longest punt return in professional football, a ninety-four-yard run against the Brooklyn Dodgers.

Casey continued his professional football career in Canada, playing a season for the Hamilton Wildcats before moving to the Winnipeg Blue Bombers, where he was the leading rusher in the Western Interprovincial Football Union in 1950. For three years running he was an All-Western Defensive Back in the Canadian league. Between conditioning and traveling for games, Casey somehow managed to find time to attend medical school in Winnipeg. He graduated third in his class and went on to become a brilliant surgeon. He also donated time to various civic committees and coached in youth leagues on the side. For his service and incredible accomplishments, the city of Winnipeg named him its citizen of the year in 1956. The many accolades Casey collected earned him a fitting nickname: Citation.

With the possible exception of Klausing's own father, there was no man in the world he admired more. He tried to pass the views he forged throughout his relationship with Casey down to his players. The Tigers were one of the few integrated squads in Allegheny County. Plenty of teams in the region had one or two black athletes, usually stars like Ben Powell or Curtis Vick whose talent rendered coaches temporarily color-blind. But few teams were open to any but the most exceptional black players. Racism and outright abuse were common, and the worst of it often came from the boys on the field. A few years earlier, a black student named Tommy Scales had joined the football team at Munhall High just across the river from Braddock. Scales, who was the only black player on the team, endured a battery of insults from his new teammates. One afternoon he returned to his locker to find his clothes missing. On a tip from a sympathetic student, he looked behind the school. Skirting the campus was a deep ravine that locals used as an illegal dumping ground. At the bottom of the ravine, half-buried under a pool of muck and fetid refuse, Scales saw his clothes. He transferred to Homestead High soon after, where at least there were a handful of other black players to insulate him.

Western Pennsylvania was a fairly representative front in the nationwide battle over race and inclusion. In 1954, the year Klausing arrived at Braddock, the U.S. Supreme Court struck down the separate-but-equal doctrine established by *Plessy v. Ferguson* more than half a century earlier. The court's new decision in *Brown v. Board of Education* brought hope that state-sponsored segregation would end. In September 1957, the NAACP registered nine black students at a previously all-white high school in Little Rock, Arkansas. After local uproar, Orval Faubus, the state's governor, ordered the Arkansas National Guard to blockade the school and bar the new students from entering. The standoff finally ended when President Eisenhower federalized the state's troops, stripping Faubus of his firepower. Eisenhower then sent the 101st Airborne to escort the Little Rock Nine past a venomous mob.

Klausing was red in the face over the Little Rock Incident, and he said as much to a roomful of coaches at a football luncheon in Pittsburgh. He would welcome the Little Rock students at Braddock High, he said, and would be especially pleased to give any ball players among them a tryout. After he gave his impromptu speech, a few close friends implored him not to make his position so public. It was still a trigger issue, they said, and not something he wanted to jump in the middle of.

A third of Klausing's 1954 Tigers had been black, and the proportion of black players to white players soon climbed to about half. From the start, the team had dealt with bitter racism outside of Braddock. In the early days, some schools had flatly refused to schedule games with the Tigers. Epithets from opposing benches and bleachers were so common that the team hardly paid any attention before long. Besides, Klausing's boys had developed a remarkably effective way of tuning them out: They beat the snot out of their opponents and then walked off the field to celebrate.

Coaches like John Zuger had less success letting the racial barbs fly by. Zuger often got into shouting matches with proselytizing locals. The prevailing football wisdom, propagated by armchair idiots up and down the Mon Valley, was that black players were physically unsuited to the sport's rough play. "Skinny nigger legs," they said by way of explanation. That the theories had held up in the face of Braddock's overwhelming success was mystifying, a testament to the depth of the adherents' ignorance.

In Braddock itself, long-standing racial barriers remained stubbornly in place. Braddock High had no black teachers, and some faculty members were open bigots. One government teacher discouraged black students from joining the debate club, maintaining that non-white students smelled funny. Black and white dances were still held separately, and it had taken Klausing all of his political capital to orchestrate an all-student sock hop in the gym in 1958. To get final approval, he'd had to promise to put a strip of tape down the middle of the floor to keep black and white students separated.

There were good educators at the school, too, men and women who fought for inclusion. Tom Horan, an English teacher, broke with the curriculum and wrote his own plays for students to read and perform, always including prominent roles for black actors. Rita McGinley was revered for her patience and kindness. She had tutored dozens of black students who might otherwise have slipped through four years of high school with poor grades and lousy prospects. Klausing's football team was the gold standard for cooperation and equality in town, and he made sure that every assistant who coached under him shared his progressive views on race. But those good eggs were the exception, not the rule. And Braddock High was far from the only discriminating institution that players had to deal with.

At the Carnegie Library, Braddock's architectural and cultural gem, black patrons still suffered embarrassing exclusions. Vernon Stanfield, the Tigers starting offensive guard, would never forget the shame of being denied permission to use the library's grand swimming pool, its steam room, or its basketball court. Black patrons couldn't use the drinking fountains, and books were lent to them on a provisional basis. Most of the white players didn't even know these rules existed. After entering the library with a black classmate on a hot day back in junior high, Mark Rutkowski had been shocked to hear the librarian say that his friend was "the wrong color" to use the fountain. The future Braddock High all-star racked his brain trying to figure out just what in the hell skin color had to do with the way a person drank water.

Rules concerning race were unstated, inferred, and subject to indiscriminate enforcement. They weren't posted anywhere, and for that reason they were even harder to fight than the overt policies of the South. It would take more than a court ruling to change the way things worked in Western Pennsylvania. In Braddock, at least, the success of the Tigers, the strong bond among the players, had helped race relations more than any effort of the last fifty years. Braddock High football players were princes in town, and on game day, the parents of princes mingled freely in the stands. Black or white, they always laid claim to the best seats in the house.

The Homestead massacre had buoyed spirits all over town. It was exactly the start people had hoped for. Any hesitation about talking up the record, mute deference to jinxes and chance, was gone now. By Wednesday, the countdown had begun.

"It's a tough two games coming up, Hopewell and Midland," John Smonski, the sports reporter for the Braddock *Free Press,* told a group of men who cornered him on Braddock Avenue. "But if one team is going to upset our boys this year, it'll be Scott."

Storeowners and checkout clerks, the foremost purveyors of news and gossip in town, became sounding boards for unsubstantiated rumors. Speculation abounded that Klausing might bring out a battery of new tricks during the home opener on the following Saturday. Braddock would be playing Hopewell, a dangerous opponent whose coach, Bill McDonald, had spent two years as a Tigers assistant under Klausing. McDonald knew Braddock's playbook, and he knew how the famed Chuck Klausing thought.

The strike had entered its eleventh week. Despite the steady stream of bored passersby who popped in at corner stores to chat about the Tigers, there wasn't much actual shopping going on along Braddock Avenue. Except in cases where families had squirreled away some savings, steelworkers couldn't afford to spend money on groceries; they were surviving on aid. Local 1219 of the United Steelworkers of America had been distributing rations to augment the county's food program. Every two weeks, workers walked to the David J. McDonald Union Hall on Braddock Avenue to pick up provisions. The strikers considered the food charity, which made accepting it difficult. For proud men who had always taken care of their families, waiting for free food felt like standing in a soup line. Workers kept to themselves while they queued up two hundred deep. With sons and daughters in tow, they quietly loaded their bags with bulk offerings of flour, sugar, dried eggs, powdered milk, corn meal, rice, and potatoes. With their sacks full, they trudged home to turn the food over to their wives, who had become artists with that limited bounty.

On the other hand, there were advantages to the strike. With idle hours every afternoon, and when they weren't scheduled to walk the picket line, fans could indulge one of their favorite fall pastimes: watching the Tigers practice.

On Wednesday, spectators lined up along the fence enclosing ET Field. Onlookers drank Yuengling and Iron City beer out of cans, sagely appraising the boys' play. Few skills garnered respect in Braddock like an insider's ability to dissect Klausing's thinking. The most committed fans knew the Braddock playbook cover to cover. Whenever Klausing introduced a new play or dusted off a little-used gem in practice, aficionados perked up, traded glances, and added notes to their mental logbooks.

"John Jacobs looks good," said Vincent Cataldi, a steelworker, as he leaned into the fence. "He's not the same kind of passer Mark was, but he's one hell of a quarterback, all the same."

"Well, Klausing knows how to use him," said Harry Stuhldreher, a man whose opinion carried weight. "Look at that option. That's a thing of beauty. It plays right to the kid's strengths."

Stuhldreher had been an all-American running back at Notre Dame, a member of the famed Four Horsemen backfield in 1924. Coincidentally, he'd also played for Massillon Washington High School in the years before Paul Brown took over and transformed the team into a record-setting powerhouse. Stuhldreher was a supervisor with U.S. Steel now. Although he was management, he enjoyed ducking out of his office in Pittsburgh from time to time to join the strikers as they diagnosed the Tigers' chances. He was a great supporter of Klausing's. Years earlier he had enlisted a crew of steelworkers to weld together Big Bertha, the enormous seven-man driving sled that would teach generations of Tigers that if they worked together, they could move mountains. Players had him to thank for their sore necks and shoulders.

Braddock's bettors mingled on the perimeter of the group of afternoon gawkers, each looking for clues about the team's readiness. Bookies had been laying odds on the record since the Tigers left for summer camp. Even for men who didn't have a dime to wager, the thought of a windfall was damned attractive. Men bet on credit, staking money they wouldn't be able to pay back. But it was worth it. Braddock hadn't lost in forty-seven games, five shy of Massillon's record. The Tigers had seven regular-season games left. Numbers like that excited the blood, and they easily overwhelmed a weak man's impulse control.

"Grudowski!" Coach Zuger barked on the practice field. "Did someone tell you this was a walk-through?"

The boys had their helmets on for contact drills. A play had just broken up, and a few suicide-squad players, who had been blocked clean onto their backs, were picking themselves off the soot-black ground. Ray Grudowski, the starting offensive guard, had hardly touched his man, who was conspicuously clean.

"Sorry, Coach," he said. "The play was away from me."

"Away from you?" Zuger asked. "Boy, if you ever throw a block like that in practice again, I guarantee you won't see another one in your direction. Do you get my meaning?"

Klausing watched the exchange quietly. He had asked his assistants to crack down on laziness. His biggest fear after the Homestead win was overconfidence, which bred sloppy play.

"They've got to be feeling pretty good about that last game," he said at a coach's meeting two days earlier. "But I don't want you to give them an inch. The last thing we need right now is a team full of big egos."

After live drills, the players split out by offensive position. Linemen ran blocking drills without running backs. Thirty yards away, on another part of the field, the ends ran screaming patterns against ghost defenders. A looped track of coaches' admonitions—"Faster! Hit the gap! Watch your feet!"—rose over ET Field.

On defense, coaches were most concerned with stopping the run. A few ground attempts early in the Homestead game had resulted in big gains. The Tigers had a small defensive line in Ray Grudowski, Vernon Stanfield, John Plisco, and Roland Mudd. The boys averaged just 190 pounds, and it had taken them a full quarter against the larger Homestead offensive line to remember the lessons of summer camp: speed and sound technique.

"Get low, Stanfield!" Zuger yelled. "And get off your heels!"

Vernon Stanfield, the senior guard, had come a long way since his first season as a scrub sophomore on the suicide squad. During one of his first practices two years ago, Stanfield had fallen down on a play and was slow to get up.

"What's the matter with you?" Larry Reaves, the Arizona State–bound senior tackle, had asked.

"Someone stepped on my foot."

Reaves, incredulous, leaned over and glared down at the underclassman. "You better get your ass up," he said.

Stanfield had since become a two-way threat, menacing blockers on defense and sealing the line as effectively as anyone in the WPIAL as offensive guard. There was always something to improve upon, though, and Zuger wasn't cutting his front wall any slack. Klausing wanted discipline, and Zuger was just the man to squeeze it out of these boys.

At the end of regular practice, which let out close to six o'clock, the coaches stayed to work with the quarterbacks and the special teams players. While the rest of the Tigers, exhausted after their rigorous workout, hauled the tackling dummies back to the high school, a handful of boys sipped ladles of water from the zinc practice bucket, windmilled their arms and torqued their backs to loosen up sore bodies, and then returned to the field to make use of the last minutes of remaining daylight.

Ray "Butch" Henderson stayed behind to work on punt blocking. His tall frame and long arms were well suited to the task. He lined up opposite Klausing, who took off his Notre Dame hat and held it out in the air.

"Now!" Klausing yelled, miming the body motions of a punter going through his steps.

Henderson ran at his coach like a banshee and sprawled out in the air, flying just to the side of Klausing and landing on the hard-packed dirt. When he picked himself up, his knees and elbows were scraped to hell. A fresh raspberry formed where a week-old scab had torn away.

On the other side of the misshapen field, Roland Mudd, the starting tackle, worked on his placekicking. After belting a field goal in the 9–6 win over Scott the previous season, he'd been feted all over town.

One storeowner tossed a bag of candy across the counter with a grin. "On the house," the man said, "and there's plenty more where that came from."

"What's this for?" Mudd asked.

"Kid, you won me a bundle last week."

There was no goalpost on the practice field, so Mudd kicked balls against a brick wall. Just beyond a single section of run-down bleach-ers, the side of a three-story building made a natural backstop. During Klausing's first season at Braddock, he'd asked a maintenance man to paint white lines on the wall to approximate uprights. Mudd practiced driving footballs into the sweet spot between those fading vertical lines. The impact made a loud *thud,* and sometimes the balls bounced straight back at the kicker and forced Mike Pratko, the holder, to take cover. During games, it was doubly satisfying for the pair to watch a well-kicked ball go sailing through the uprights. It was a relief not to have to worry about it hurtling back into their faces.

Quarterbacks didn't get much chance to throw during normal practice hours. With only seven or eight passing plays each game, it didn't make sense to use valuable practice time perfecting the air game. But throwing was too important to ignore completely, so Jacobs and his backups, Ron Davis and sophomore Ken Reaves, stayed after to work on their accuracy. Ben Powell, Elbow Smith, and Joel Peoples ran routes for the quarterbacks, and Zuger critiqued the technique of each ball slinger.

"Jake, keep that arm up," Zuger said. "It's dropping to the side again. Scan the field, Davis. Don't follow the flanker with your eyes."

When he had finished with Klausing, Butch Henderson joined the group of quarterbacks and pass receivers. Sometimes his mitts felt like tennis rackets lashed to his wrists. He was a power player, all size and strength, and like most power players he had trouble with his touch. The offensive end hoped to regain Jacobs's trust after drop-ping an easy pass in the Homestead game. Elbow Smith, the end on the other side of the line, had better hands, and Henderson would have to prove he could catch to earn another chance in the limelight.

John Jacobs had started the week with a scratchy throat, but before long, his lungs were ablaze. By Friday afternoon, he had a raging fever.

His body ached and he felt clammy all over. Worse, his back, which hadn't bothered him at all during summer camp or in the previous week's game, felt strange. His spine tingled every time he stepped, and the muscles in his lumbar region had tightened into a protective knot. He didn't mention any of this to Klausing—he wanted to play in Saturday's game and he damn sure wasn't going to let a little cold stop him. By late afternoon, though, his worsening condition was impossible to conceal.

"You don't look good," Klausing said gravely before the pep rally in the high school gymnasium on Friday.

"I'll be fine, Coach."

The Tigers were about to make their entrance before the applauding student body, and Jacobs, visibly pale, was slouched over against a wall in the hallway. Klausing knew flu when he saw it. A bug had been going around the school, and it was just a matter of time before it got to his players. He just wished it wasn't his starting quarterback who had finally picked it up.

"Go to the trainer for a whirlpool after our walk-through this afternoon. And be sure to get lots of rest tonight. I need you fresh tomorrow."

Jacobs promised that he would. Before the Tigers ran out onto the basketball court, where the cheerleaders were already busy warming up the crowd, Klausing made his way over to John Zuger and quietly told him what he'd seen.

"We'll need Davis ready, just in case."

On Saturday, Klausing dressed in black slacks, a collared shirt, and a Tigers letterman jacket. He put on black boots and finished by placing his lucky Notre Dame hat on his head. Then he drove to St. Michael's Church in Pitcairn, where his family attended Mass each week. Klausing made confession every Saturday afternoon. In his first years coaching at Pitcairn he had waited in excruciatingly long lines at church before dashing off to the occasional Saturday game. Now that everyone in the area knew who he was, churchgoers usually implored him to jump to the front of the line so he wouldn't risk being late when the Tigers played on Saturday. It was one of the many perks of being a successful coach.

After confession, Klausing drove to Braddock High. He descended into his basement office and sat down at his desk to review his game plan. The subplot of this game had stirred excitement all over the Mon Valley. Hopewell's head coach, Bill McDonald, had been an assistant at Braddock in 1956 and 1957. Now he was challenging his old mentor. Adding to that high drama, McDonald and Zuger hadn't gotten along well. There was no love lost going into that afternoon's game.

McDonald's Hopewell squad was 2–0 on the season and looked like real competition for the Tigers. They had just beaten New Brighton, a team they hadn't had success against in twelve previous meetings. On average, Hopewell's linemen were ten pounds heavier than the Tigers' front wall. Senior Hopewell tackle Jim Harvey alone weighed 240 pounds. Worse, McDonald knew Braddock's playbook inside and out. He'd been friends with Klausing for years, had coached under him, and had as much insight into his strategic thinking as any man in Western Pennsylvania. The game looked like it would test both men's strategic abilities.

Players began to arrive at the high school by midafternoon.

"Hi, Coach," Roland Mudd said, taking a football out of a bag in the training room and tossing it up appraisingly. "I got a B-plus on my English quiz."

"That's good, Roland. Rita told me she was working with you. I'm glad it's helping."

"She's not too tough. You know what she told me? She told me the Steelers are going to be hot this year."

Klausing gave Mudd a doubtful look. "Let's just worry about our season."

More players arrived and milled around the equipment room. When everyone had assembled, the team left the dim basement and walked down to Library Street. They filed into a narrow alley to the side of a large church and reappeared in front of a squat cinder block building on the other side: the Braddock Elks Lodge. Klausing always made sure to feed his boys before games, and when they played at home, the Tigers ate at the Elks Lodge. Klausing considered the meals a vital part of his pregame ritual. He knew that many of his players wouldn't eat as well again for another week.

The team gathered at the back of the long, open lodge. They sat away from the front section of the building, where a bar area catered to a dozen early-day drunks. The buffet had already been laid out for them, and the mingling aromas of hot, wholesome food crept out beneath a dozen metal cafeteria lids. In his early years at Braddock, Klausing had noticed that black players and white players liked different foods. Reliably, his black players would scarf down roast beef, baked potatoes, and peas while the white players, and particularly the Catholics, preferred fish, big globs of mac and cheese, and buttery rolls. Klausing got the Elks Lodge kitchen to serve two options at every meal. Presented with a choice, the boys started experimenting, nibbling unfamiliar side dishes and trading portions of meat. Before long, mothers all over town were fielding new requests for dinner items. On the advice of their Catholic counterparts, black players started staking out Friday fish fries at churches all over town.

After the meal, the Tigers crossed Braddock Avenue and headed into the lobby of the Paramount Theater. Klausing always reserved the balcony on game day, and the theater always made sure to have something action-packed ready for his boys—although Klausing insisted on checking in with a local Catholic organization to be sure the films were suitable for high schoolers. In the balcony, the players settled in for a Jack Lemmon and Rita Hayworth adventure movie about smugglers in the Caribbean, *Fire Down Below*. The boys whispered back and forth to each other, but teenage high jinks were restrained by their code of discipline and by the nerves of the pending game.

As players watched the film, Klausing and Bobby Williams, the trainer, called groups of boys into the lobby by position. There, with popcorn-nibbling patrons stopping to wish the players and their coach good luck, the two men taped ankles and knees. Silently, the players who wound up sitting down in front of Klausing cursed their bad luck and prepared for one of their coach's famously tight ankle jobs. After the movie, and when all the Tigers had been taped, the team made its way back up the hill to Braddock High. The boys returned to the basement equipment room to dress and gather their gear. Players examined pads and adjusted straps; in corners, they repositioned finicky jock straps. Last, the players stretched their tight home jerseys over their shoulder pads. With their jerseys on, the attitude of every player, the very air in the equipment room, changed in an ineffable but undeniable way. The jerseys still held some of the magic of the past, some essence of the skill of each young man who'd worn them before. Those jerseys had never known a loss, and the players were changed when they wore them.

Carrying their cleats, the Tigers began their walk into North Braddock. With no stadium of its own, Braddock High played its home games at North Braddock Scott Field. To avoid scheduling conflicts, the Tigers played on Thursday or Saturday when Scott also played at home. Scott Field had been one of the first stadiums in the area to have lights for night games, and it was still considered one of the nicer venues for high school sports in the region. Concrete bleachers ringed the outside of the grass surface, which was sunk down into the ground like the bottom of a deep swimming pool. There were enough seats in the bleachers for eight thousand fans, and many more squeezed in whenever Braddock and North Braddock faced off. Like most structures along the Monongahela River, the stadium clung to the side of the valley's steep slope. Standing in the top row of bleachers, fans could look down at the Edgar Thomson Works to the left, scan the length of the valley, and follow the cars beading silently across the Rankin Bridge far off to the right.

The Scott High grounds crew was prepping the stadium when

the Tigers arrived and the first fans were already finding their seats. The team walked silently into the home locker room, where a big Scott Raiders emblem took up an entire wall. There, with tumbling butterflies in their stomachs, the players sat on long skinny benches running up the middle of the locker room and put on their cleats. Coaches walked the room and chatted with the boys to calm their nerves.

"What do you think, Lucarelli?" Zuger asked. "Any girls in the stands for you tonight?"

"There will be if you put me in," the sophomore answered.

The Tigers would go over their game plan in the locker room, and then each position would have a detailed review before players went out for warm-ups. Coaches never had to ask twice for attention in the locker room. Fighting pregame nausea, slapping their arms and legs to try to get rid of their gooseflesh, the players were glad for whatever distraction their coaches could offer.

Hordes of Braddock fans started their march into North Braddock around two o'clock, a mass exodus that, if not for the buoyant, expectant faces of those walking, might have suggested a terrible flood or a devastating mill fire. A thief would have had outstanding success ransacking the town during Tigers games. But then, thieves wanted to watch the Tigers play as much as anyone.

Townspeople who didn't attend the game tuned in to the live broadcast. In car lots and fill-up stations, and sitting around kitchen tables all over the Mon Valley, fans, well-wishers, and skeptics who doubted that the Tigers could keep the streak alive through the season listened to veteran sportscaster Sam Vidnovic on 1360 WMCK. A roar in the background of the broadcast told listeners that the Tigers had taken the field for warm-ups, and that's when Vidnovic read the starting lineup.

"If the Klausingmen are going to stumble," Vidnovic judged, "this is a likely game for it. Hopewell, coming off of last week's win, is primed to play the spoiler. They have size on their side, but there's one thing they don't have, and that's Chuck Klausing. He's on the field now, and the look on his face says that he will not be deterred. What's going through his mind is anybody's guess. But I can safely say that he's carrying a tremendous weight on those shoulders."

Because it was a Saturday afternoon game, Joann had brought the children. In the stands, Patti, Mary-Lou, and Tommy, the three oldest, looked around at the mass of people. Fans choked every inch of free space inside the stadium. It was hard for Klausing's kids to comprehend so many people in one place, and it was exhilarating to know that everyone was there to see their father. On the field, Klausing was conferring with his coaches while the Tigers warmed up. Now and then, he looked back into the stands, his eyes pausing on his wife and children. Though pregame preparations kept him busy, he managed to send subtle, loving waves up at them.

As warm-ups drew to a close, Klausing went out to meet Bill McDonald. He had great affection for his former assistant, even if Zuger and some of Braddock's fans felt otherwise. Zuger thought that McDonald was a climber, a careerist more dedicated to getting to the next rung than to coaching boys and turning them into young men. It was easy to forget amid the hype and hoopla that prep coaches were paid to be high school teachers. Some, like Zuger, took that role to heart, while others considered prep coaching a tryout for bigger things. It was a rare coach indeed who took his role as a teacher and mentor of high schoolers seriously, but who also had the adroitness and leadership to be a world-class coach. There weren't many Chuck Klausings in the world.

At midfield, the two opposing coaches clasped hands and embraced.

"Good luck, Coach," Klausing said.

McDonald was touched to be on equal footing with his former mentor. In the same vein, he wanted badly to beat the man he'd served under for two years, to end the Tigers' run cold. He wanted it as badly as he'd ever wanted anything in his life. No one the Tigers faced

Chuck Klausing on the practice field at Penn State University circa 1944.

Chuck Klausing with his future wife, Joann, on a date in 1945.

Chuck Klausing and teammate Bob Flick show off their missing teeth at Slippery Rock University circa 1946.

Chuck Klausing (*top row, center*) and his 1951 Pitcairn High Railroaders.

Klausing's undefeated 1954 Braddock High Tigers. Quarterback Joe DeNone is in the front row, second from the left; Joe Reaves is in the back row, third player from the right; and Jim Gilliam is sitting to his left. Trainer Mike Trusky is pictured in the white hat.

The Braddock High Tigers practice on E.T. Field circa 1957.

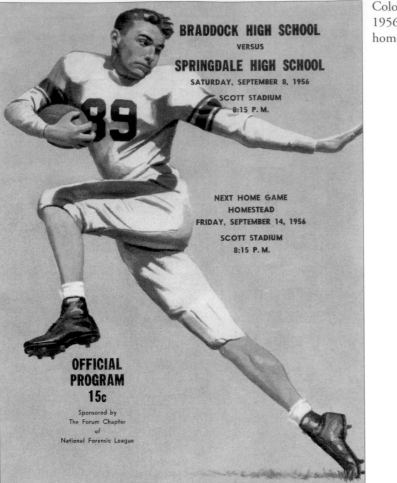

BRADDOCK HIGH SCHOOL
VERSUS
SPRINGDALE HIGH SCHOOL
SATURDAY, SEPTEMBER 8, 1956
SCOTT STADIUM
8:15 P. M.

NEXT HOME GAME
HOMESTEAD
FRIDAY, SEPTEMBER 14, 1956
SCOTT STADIUM
8:15 P. M.

OFFICIAL
PROGRAM
15c

Sponsored by
The Forum Chapter
of
National Forensic League

Color program from a
1956 Braddock High
home game.

Chuck Klausing and son
Tommy at home in 1956.

The Klausings pose for a family portrait in 1959.

Chuck Klausing, center, at the 1960 coach's clinic at Kutsher's Country Club, an event he spoke at as both a high school and college coach. From left: Tuft's Harry Arlanson, University of Washington's Jim Owens, Penn State's Rip Engle, New York Military Academy's Clair Bee, West Virginia's Fred Schaus, Rutgers' Klausing, University of California's Pete Newell, North Carolina State's Earle Edwards, University of Utah's Jack Gardner, Navy's Wayne Hardin, West Virginia Tech's Neal Baisi, Navy's Ben Carnevale, and Purdue's Jack Mollenkopf.

The 1958 Braddock High Tigers.

The 1959 Braddock High Tigers.

The unbeatable 1959 Braddock High offense.

Chuck Klausing is carried off the field after the Tigers beat Waynesburg High for a sixth-straight WPIAL Class A title in 1959.

The enormous trophy case at Braddock High School.

They Coached the Champions

CHARLES KLAUSING
Head Coach

ROBERT TEITT
Assistant Coach

JOHN ZUGER
Assistant Coach

ROBERT MATSEY
Assistant Coach

HARRY CARR
Assistant Coach

A page out of the program of one of many local banquets thrown for the 1959 Tigers.

could expect to match Klausing's streak, but every coach dreamed of being the one to stop it.

The 47–0 win over Homestead had been a warm-up, a chance for Braddock players to show off. In Hopewell the Tigers had a real opponent. Journalist John Smonski stood on the Braddock sideline. Writing for the Braddock *Free Press* two days earlier, he had front-loaded his pregame report with an ominous headline: VISITORS COULD HALT TIGERS' LONG STREAK. In his breakdown of Braddock's chances, Smonski emphasized the role Jacobs would have to play. If the quarterback put in another performance like he'd had against Homestead, running for more than fifty yards and throwing two touchdowns, the Tigers would be tough to beat. If he floundered, it was anyone's game.

On the sideline, Klausing and Bobby Williams huddled around Jacobs. His condition had not improved. He was sweating profusely, though he had hardly warmed up, and he was white as a sheet behind his face mask. His eyes had trouble focusing on any one object, which boded poorly for the Tigers' throwing game.

"Jake, I need to make a decision," Klausing said. "Do you feel like you can go out there?"

"I'm playing, Coach. I'll be fine when I get going."

"Okay, we'll see how it goes."

"Just give us a few touchdowns, Jake," Williams said, "then you can take a rest."

The Tigers captains, minus Jacobs, came back to the sideline to report that they'd lost the toss.

"Kickoff team, let's go!" Klausing yelled.

In the stands, Joann instructed the children to cheer for their father. It seemed as though the entire stadium took her cue in that instant. Sensing the start of the game, the capacity crowd roared to life, easily drowning out the Braddock High band.

Roland Mudd lined up his kicking team and then waited for the referee's signal. When he got it, Mudd made his approach, quickening his pace until his foot collided with the ball. His teammates took off like a pack of dogs after a rabbit, hurtling downfield to squash out the Hopewell return. The kick was high and deep. The Hopewell blockers tried to form a wall as the ball came down into the waiting arms of their return man, but Mudd's hang time was impressive and Braddock ran holes through their dodgy barricade. Three Tigers converged, and the home crowd screamed in approval as the Hopewell ball carrier went down in a heap. The heavy beating of drums by the Braddock drum corps punctuated the cheers of the home crowd, lending the scene an atmosphere of savageness and ritualism.

Hopewell's offense took over and a few Braddock defenders came off the bench to replace kickoff specialists. On the sideline, the Tigers players leaned forward on the bench. Klausing didn't permit his players to stand during games. Despite the occasional story, the tradition of standing on the sidelines was new to football. There was Paul Brown, who had been considered cruel for making his Massillon Washington High School players stand in the 1930s. And under Bud Wilkinson, the University of Oklahoma Sooners began standing for good luck. They won forty-seven straight between 1953 and 1957, the longest streak in NCAA history. But Klausing's boys, whose own streak now stood at forty-seven, had earned their wins sitting down.

Hopewell ran the ball on its first three tries from scrimmage, but got no traction. The massive tackle, Jim Harvey, thrust himself at defensive lineman Roland Mudd, but Mudd held firm each time. Klausing, a former center at Penn State, had been preparing the line all week for the bigger Hopewell front. Braddock's linemen got low for leverage, sticking their rear ends way out. Mudd used Harvey's weight against him, as Klausing had showed him, holding the larger player up for a split second before sidestepping, letting him plunge forward. McDonald had planned to use his players' size to run the ball straight up the gut of the Tigers' defense, but Braddock frustrated Hopewell's opening drive and forced them to kick away.

Vick returned the Hopewell punt to the Tigers' 40-yard line, and the home team offense took the field for the first time. On the sideline, the cheerleaders kicked their bare legs high in the air, freeing them momentarily from their long red and white skirts. In the stands, Braddock High students furtively passed around bottles of whiskey, which they'd smuggled in and now strained to keep out of sight of parents and school administrators. Elsewhere in the stands, steelworkers less furtively sipped from cans of beer or flasks.

In order to give his ailing quarterback time to get used to the pace of the game, Klausing decided to open his attack with running plays. Powell got room on first down and scampered for five yards. After the following play went for no gain, big Doughboy took the ball on a sweep to the left and rumbled six more yards for a first down. The Braddock High band celebrated with a loud crash of horns, but the Tigers momentum came to a halt after a promising start. Hopewell's linemen closed ranks, utilizing their size to close down the run. Hopewell tacklers broke through on the next two plays and dragged Powell and Vick down for short gains. Klausing called a quarterback option and then winced as his ailing passer failed to pitch the ball to his trailing runner in time and got buried under a pile of defenders. To his relief, Jacobs was quick to get up. The quarterback jogged off the field and the punt team got in formation.

If the offense looked less than convincing, Braddock's defense seemed to have improved after the slow start against Homestead. The Tigers stymied Hopewell on the next series. Runners lost yards on consecutive plays, and the Tigers managed to pin McDonald's boys inside their own 10-yard line. The first half was shaping up to be a defensive grind, but just then Braddock got a gift. Hopewell's punter, Charles Lundy, backed up to boot the ball out of his own end zone. He caught the long snap cleanly, but he bobbled the ball on the drop and it thudded awkwardly off his foot. The result was a sixteen-yard dink. When the ball landed, a gang of Braddock players pounced on it.

The Tigers were geniuses at scoring on long plays, but Braddock had a reputation for choking from short distances. It was a problem that had nagged Klausing since his first season with the Tigers. Because field goals were virtually unused in high school football—most teams assigned kicking duties to players who already had starting offensive or defensive positions, which meant kickers spent little time in practice developing leg strength or accuracy—Braddock fans had seen plenty of turnovers on fourth-and-goal over the years.

Taking over with sixteen yards to goal, Jacobs lined up under center. At the snap, he handed the ball to Doughboy, who ran up the middle. The bruiser advanced one yard before succumbing to the large Hopewell wall. Klausing called the same play on second down, but again Doughboy advanced for a short gain.

Frustrated yells went up from the stands, but Klausing knew what he was doing. He had set the trap. On third down, the ball again went to Doughboy. This time, after feinting up the middle, the running back swung wide to the right. Ray Henderson put a strong outside block on the Hopewell defensive end and Gay opened up, rumbling like a bowling ball for a Tigers touchdown. With 7:12 gone in the first quarter, the Tigers had drawn first blood.

After fruitless tries from both sides, the first quarter came to a close. Klausing walked over to the Tigers sideline phone and grabbed the handset. He looked up into the Scott High classroom building overlooking the field. There, in the window, Coach Zuger looked back at him.

"How are they up the middle?" Klausing asked.

"Soft," Zuger said. "Elbow can get free."

Klausing had stuck to the run in the first quarter largely to protect Jacobs. But his team's offensive production hadn't inspired much confidence. It was risky to start throwing. A quarterback opened himself up to injury anytime he held on to the ball long enough for his target to get loose, and that risk only increased with illness clouding his judgment. Against the larger Hopewell defenders, hesitation or indecision could leave Jacobs at the bottom of a heavy pile. Mark Rutkowski's knee injury in the all-star game a few weeks earlier had reminded the Tigers just how fragile quarterbacks could be.

Klausing hung up and walked over to Jacobs, who was sitting on the bench guzzling water. He looked exhausted.

"I'm fine, Coach, nothing to it."

"They're dropping coverage in the middle, playing off their man. But if you don't see anything, get rid of it fast. I don't want to see you get hit."

Jacobs finished his water and put his helmet on. After the brief intermission, the Tigers took the field on offense. Breaking the huddle, Jacobs lined up under center. He had always been confident at the line, bordering on cocky. He made an art of staring down the defenders, baiting them with his eyes. *You think you can catch me? You can't catch me. I'm too damned good.* He owned the field in the seconds before the snap. To look at him scanning the defense now, no one could tell that he had the flu. Jacobs was a competitor, and illness couldn't drain that instinct. He had intestinal fortitude.

At the snap, Elbow Smith, the lanky left end, ran ten yards on an inside slant. The coverage was sloppy and Jacobs delivered a tight spiral, which Elbow hauled in for a gain of fifteen. Jacobs lined the offense up quickly. While the defense was still getting set, center Dan O'Shea snapped the ball. Jacobs dropped back and released a wobbly pass, hitting Elbow again, this time for eleven yards. Braddock fans, witnessing the reincarnation of the rapid-fire offense that had characterized the Tigers' attack under Rutkowski, applauded the back-to-back passes and cheered for more.

Hopewell stopped a run on the next play, so Klausing decided to get creative. He sent in Tony Thompson, the backup halfback, to give Doughboy a rest. On the next play, Jacobs handed off to Thomson, who ran around Elbow Smith on the left end. A few yards downfield, Thomson lateraled back to Ben Powell, who was trailing on the outside. Powell caught the ball at full stride. There wasn't a player in the WPIAL who could catch Powell in the open field, and he easily skirted a Hopewell safety for eleven yards and a touchdown.

The Tigers now led 13–0. After another stop on defense, Jacobs again hit Elbow Smith for long yards. The Tigers ran in the touchdown, and Mudd's extra point made the score 20–0 heading into halftime. Bill McDonald's team had gained only thirty-eight yards of total offense in the first half, and had earned no first downs. McDonald had bet on his boys being able to push the smaller Tigers around, but Klausing's line held its ground. If Hopewell had any chance of coming back, McDonald would need to drastically change his team's strategy.

At halftime, spurred by adrenaline and his innate showmanship, Jacobs walked the locker room and riled up his teammates. "Elbow, you got better hands than a poker player! Ben, you better give them a little bit of a head start to make this even. All the fans are going to leave!"

Suddenly the Tigers quarterback didn't seem sick at all. Klausing decided to keep him in to build the lead. After the break, the Tigers retook the field. Hopewell kicked off to start the third period. Invigorated by their first-half domination, the Tigers confidently moved down the field on their first possession. With methodical running and a few short passes, Braddock advanced the ball to Hopewell's 8-yard line. But Jacobs and company couldn't break through from close range. A holding penalty sent the Tigers back ten yards, and then the drive fell apart completely. Once again, the Tigers couldn't score with the end zone under their noses.

Braddock held on to its 20–0 lead into the fourth quarter. That's when McDonald finally abandoned the run and tried something else. The Tigers' secondary hadn't seen much action all afternoon, and now they were caught off guard. Twice Hopewell made big gains with quarterback Bill Gedris throwing down the sidelines. After three more Gedris throws for short gains, Hopewell broke through for their first touchdown of the afternoon. The point after gave them seven.

Jacobs, meanwhile, had lost his jauntiness. He had managed to stave off the worst of his illness by sheer force of confidence, but now his body was starting to fail him. On the previous series, he'd groped for his back after each snap, massaging the muscles in an effort to work them loose. Sitting on the sidelines, waiting for the offense to go back in, he again looked spent. Klausing would have preferred to keep him out, but 20–7 wasn't a comfortable lead with Hopewell rallying.

"I need one more touchdown," he told his quarterback.

Jacobs nodded, queasy now. Hopewell kicked off, and Curtis Vick's return set the Tigers up nicely on their own 40-yard line. Klausing called a pitch play to Powell to start the series. Jacobs ran the play to perfection, and Powell managed to scramble for five yards on the outside. Klausing called the same play on the next series. Jacobs again pitched back cleanly, and this time Powell broke free. With the home crowd screaming him forward, Powell sprinted fifty-five yards down the sideline.

The touchdown came at a price. Jacobs tried to stagger off the field, but after the final exertion, he dropped to his knees. Teammates helped him to the sideline, where he sat on the bench and took off his helmet. Bobby Williams walked over to evaluate him.

"Coach," Williams told Klausing, "Jake doesn't look so good."

Klausing looked at his quarterback, who was slumped forward limply.

Bill Gedris guided Hopewell eighty yards for another quick touchdown. McDonald seemed to have found the Tigers number, but he was a quarter too late. Time ran out not long after Hopewell's final touchdown. Klausing's boys had won 27–13. It was a strong showing, but the Tigers had exposed a critical vulnerability to the passing game. It was a sure bet that scouts from Midland High, the Tigers next opponent, were taking careful notes from the stands.

Jacobs was a wreck. His back had tightened so badly that he

couldn't walk on his own. With the help of center Dan O'Shea, he limped off the field and into the Scott locker room. He was shivering violently and had trouble taking off his pads. Klausing congratulated the team on the win. Then he had a student manager go see if he could find Jacobs's parents. A few minutes later, Klausing was pulling up outside of Braddock Hospital. The nurse on duty recognized Klausing and immediately sent a gurney out for Jacobs. Klausing talked with the nurse while the hospital staff wheeled Jacobs through two swinging doors. Jacobs's parents showed up at the hospital not long after. Klausing saw the terror on Mrs. Jacobs's face, and he found himself looking away, guilty that he'd kept her son in the game so long and that he had played him at all.

Chapter Seven

DEVOTION

RUMORS ABOUT JACOBS TRICKLED OUT slowly over the weekend, then flooded the town all at once. Without concrete information, worried residents assumed the worst: The Tigers had lost their starting quarterback, and no one could say for how long. Unsubstantiated time frames—three weeks, the rest of the season—passed from person to person like a speculative game of telephone. Though none of these estimates carried the weight of attribution or substantiation, each succeeded in frightening the pants off loyal fans.

In the halls at Braddock High, paper banners testified to a firm resolve and a fighting spirit that had been deeply bruised. A pall had fallen over the school. Jacobs hadn't shown up for classes on Monday, hadn't been in Klausing's car pool with the other North Versailles boys. His solid performance against Hopewell made the news that he'd been playing sick, had collapsed after the game, and had been rushed to Braddock Hospital all the more jarring. With the record in sight, a curse seemed to have struck the town. This was Western Pennsylvania, after all, where a hundred thousand frontier ghosts amused themselves with the living.

In the cafeteria at lunch, students compared notes and dealt the latest gossip. In the background, doo-wop music poured from the personal address speakers, an incongruously cheerful underlay to the sober exchanges. Principal Stukus always played doo-wop at lunch, taking his cue from a record store owner on Braddock Avenue who piped popular music outside to pacify the teens waiting there. The owner didn't trust teenagers and let only one of them in his shop at a time. Principal Stukus needn't have bothered with the music today. Students bled Braddock red and white, and the bad news about Jacobs had everyone preoccupied. Girls with crushes exaggerated their access to Jacobs and bluffed through detailed accounts of his recuperation. There were implications of private bedside vigils, late-night phone calls, and touch-and-go moments when the quarterback had asked for one or another of them by name.

The boys on the team were feeling especially somber.

"I heard he spent the night in the hospital," Ray Grudowski said to a table of his teammates.

"Sure didn't look like the flu," Dan O'Shea said gravely. "He looked like he was dying."

The boys contemplated O'Shea's grim assessment. It wasn't just the loss of the starting quarterback. Jacobs was adored by his team, as much a mascot as the offensive leader. Without his dancing, his predictions of outlandish passing totals, and his ceaseless belief in the happy outcome—the assured win—players felt deflated.

Strategically, Jacobs couldn't have been sidelined at a worse time. On Friday, Braddock would play Midland High, a perennial thorn in its side and the only team to blemish its long streak with a 7–7 tie in the 1954 WPIAL championship game. The record no longer seemed like a forgone conclusion, and a new fear crept into the bellies of a group of high school football players who had never known defeat: They were vulnerable.

———

After practice on Monday, and after he had dropped off the North Versailles crew, Klausing drove out to see his father. Charles Sr. was the mayor of the small Borough of Wilmerding and the superintendent of the town's Lutheran Sunday school, though he had only an eighth-grade education himself. He'd gone to work at the Westinghouse Air Brake when he was fourteen years old as a machinist. He got paid a piece rate for every part he turned out, and he soon got so good that he could complete a normal day's work in just an hour. The older men felt he was making them look bad, so they advised him to take longer-than-normal breaks and to participate in the various coffee clubs that met in different break rooms throughout the day. He developed a reputation as a smart kid who could solve problems, and he became enormously popular. Later he ran for a Wilmerding city council seat, using his network of friends from the Air Brake as his base of support. Soon he was mayor. Charles Sr. had built a life around counseling others. In anxious moments, Klausing drew calm from his father's wisdom, from the way he judiciously smoked his cigarettes and parsed life's mysteries.

Wilmerding was a gerrymandered blip, a company town hugging the Westinghouse Air Brake, the enormous manufacturing plant built by industrialist George Westinghouse to make hissing brake systems for locomotives. The town had been little more than a farming tract before industry and modernity arrived late in the nineteenth century. In 1889, Westinghouse began building infrastructure to attract workers to his new factory. He offered affordable, modern homes that could be rented directly from the company. If something broke, tenants called a Westinghouse operator, who would dispatch a standing army of plumbers, carpenters, electricians, and repairmen, all Westinghouse employees. Residents wanted for nothing, and so had no reason to stray far from work.

Everyone in Wilmerding had some connection to Westinghouse, just as every resident of Braddock could be linked by a cousin or a brother to the Edgar Thomson Works. Klausing's grandfather, William

Klausing, had worked as a patternmaker at Westinghouse's original plant in Pittsburgh. His job was to transform complex mechanical designs into the wooden forms used for sand casting. To entice William to uproot and move to Wilmerding, located about fifteen miles outside of Pittsburgh, George Westinghouse offered him a three-story brick home perched prominently on Westinghouse Avenue. Among other modern amenities, the new house had a freshwater spring running through the basement. The spring offered a constant, chilly bath to keep food cold long before the advent of mechanical refrigeration.

William Klausing had a son, Charles, who married a Swedish girl named Alma. These were Klausing's parents. Before embarking on a life in politics and service to God, Charles worked at the Westinghouse Air Brake as a skilled machinist. The young couple lived on the third floor of the brick house on Westinghouse Avenue and began planning for a family. They had a little girl, Dorothy, and then, five years later, a boy, the future Tigers coach.

Klausing attributed his personality and integrity to his father's influence. He believed that an inheritance of character was fundamental to any young man's development, and so had always been deeply vexed by the troubling family lives of many of his players. He tried to be a model for the boys on his team, a surrogate guardian to rough-and-tumble teens who often faced misery at home. His players, in turn, loved him like a father, would move heaven and earth to make him happy.

With the windows down to the chilly fall air, Klausing drove along familiar streets. Lately, the town where he'd grown up seemed sleepier to him, smaller than it once did. He didn't feel any different than he had when he'd taken the Braddock job five seasons earlier. But of course, he was not the same man. He had become a success, a nationally known coach. He had a beautiful family and adoring supporters. He had more confidence in himself, in his ability as a coach, than he'd ever had before.

Most of the changes of the past five seasons were positive, but there were others that concerned him. Small fissures had opened around the edges of Klausing's happy demeanor. He had started putting more pressure on the people around him, expecting perfection, feeling less tolerant of those who couldn't deliver. He had asked Coach Zuger to skip church that week to finish a scouting report on Midland. Braddock had survived a 9–7 scare against Midland High in 1958. That narrow victory had been delivered by a healthy Mark Rutkowski. With Jacobs questionable for Friday's game, Klausing needed to be even more prepared than usual. Religion was dearly important to him, and a few seasons earlier, he never would have asked an assistant to skip church. But the streak was a kind of religion, too, and it demanded piety.

In the car, Klausing passed the office building where his sister, Dorothy, had once saved his life. The old brickwork had been freshly pointed, and the new mortar stood out between the weathered masonry. He and Dorothy had been sledding together down a steep slope when they lost control. He was five and she was ten. Dorothy had been sitting upright at the back of the sled while Klausing lay headfirst on his belly. The sled jumped a curb at the bottom of the hill, and as they careened toward the side of the building, Dorothy stuck her legs out to absorb the impact and shield Klausing from a fatal collision. She fractured her hip in the crash, and it would have to be set by a Westinghouse doctor. She would walk with a limp for the rest of her life.

Intestinal fortitude—how often had Klausing praised that self-sacrificing trait? Dorothy's heroic act was the antecedent to dozens of sprains, dislocations, and bouts of exhaustion, the bodily offerings of loyal players who would do anything for him. Klausing was a great coach in part because he demanded that others rise to his high expectations, that they give him everything. Tigers often played through illness and injury, ignoring the better judgment of their own exhausted bodies. In 1958, Wayne Davis had taken the field with a broken collar bone against North Braddock Scott, played so hard that the fractured bone burst through the skin. Jim Hux had bounced back days after being diagnosed with a hip pointer, though everyone knew he was playing with immense pain. Intestinal fortitude. Boys played with broken fingers and joints held together by trainer's tape. John Jacobs was sick now, laid up after offering his last reserves of energy against Hopewell. That devotion had brought the Tigers uncommon success. But in quiet moments, the consequences haunted him.

Klausing edged the station wagon along a grassy park dotted with trees. The trees were vibrant in the brittle bloom of fall. He had played countless neighborhood games here as a boy and had been tackled over every inch of that lush grass. Most of his old friends worked at Westinghouse now. Others had died in the war, and a very few, like Tom Casey, had gone off into the wider world. He couldn't help thinking that he, too, was ready for a leap into the wide world.

Klausing turned onto Air Brake Avenue, which was right across from the Westinghouse plant. A block farther on he pulled to the curb in front of his childhood home. His father had moved to Air Brake Avenue to eliminate the time it took him to get to work. Charles Sr. didn't drive, and so had always arranged rides or used public transportation. When he became mayor, he got a personal chauffer: Wilmerding's chief of police.

The Tigers coach got out and walked across the lawn to the front door, which was never locked. When he opened it, nostalgic smells—stewing meat and loamy tobacco—drifted out. His mother called from the kitchen. She was laboring at the cutting board when he entered, and was happy to see him. He apologized that he couldn't stay for dinner. Joann was expecting him.

In the den, Klausing found his father reading. Charles Sr. got up to greet him, and they stood and chatted a few moments, each enacting a small deference to the other man.

The two sat together at last, and Charles Sr., sensing an anxious motive for the visit, put on a gentle face. "How is your quarterback doing?" he asked. "Is he going to be okay?"

"He should be. He's out of the hospital, at least. His parents took him home."

Jacobs had a bad flu. Three quarters of hard playing had exacerbated the illness and left him dehydrated and weak. There was another concern: Jacobs's back. In his weakened condition, there was a real possibility that he'd strained it.

"Well," Charles Sr. said, retrieving a lit cigarette from its resting place between the small battlements of an ash tray, "we'll wait and see. He's a strong player, a tough kid. He'll bounce back."

After a meditative draw, Charles Sr. abruptly changed the subject. "Have I told you about the 1916 Canton Bulldogs?"

He had, many times. Charles Sr. was a die-hard football fan, possessor of a vast mental archive of games, scores, and plays. His obsession had sprouted out of his friendship with Bob Shiring, one of the most celebrated players in the early years of the game. After Shiring retired from the Ohio League, a loose association of top professional clubs in Ohio, the Wilmerding native used to take the younger Charles Klausing by train to Canton every Saturday to watch the big matchups. In the beer garden at the stadium, they met the football greats of the day, including Jim Thorpe, who played for the Canton Bulldogs, and Knute Rockne, who played for the Massillon Tigers, a pro club that shared a name with the high school that would later be made famous by Paul Brown.

Charles Sr. passed his love of football on to his son. When Klausing was a boy, his father would take him on long walks after church to anoint him in the waters of gridiron glory. They would stroll down the hill into East McKeesport, and then down Route 30 to the Westinghouse Bridge, which had just opened. At 450 feet, spanning the vast profundity of the Turtle Creek valley, it was the longest concrete arch bridge in the country. The pair would cross it on foot, then head down through East Pittsburgh, into Turtle Creek, and back up to

Wilmerding, a loop of more than nine miles. Along the way they talked about football, and Charles Sr. recounted every play from the greatest games he'd seen. He carefully explained the role of each position, and illustrated how deceit and strategy often trumped size and strength. They were lessons Klausing would draw on again and again when he became a coach.

In the den all these years later, Klausing listened to the story of the 1916 Bulldogs once more. Just as when he was a boy, he drifted easily along to the steady cadence of his father's voice. Toward the end of the 1916 season, the undefeated Bulldogs met the Massillon Tigers, their longtime rival. The game ended in a tie, which rankled the Bulldogs. The following week, more than eight thousand fans—a huge number for the era—turned out to watch a rematch. The Bulldogs had never won an Ohio League championship, and the team's head coach and star player, Jim Thorpe, the world-famous athlete, was determined to break the unsuccessful run. Thorpe rallied the team behind him, getting more out of his boys than even they knew they could give. Canton won 24–0.

"It was a thing to behold," Charles Sr. said, looking at his son. "Thorpe was a great leader."

The two continued talking until the younger Klausing had to go home to dinner. As always when he spent time alone with his father, he left feeling lightened. Charles Sr. had a rare gift for leading people to insight. If he were a boxer, he would be the kind to finesse his opponents with a thousand glancing blows, the sum of which would be more powerful than any sudden punch.

John Jacobs's house was fragrant with the smell of his mother's freshly baked nut rolls. For a woman who cooked Spam with religious devotion, Jacobs's mom could turn out surprisingly delectable baked goods. Girls at Braddock High had come close to proposing marriage to Jake to get their hands on that recipe.

After two nights in the hospital and a visit from the chiropractor, the ailing Tigers quarterback was recuperating back at home in North Versailles. His fever had broken and his strength was starting to return. His sore back still kept him off his feet, but he wasn't uncomfortable. If not for the prospect of missing playing time, which was unacceptable to him, he might have enjoyed his convalescence. His mother and two sisters were being sweet, carting in food and fluffing his pillows. Even his father had been conciliatory, a welcome and abrupt change from the normal tense routine.

To the family's irritation, and to Jacobs's great satisfaction, people had been calling incessantly to check on the quarterback's condition. Along with coaches and concerned teammates, complete strangers were ringing for news. Many of them were bettors who disguised their interested prying with flowery well-wishes. Even so, local girls made up the largest bloc of callers. Jacobs was enormously popular with young women in town, and he dated widely and noncommittally. If his good looks and role as Braddock's starting quarterback entitled him to a degree of built-in popularity, his romantic success had more to do with the way he carried himself. Jacobs was an unrepentant braggart. He was also such a hopeless joker that he simply overwhelmed the most high-bred girls' best defenses. "I've seen better legs in a bucket of chicken," he once told a date, and instead of smacking him, she laughed the gum right out of her mouth.

For as long as he could remember, Jacobs had felt special. He'd always been praised as a natural leader and a gifted athlete. When he played quarterback in junior high, his team went undefeated both years. He hadn't lost a football game since, and so had reason to be confident.

Still, Jacobs's arrogance didn't stem from his success on the field. Just the opposite, he believed fundamentally in his own ability, and that belief drove him to excel. What set Jacobs apart from the typical jock was the unyielding nature of his self-esteem. Where the former wore a mask of confidence cobbled from a few newspaper clippings and a date with the head cheerleader, Jacobs was nakedly, unabashedly confident. When he burst into spontaneous fits of dancing, and when he wore all-purple outfits that the most stylish men in Braddock wouldn't dare trot out, he was being true to character, giving expression to the bright vision he had of himself. In the face of that confidence, and unable to beat it back, the world at large made the correction and came around to Jacobs's vision.

Jacobs wanted to leave Braddock, and so he would. He had taken a tour of the Edgar Thomson Works with his classmates a few years earlier, and the heat of the place, the unrelenting monotony, revolted him. He wanted to hit the road, to get away from the town and from his father, to test the waters of a bigger pond. That meant a scholarship. He had watched recruiters from half the colleges in the nation hound Mark Rutkowski a year earlier. Now it was his turn. Lying in bed was a torment, no matter how many batches of rolls his mother whipped up. His destiny was waiting for him, and he knew all he had to do was claim it. He couldn't do that from bed.

Far away from Jacobs and Klausing, and a world away from the adoring embrace of Western Pennsylvania, in a dorm room in Hanover, New Hampshire, Mark Rutkowski was pensive. A few long weeks had passed since the former all-star quarterback of the Braddock High Tigers had torn the ligaments in his left knee. The bodily damage seemed to have spread now, crossing some invisible divide between the corporeal and the existential. It was as if the connective tissues bonding him with his bright future and lofty dreams had also ripped, and with them the fragile threads of his self-confidence. He was a different person than he had been a short while ago. He felt like a fraud standing in some other Mark Rutkowski's shoes.

He played the injury over and over in his head. It was a kind of torture, and also a mad attempt to change the outcome, to reason his way to a better result. He'd always been able to do that—sit and think about a problem, exhausting the angles, until a solution emerged. The injury happened in a scrimmage, of all things, a prelude to the celebratory matchup that was supposed to be the final hurrah of his high school sports career. It was a meaningless moment in August, a blip at the end of the summer before college and freedom. But it had meant everything.

The Big 33 game was an annual contest for interstate bragging rights. The thirty-three best prep players in Pennsylvania faced Ohio's top thirty-three. Football fanatics had long debated which state nurtured the best football talent in the country. Texas had a legitimate claim to a top slot, and some of the Southern states were contenders, but any list had to include Pennsylvania and Ohio in the top three.

Of course, Rutkowksi was selected—it would have seemed ridiculous to him, to everyone, if he hadn't been. He had started for the Tigers since his sophomore year. That's when the coaches discovered he could throw a ball thirty yards without any arc, could fire a bullet that didn't just hit a man in stride, but hit a specific portion of that man, the smallest window beyond the outstretched fingertips of the defender. The receivers learned his rhythms, learned to trust him. They only needed to run their routes perfectly, uncreatively, and they would score touchdowns. Rutkowski had no foot speed, no moves outside the pocket. He never needed any. His was a singular skill: He could throw the ball to perfection.

And that was why the practices leading up to the Big 33 game felt wrong to him. The coach of the Pennsylvania team, Carl Snavely, had just retired as the head coach of Washington University in St. Louis. Snavely was a devotee of single-wing football, an offensive set that worked best when quarterbacks had talent in the pocket *and* on the run. Rutkowski didn't complain, even when asked to tuck the ball, even when he started getting knocked around. He didn't complain when Snavely reamed into him for being slow as molasses. He just bit down. He had never been anything but perfect on the field, and in his gut he believed he would figure this out, too.

There was a giant tackle out of Philadelphia on the Pennsylvania team. John Sherrer was a man-child, a born quarterback killer. He would eventually be named the top lineman of the Big 33 game, and no surprise there, because he was the kind of guy who smelled blood and lived for the sack. It was just an intra-squad scrimmage, preparation for the big game. But those boys were competitors, and for competitors there was no such thing as three-quarters speed.

Rutkowski was in at quarterback. He stood over center as he'd done ten thousand times before, and he scanned the defense quickly, efficiently. He dropped back after the snap, and then, intent on making his legs work, on figuring out how to overcome the obstacle before him, he ran. A hole opened up. It was like magic, like charging toward an unscalable mountain only to realize that the rock face was really two walls, offset and overlapping, with a perfect passage in between. Rutkowski bolted through, the football cradled awkwardly to his body. He saw the green field, the end zone.

It was a trap. There was Sherrer, lying in wait like a bandit by the roadside. He grabbed Rutkowski by the shoulder. There was a violent torquing of bones, a scampering of legs. Something felt wrong to Rutkwoski when he landed. It was an academic realization as much as a physical one, a slow accounting of the body crumpled beneath its own weight. When he gazed down, his leg didn't look familiar. It took a second, lying there, registering the horror on the faces of his teammates, to realize what was wrong. His left leg was bent the wrong way at the knee.

That's the moment life stopped making sense, the moment the old Mark Rutkowski began fading. When he returned to Braddock after the Big 33 game, he limped into the house and collapsed onto his bed. It was mid-August, and Coach Klausing and the 1959 Tigers had just left for summer camp. He didn't think he'd be nostalgic, but he was. He would miss the ride up on the bus, the camaraderie, and even the discipline. He would miss being a Tiger, which had been his only aspiration since childhood and his only identity since tenth grade.

Rutkowksi looked at the stack of offer letters in his room: Ohio State, Michigan State, Penn State, Dartmouth, Brown. There were so many, he had lost track of the schools that were courting him. He planned to make his decision at the last minute. He was a quick thinker on the field, but methodical off it. Only now he couldn't muster any clarity. He hadn't been to see a doctor yet, petrified of what he might learn, of what he would then have to confess to the recruiters. Schools were calling. Most were holding an open spot for him, but he had to make his decision before the first day of classes.

A few days after his injury, the pressure became too great. Rutkowksi was standing in his room, thinking about his future. It was scorching-hot inside, and Rutkowski passed out. He hit the floor like a ton of bricks and came to in the hospital hours later. Doctors said it was nervous exhaustion.

He had to get away from the recruiters, from the Braddock High fans, and even from his friends, who couldn't stop asking about his bright future. His knee was a mess. At best, he reasoned, he'd have to sit out a portion of the upcoming season. Most schools would take one look at the knee and send him packing. He needed a scholarship to go to college. He couldn't risk having his funding revoked. When he got out of the hospital, he fled to an uncle's house in Cleveland to think.

Aid packages at the Ivy League schools were based on academic merit and financial need, and not on athletic performance. Coaches gamed the system easily enough when it came to recruiting top football talent, but for Rutkowski the upside was clear: His funding at an Ivy League school wouldn't be conditional on his readiness to play. Dartmouth had flown him to campus earlier that summer on a private plane. He liked the school well enough, though it had never been one of his top choices. Now it seemed like his only bet.

Rutkowski phoned the Dartmouth recruiter. The man told him to get on a bus immediately—not to Hanover, but to New York City. The student aid package didn't cover room and board, so the athletic department sent financially strapped athletes to work short-term jobs that were arranged by sympathetic alumni. It was late August when he got on the bus. He was pouring sweat and his knee throbbed at every pothole. It was the longest ride of his life, and when he arrived, he felt small standing in New York City.

Rutkowski stayed at the Dartmouth Club, a hangout for rich alumni. His first night, the concierge stopped him from entering the polished dining room. He would need a jacket and tie if he wanted to eat, the man informed him. Rutkowski didn't have much of an appetite anyway, but the club arranged loaners. The size 48 jacket hung like a tarp from his size 40 frame. When he was seated, Rutkowski looked around. It was the most elegant group of people he'd seen outside of a movie. He felt certain that he could read their minds and that collectively they were wondering what he was doing among them. It was one year, almost to the day, since he'd returned from his summer job at Camp Iroquois with a Mohawk haircut and a clear vision of his future.

Rutkowski spent the next two weeks working construction alongside two other athletes at a local airport. He wrapped his knee as best he could and got used to hopping around on his good leg. He finally made it to Dartmouth a week after classes started, though it seemed like he'd missed an entire semester. He didn't understand a word that his German professor said. The other students, prep school kids who had already had extensive language preparation, didn't seem to have any trouble. Rutkowski kept quiet, kept his head down. For the first time in his life, the academic standout felt stupid.

Football went no better. The Dartmouth trainer outfitted Rutkowski with an enormous brace made of metal and leather. The quarterback limped to practice on the second week of school and met the team on the field. The head coach wanted to see what his freshman recruit could do. He called out a play and told him to step to the line. Rutkowski stared back blankly. He'd been sent a playbook months earlier as a recruiting enticement, but the school had been low on Rutkowski's list then, and on a lark he'd given the playbook to Coach Zuger. He had forgotten all about it until that moment. He didn't know any of the plays.

The coach's face turned red as Rutkowski stammered to explain himself. Being unprepared was bad enough, but the freshman had given away the team's offensive playbook. Few betrayals cut deeper in the locker room, and Rutkowski wouldn't be issued another playbook. If he wanted to learn, he'd have to watch during practice. Not that it mattered much. Even buckled into the brace, his knee was in no shape to play football. He returned to his dorm room each day after practice and sat on his bed. He massaged his aching leg, thought of glory days that now seemed years behind him, and tried to find that other Mark Rutkowski, whose slippery image receded a little more with each passing hour.

Klausing met with his assistants at lunch on Monday. Hopewell had discovered a glaring vulnerability in the Tigers secondary. Midland High had a talented senior quarterback in Ken Russell, and it was a safe bet that the Leopards would try a passing onslaught. Head Coach John Petchell had been at Midland High since 1951, and he had been facing Klausing-led teams for years. With a tie in the 1954 championship game and a nail-biting loss by two points the previous season, his teams had come closer than any other to ending the Tigers' streak.

The 1958 game had gone in Braddock's favor on a valiant last-ditch effort. Until the closing minutes of the final quarter, Braddock's only score had been a safety, a fluke that resulted from a botched Midland punt. With precious minutes left before the final whistle, and trailing Midland 7–2, Mark Rutkowski and Ben Powell, then a junior, had masterminded a sixty-four-yard drive in twelve plays. A twenty-yard pass from Rutkowski to Powell put the Tigers on the 14-yard line, and two plays later Powell lunged in for the go-ahead score. Midland fans were incredulous. It seemed like a stroke of bad luck, a lousy safety, had done them in.

This year, Midland's experience extended well beyond its coaching staff. With eight senior lettermen in the starting lineup, the Leopards were seasoned. Aside from Ken Russell, the quarterback, the biggest concern for Klausing was a six-foot-five-inch, 210-pound All-State senior offensive and defensive lineman named Movie Smith. After debating how to pronounce Smith's first name—opinions were split between *MOE-vee* and *MOO-vee*—Klausing and his assistants tried to figure out how they could beat him.

The thinking went like this: If Jacobs bounced back, his greatest asset would be his mobility. With a shifty quarterback, a defensive lineman's speed and agility mattered more than his size. But backup Ron Davis didn't have Jacobs's legs, and if he got the start, he would be a sitting duck whenever Smith broke through the line. With the Tigers' undersized front wall, that was bound to happen throughout the game. Klausing would have to call running plays to get the ball out of Davis's hands quickly. If the All-State lineman proved as fearsome as the game film suggested, those runs would have to be directed away from him. Coach Petchell's team would just need to defend one side of the field, as a result, and even Ben Powell and Curtis Vick wouldn't be able to rack up big yards against a defense that knew where they were going.

After much discussion, the coaching staff drew up two plans: one for use if Jacobs bounced back, and one to use if Davis got the start. When they broke at the end of lunch, no one was brimming with confidence.

On Tuesday and Wednesday, Klausing approached his basement office cautiously. Nervous visitors had taken to camping out there in hopes of getting an update on Jacobs. Dan Rice, the athletic director, and Mike Sullivan, the school board president, both stopped by several times each day to get the latest news on Jacobs's condition. Klausing urged patience, though that hardly calmed his bosses.

A few well-known bookies had popped into Klausing's office, as well. These men Klausing turned away cold. Bookies operated out of newsstands and corner markets on Braddock Avenue. Cops on the take looked the other way as patrons streamed into unkempt, understocked shops and emerged with cocksure grins and no groceries. Many bookies had been extending credit to striking workers into the hundreds of dollars, and each passing game etched deeper lines of desperation onto the faces of the biggest losers. Action on the Midland game, which promised to be a real contest, was already hotter than on any game played that season. With Jacobs out of school, the temptation to bet against Braddock was too great for many strikers looking to settle their debts on one lucky take. It was blasphemy to bet against the Tigers, but a bookie's oath was at least as strong as a lawyer's or a priest's.

Klausing had been telling people not to worry, but he was as eager for updates as anyone. He had been in regular phone contact with Mrs. Jacobs. Her son had been feeling better, she said, but his back still ached and kept him in bed. With the game two days away, the hours available for recuperation were waning.

On Thursday afternoon, after a long week of contingency-planning, Klausing called the Jacobs residence one last time. District policy dictated that all athletes had to attend school on the day of a game in order to suit up. Though it might have been easy enough to cook the attendance books to secure another morning of rest, Principal Stukus was not a man to bend the rules. If Jacobs stayed home on Friday, the Tigers' hopes would be riding on the arm of junior Ron Davis. After a few rings, Klausing got Jacobs directly. That was a good sign.

"I'll be waiting for you in the morning, Coach," Jacobs assured him.

Klausing told him not to push himself, but Jacobs said he felt fine. The Tigers coach hung up the phone. He knew Jacobs was putting up a front, and he'd have to wait and see for himself how his quarterback was faring.

In the morning, Klausing and his two school-age daughters drove the usual route through North Versailles. When they crested the hill, Klausing was relieved to see Jacobs standing in his normal spot, his book bag by his feet. After the previous Saturday's frantic trip to the hospital, it was a welcomed sight. Klausing pulled over and Jacobs slid gingerly into the station wagon.

"How are you feeling?" Klausing asked.

Jacobs grinned weakly and said he was fine. Klausing admired the boy's determination, though he was hardly convinced of his health. They continued the route, and soon Klausing had a full car that bottomed out at every dip. The others razzed Jacobs about missing practice, though they were all relieved to see him in the car.

"Enjoy your vacation, Jake?" Curtis Vick asked him, grinning.

When the familiar station wagon pulled up in front of the high school, dozens of students waiting for the bell caught sight of Jacobs. A ripple of excited chatter shot through the throng. Jacobs swung the door open and stepped out. A moment later, before he knew what was happening, the students in front of the high school began applauding. Even Jacobs, with his supreme confidence and his unerring belief in himself, was taken aback. He walked toward the school through a corridor of happy, cheering faces. He had a sense even then that it was a moment he would never forget, one he would replay over and over for years to come.

The morning reception at Braddock High had a tremendous effect on Jacobs. Hungover from the flu and achy down his back, he nonetheless felt the old Friday buzz, the familiar rush that, if timed right, would crest with the opening whistle and carry him through four spirited quarters. Later that afternoon, while fans drove nervously

out to Beaver County, about an hour away, and while Jacobs's teammates didn't know for certain whether he would get the start, the
quarterback was already mentally preparing for the Midland secondary, running touchdowns in his mind.

The team bus arched over the Monongahela River at its confluence
with the Allegheny, and then wended north away from Pittsburgh.
Beaver County, home of the Midland Leopards, had opened the
nation's first atomic power plant two years earlier. Nestled on a flat
stretch behind the Ohio River, surrounded by thick woods, the Ship-
pingport Atomic Power Station had ushered America into the nuclear
age. A lot of history had been made since the Tigers streak began
more than five years earlier. With six games left in the regular season
and only five needed to break Massillon's record, the Tigers were hoping to make a bit of their own history before long. If they were going
to stumble, it was a good chance it would be at the hands of Midland.

When they arrived at the stadium, the Tigers got a nasty surprise.
Midland's field was sopping wet. The water was so deep in places that
only pin tips of grass were visible. Klausing glared out at the reflecting
pool from under the brim of his ND hat. It hadn't rained a drop in
two days, but he hardly needed to ask what had happened. John
Petchell, Midland's coach, was a feisty son of a gun. The Midland fire
department had been out with a pump truck all week. Midland had
intentionally soaked its field to slow Braddock's running game, and
Petchell's team had been practicing in the muck all week to get accustomed to playing in the slop. This was football in Western Pennsylvania. Within the bounds of the hole-filled rule book, anything was
fair game.

With the wet gridiron, Klausing wanted to get the boys into warm-
ups quickly. They hadn't expected wet weather, and they'd need time to
find their footing. In a brief speech in the locker room, Klausing told
his players they'd be sticking to the game plan.

When Doughboy complained about the field, Klausing snapped
at him. "Hellfire! It's wet for them, too!"

Klausing was no Vince Lombardi in the locker room.

After going over the game plan, players ran out onto the sodden pitch. Their cleats sank in the mire, and after a few minutes, the Tigers' pristine game pants were completely covered in mud. Balls landed with a cold *plop* on the wet earth. It was like playing football in a swamp.

In the stands, arriving Braddock fans caught up on the latest Tigers gossip. To save money on gas, striking workers had packed six or seven to a car. The close quarters during the thirty-minute trip, along with the smuggled hooch that men passed liberally back and forth, worked to kindle a deep fraternity. Fans carried the clubhouse air of Braddock Avenue with them wherever they went. Even an away game at an unfriendly stadium was a haven from the bigger problems awaiting them at home.

Toward the front of the visitors' side, the bass drummer of the Braddock High band pounded a steady beat. With that prompting, a chorus of loyal students let loose with the opening lines of the Braddock High fight song.

We are—Braddock
We are—Braddock
Cheer—Oski
Wow—Oski
WE WE—Eat up
Tigers—Raw Raw Raw.

Like a counterpoint to the easy comradeship of the Braddock sideline, the Midland Leopards took the field for warm-ups to the thunderous foot stomping of the home crowd. Klausing wasn't worried too much about the wet field—his Tigers practiced on a swath of dirt so bare that even a light drizzle turned it to quicksand. He was worried about facing a tough Midland team on its own turf. The Leopards hadn't lost at home in twenty-three straight contests. The

Tigers had bested the Leopards at Scott Field in 1958, but that meeting was the first the two teams had had since fighting to a tie in the 1954 championship game. Tricks like the soaked field accounted for some of Midland's home stadium success, but an excellent coaching staff and intensely loyal fans were the biggest reasons for the team's sterling record. The town was as rabid about football as any in Western Pennsylvania.

Midland lost the toss and Braddock elected to receive. Stomping Midland fans tried to intimidate the Tigers with sheer volume. Though no place in Western Pennsylvania was louder than North Braddock Scott Field during a Braddock–North Braddock game, Midland's field came close.

The Leopards' kickoff man ran ahead for the kick. He booted a long ball that barely bounced when it landed. Curtis Vick fell trying to scoop it up and got half-buried in mud. He couldn't get his footing before a pack of Midland defenders jumped on him. One player fell on Vick's helmet, forcing the running back's face straight into the wet muck. For a moment he couldn't breathe. Though only a few seconds elapsed, it felt like a full minute. When Vick got free, he took a big breath and put his hands on his knees.

"What's wrong, Curt?" Roland Mudd asked.

"Nothing," Vick said, demonstrating that workmanlike attitude that Klausing admired.

With the Tigers specialists trotting to the sidelines, fans on both sides craned to see whether number nineteen, John Jacobs, would take the field. When he ran out, stepping gingerly in the soggy turf but looking healthy, the visiting Braddock fans let out a roar. They had pinned their hopes on the brash kid from North Versailles, and with good reason. With Jacobs in as quarterback, Braddock's backfield had four dangerous runners. With the quarterback option and the possibility of laterals and reverses, there was no way for a defender—even one as imposing as Movie Smith—to cut off every attack.

Jacobs broke the huddle and trotted to the line. When he looked up, he found himself staring at Movie Smith. The tackle was so tall, it looked like he could step right over guard Ray Grudowski, who was just getting into his stance.

"Movie," Jacobs said, pronouncing the name *MOO-vee,* "we're going to run all over you."

The All-State tackle looked insulted. "My name isn't *MOO-vee,*" he responded in a deep baritone. "It's *MOE-vee.*"

Flying on adrenaline, Jacobs made quick work of the snap count and took the ball from center Dan O'Shea. A week without practice had taken its toll. Jacobs bobbled the ball, which fell loose on the ground. Quick-handed, he bent and scooped it up, and then tried to scramble forward. The Midland wall converged, and Jacobs fell at the line of scrimmage for no gain. In the stands, nervous steelworkers groaned. Jacobs's recovery from illness had been a talisman, a sign that all was right with the football universe. Few had considered that the boy could still have a bad game.

Klausing gave Jacobs a chance to redeem himself on the next play. Jacobs took the snap and light-footed it behind center for a moment. Klausing had called a quarterback keeper, and now Jacobs saw an opening between Stanfield, the piano-playing guard, and center Dan O'Shea. But when he tried to slither through, his cleats lost their grip in the mud. He slipped again and fell for no gain. Midland's wet field was taking a toll.

On the Braddock sideline, Klausing picked up the phone to confer with Zuger. From the assistant coach's vantage in the bleachers, the field looked like a mud pit. Two plays into the game, it was virtually impossible to distinguish one jersey from another. Zuger had seen that Midland's defense was cheating to the middle, though, anticipating the inside run with the wet field. Klausing chose the next play accordingly.

Jacobs took the snap and pitched back to Ben Powell on a sweep. Floating over the mud like a bug on water, Powell sprinted parallel to the line and then broke upfield off a containment block by Ray Henderson. Powell switched direction twice to avoid defenders, bounding nineteen yards before hydroplaning to a stop with a Leopard hanging on his legs.

Vick pounded out five hard yards up the middle on the following play. Then it was all Powell. The halfback finished the opening drive with a twenty-five-yard sprint around end for pay dirt, coasting to a stop after he crossed the goal line and letting the ball fall gently to the ground. A less ostentatious star would have been hard to find. Jacobs made up for Powell's restrained demeanor by dancing downfield with his arms held up. Despite the early hiccups, he felt strong. His mother's nut rolls had done the trick.

Midland couldn't do anything against Braddock's defense on the following series, and Petchell's team punted away after losing three yards in three plays. Braddock took advantage with another long drive on the ground. With Jacobs rusty after a week's rest, and with the sloppy conditions, Klausing didn't want to tempt fate with a lot of passing. He interchanged sweeps to either side with hard running up the middle. The latter was Vick's specialty. After powering for small gains, the fullback smashed through Movie Smith for an eleven-yard touchdown on the Tigers second possession. Braddock surged ahead 13–0.

Both teams were quiet for most of the second quarter, but Midland responded in the waning minutes when quarterback Ken Russell hurled a forty-four-yard pass to end Ken Lake for a quick touchdown. The extra point kept Midland very much alive at halftime and left the visitors feeling vulnerable. Braddock's safeties weren't getting any traction in the mud, and Midland's ends just needed a quick jump off the line to get free.

In the locker room, Klausing conferred with his assistants. He was impressed by how capably his front line had handled Smith. If the undersized wall could keep shoving the tackle around, he was going to keep calling plays up the gut. Speaking briefly to his team,

Klausing emphasized pass defense. After the effortless touchdown a few minutes earlier, Midland was sure to throw the ball again. Braddock's defenders would have to figure out how to backpedal in the mud.

Smith lived up to his reputation on offense during Midland's first possession of the half, opening several holes that allowed the Leopards to advance the ball past midfield. But to Klausing's relief, the Midland aerial game didn't go anywhere. The Braddock secondary played it tight, adjusting well to the wet conditions. Midland turned the ball over on downs deep in Braddock territory.

As John Jacobs bent under center, a voice in the stands rang out: "Kill the quarterback!"

It was Jacobs's mother, of all people. She had never understood football and didn't know the difference between the positions. The Braddock loyal thought that they had an enemy in their midst, but when they spun around, they saw a confused Mrs. Jacobs and laughed.

Halfway through the third quarter, Powell took a handoff on the Midland twenty-six-yard line and got a chance to demonstrate just how talented he was. He was immediately met by a Midland defender behind the line of scrimmage, but he shook the player with a quick juke. Another defender had a clear shot at the line of scrimmage, but Powell spun so quick that the boy came up with air. A third man had Powell dead to rights for a short gain, but the running back kept his feet, twirled through a hole in the converging defense, and contorted over the goal line for another touchdown. If there had been any doubt about Powell's rightful claim to being the best runner in the state, his performance in the sloppy conditions at Midland put it to rest for good.

Doughboy scored the final touchdown of the evening, extending Braddock's lead to 25–7. Midland never recovered, and the team's aerial attack, which was its only hope against the Tigers, never materialized. At the end of the game, Klausing and Petchell met at midfield to shake hands. The older coach wished Klausing luck with the rest of the season. Then, in the dignified way that losing coaches have of putting on a brave face, he strode back to his sideline and gathered his down-trodden players around him. They would learn from the game, he said, avoiding the painful truth that the loss had once again knocked them out of contention of an appearance in the WPIAL championship game. For the eight senior lettermen, the goal they had worked so hard for since sophomore year had slipped irrevocably out of reach.

The Tigers, on the other hand, had survived, and their hopes were alive and well. On the bus, exhausted but in good spirits, Jacobs sat with his North Versailles friends. They sang doo-wop tunes by the Flamingos and the Sheppards, standing in the aisles and unleashing vocal solos. Some of the Tigers were decent singers, and Jacobs was sure that he could make big bucks if he had a tape recorder. At the front of the bus, Klausing chuckled. As long as the team won, the players could do whatever they liked on the bus ride home. They'd been winning so long that no one knew what they would do on the ride home if they lost.

Chapter Eight

A TOWN AND ITS TEAM

IT WAS MIDMORNING on Monday when Ernie Vida, a short, balding man in a thick coat, scurried down Braddock Avenue. Beneath wispy hair, which fluttered in the fall breeze, Vida's eyes searched back and forth. He greeted no one along his path, and no passersby stopped to chat about the weather. Most people avoided making eye contact entirely.

Vida was an enigma. Everyone in Braddock recognized him by sight, but few had any idea what he did for a living. He was in his mid-forties, small-framed, and cagey, and he had the unique talent of being both ubiquitous in town and almost completely unknown. He seemed to be at every street corner summit, barroom assembly, and shadowy rendezvous on Braddock Avenue, always clinging to the outside of tight, close-shouldered circles, no one present ever sure who had invited him or why. He was too squirrelly to be a politician, even in a town full of squirrelly politicians, yet his personality and demeanor suggested that he was someone close to power. He also suggested this—quite vocally. At various times he'd claimed to be a lifelong friend of Steelers owner Art Rooney Sr., an acquaintance of Senator John F. Kennedy, and a spy for the FBI. None of it would have surprised anybody, but neither did most residents give him the satisfaction of believing his stories outright.

The only thing anyone seemed to know for certain about Vida was that he loved football and was loyal to Coach Klausing. Vida had been around since the early days of the 1954 season, was one of the longest-serving members of the unofficial club of hangers-on that had coalesced around the Tigers coach. He ran errands for the team, shuttling equipment and giving rides to VIPs during away games. His real contribution, though, was his resourcefulness. He was a man who knew how to cut corners. For example, he had drastically reduced the time it took the Tigers to get their game film developed, which gave Klausing a fantastic strategic advantage. With no commercial labs nearby, high school teams in the region had to send their film canisters to the Eastman Kodak Company in Rochester, New York, to be processed. Even with rush shipping, Friday's game films didn't make it back until the following Wednesday. That hardly left enough time for coaches to analyze the footage and make the necessary corrections. But Vida found a television studio in Pittsburgh that had its own processing equipment. He struck a deal, and the Tigers had been getting their film developed overnight ever since. The man was a born hustler, and Klausing loved him for it.

Walking down Braddock Avenue, Vida spotted an unoccupied pay phone. He took a crumpled sheet of paper out of his coat pocket and smoothed the creases. Lifting the receiver, he scanned his list and waited for the operator.

"Offices of *The Saturday Evening Post*—Philadelphia," he said when she came on.

Vida spent the next two hours crossing magazines off his list. Whenever he managed to get an editor on the phone, he began talking hurriedly, spilling headlong into his pitch. He asked if the editor had heard of the Braddock High Tigers, explained that the scrappy group was barreling toward a national record, and said that he was willing to offer the magazine—whichever he happened to be talking to—an exclusive. He brought up the steel strike, masterfully overlaying the Tigers' inspirational march, the region's economic crisis, and the nation's uncertainty. He was a world-class bullshitter, a champion wise guy, and he knew how to grease the wheels.

As a finishing touch, Vida made sure to mention all the other publications that wanted a piece of the Braddock story. Speaking with an editor at *The Saturday Evening Post*, he let slip that *Life* and *Time* had expressed interest. When he got through to *Sports Illustrated,* he mentioned *SPORT.* He collected editors' names along the way and mentioned them in subsequent phone calls, lending credibility to his claims. None of the editors he spoke with gave a firm answer, but neither did they pass on the story outright. By early afternoon, after two hours working the phones, the hustler was fairly certain he had secured some big-time coverage for his friend Chuck Klausing.

It had been three months since the strike began, and President Eisenhower was getting anxious. The country needed building girders, sewer grates, and thumbtacks, to say nothing of tanks and Polaris missiles. All of it required steel. Whatever quantities manufacturers had stockpiled before the strike were now depleted. American automakers, which consumed about 20 percent of the country's steel, had already begun laying off workers. General Motors alone let go of sixty thousand of its production employees, and the company was announcing that another sixty thousand layoffs were on the way. The economy had slowed, and now the Pentagon was warning of declining military preparedness. To top it off, the country was heading into an election year.

The president had been trying to avoid direct intervention for weeks. There was no political upshot to wading into the murky waters of a labor dispute. The United Steelworkers of America was a solidly Democratic organization, and its members weren't likely to vote Republican regardless of the president's actions. But if the union felt strong-armed by the White House, opposition turnout by labor groups would be higher and more vociferous in the 1960 elections than it might otherwise have been. On the other hand, if the steel industry felt cheated, Eisenhower risked alienating a Republican base that was allergic to government encroachment into private industry. Many Republicans were already disappointed that his administration hadn't rolled back more of President Roosevelt's New Deal, and Vice President Richard Nixon was hoping to keep the Grand Old Party in the executive suite for another eight years. He would need staunch support from the party faithful to do so.

Even with his aversion to direct intervention, Eisenhower knew he couldn't stand by and watch the country spiral into economic stagnation. There was no political upside *there,* either. Incredibly, industry and union negotiators seemed no closer to a deal than they had been in mid-July, when the strike began. The time had come for the president to take action. The Taft–Hartley Act authorized the federal government to order strikers back to work if their action posed a threat to national security. Now, in early October, the president could see no alternative.

Negotiations between the USWA and the steel industry representatives hadn't gone anywhere for one simple reason: The two sides weren't interested in settling the strike—at least, not yet. The steel industry's lead negotiator, R. Conrad Cooper, had been betting that a protracted fight would work to management's advantage. Months before the union's contract expired, Cooper gave numerous interviews in which he threw into grave doubt any hope of a smooth contract renegotiation. He made it clear that he was spoiling for a fight, and his saber-rattling tipped off customers, such as the country's auto manufacturers, that a strike was imminent. Those customers began ordering huge amounts of steel to weather a probable industry shutdown, and demand soared in the first half of 1959. With those profits accounted for, the major steel companies were well situated to survive a few weeks of lost revenue.

Cooper had a hunch that the steelworkers wouldn't be nearly so resilient, particularly since their confidence in David McDonald, the union's playboy president, was already so low. Until then, the longest strike USWA members had ever mounted lasted just fifty-eight days, and that was in 1952, when beloved former president Philip Murray was at the helm. If the steel companies could hold out for two months in 1959, Cooper bet union members with families to feed would break ranks with McDonald and demand a swift settlement. When that happened, management would win massive concessions and roll back some of the gains labor had made in the previous decade.

The industry's plan wasn't exactly a secret. In August, President Eisenhower had invited Cooper and McDonald to the White House for separate sit-downs. By that point, McDonald and the union negotiators had been trying to reach the industry negotiating committee for weeks, but to no avail. Satisfied that time was their friend, the industry reps had been lying low, accepting the president's invitation only to avoid the public appearance that they were intransigent. Not surprisingly, the talks with Eisenhower went nowhere—the steel industry didn't want to settle, and the USWA wouldn't offer concessions without proportional commitments from management—but McDonald did end up meeting with Cooper's team. The parties had booked the same hotel in Washington, D.C., and when the elevator doors parted one afternoon, McDonald found himself staring right at the entire steel-industry entourage.

"What a remarkable coincidence," McDonald said. "I've been trying to reach you people for weeks, and now we meet in an elevator."

The union president climbed aboard, savoring the chance to make his foes uncomfortable. The group rode down to the lobby in silence. Before the others could disembark, McDonald jumped out and offered his hand, forcing each man to shake it before escaping.

Cooper's strategy of dragging his feet was tactically sharp, but he had miscalculated the depth of the steelworkers' resolve. Far from wavering, striking men grew more committed as the weeks and months trudged on. Massive pickets, which at first had been pro forma, a rehearsed show of solidarity by the union faithful, became the front lines in a larger battle for the future of organized labor. In Chicago, one plant began charging mill supervisors—the nonunionized company men who continued to report to work each day—two dollars to cross their picket line.

"Dump the bosses off your back!" union leaders yelled to irate crowds in front of the gates.

Union fervor was equally strong in Western Pennsylvania. In Homestead, just across the Monongahela River from Braddock, picketers blockaded a U.S. Steel plant and were refusing entry to managers and maintenance workers. U.S. Steel sought an injunction to limit the number of picketers at each gate to just two, but the courts were reluctant to encroach on the strikers' freedom to assemble, particularly in a place as symbolic to the labor movement as Homestead. In 1892, Andrew Carnegie's Homestead Steel Works had been the stage for the most dramatic face-off between management and labor in U.S. history. After plant managers physically locked union workers out, townspeople surrounded the plant in a bid to keep production shut down. Andrew Carnegie's lieutenant, Henry Clay Frick, turned to a private police force called the Pinkerton National Detective Agency to secure the property. In the predawn hours of July 6, three hundred armed Pinkertons floated up the Monongahela River on barges, hoping to catch the strikers off guard. Word of Frick's plan leaked out, however, and armed strikers rushed to stop the invading force. Shots were exchanged. All told, sixteen people died in the daylong battle that followed, with high casualties on both sides. It was one of the most well-publicized labor tragedies in history, and it irrevocably tarnished Andrew Carnegie's reputation.

Sixty-seven years later, with the 1959 stoppage twelve weeks old, workers across the country felt a tug of allegiance to their armed Homestead forebears. With that bloody history reminding them of all they had gained in the intervening generations—and all they stood to lose—the strikers' resolve had stiffened.

With the stoppage nearing its third month, the USWA had turned the tables on Cooper. As the country's steel consumers burned through their stockpiles and started turning to foreign imports, the American steel industry finally felt the sting of lost revenue. If the union could stay on strike long enough to convince even one steel company to negotiate a favorable settlement, McDonald wagered that the other companies would cave and follow suit. Steel producers would be reluctant to let one of their competitors capture the market while they held out for a tougher contract with the union. Just as the USWA was only as strong as the solidarity of its members, the industry's leverage depended on the twelve major companies acting as a bloc. The strike had become a battle of endurance on both sides.

Sensing the futility of further talks, President Eisenhower made his decision. Citing warnings from the Pentagon about the country's military preparedness, and noting the potentially devastating economic consequences in the offing for industries that relied on a steady flow of steel, he appointed a board of inquiry on October 7, 1959. This was a required step before the back-to-work provisions of the Taft–Hartley Act could go into effect. The board would seek to clarify the issues under discussion by labor and management and to ensure that every effort toward compromise had been exhausted. As the board convened, workers around the country waited to see if Eisenhower would bring their fight to a political end.

The Tigers would play the Derry Area Trojans on Friday. Derry Area had lost three of four games on the season and looked thin on film, but Klausing wasn't taking any chances. To see his team practice, a visitor could be forgiven for thinking they were preparing for the Pittsburgh Steelers.

Klausing was tired of watching his boys play brilliantly, only to make the sorts of small mistakes that could resurrect an opponent's hopes. It had happened when Midland scored a forty-four-yard touchdown to end the second half, and it had happened with fumbles and holding penalties in each of the Tigers' first three matchups. Braddock would play away on Friday, and even a weak team could muster a command performance at home. With nothing else to play for, the Trojans would be foaming at the mouth to upset the Tigers' hopes.

After a solid performance in the mud at Midland, John Jacobs was back in practice and healthy.

"Must be nice," Roland Mudd kidded him, "to only work Fridays."

Jacobs smiled. "I'm that good."

Coach Zuger, working with the backfield, made it a point to tighten Jacobs's timing, particularly on the Tigers highly effective option play. The quarterback had a tendency to hold the ball for just a second too long, juking and jiving to see if the defender would bite. It made the coaches very nervous.

"Jake," Zuger shouted during a live drill, "if you want to dance with him, buy him a nice dinner first!"

The quarterback had been lucky so far, but a well-trained linebacker would surely crack him square in the jaw if he kept light-footing it. After his scare the previous week, the Tigers were more conscious than ever of how quickly an injury to a key player could dim their prospects.

Aside from Jacobs's illness, the team had remained healthy so far. But "healthy" was a relative term. Vick, Powell, and Gay, the Tigers potent backfield, had so many bruises on their arms and thighs that it looked like someone had gone at them with a ball-peen hammer. Twenty-plus carries per week made their heads swell so badly that it could be difficult for them to remove their helmets after the final whistle. To give his boys a chance to recover, and to keep them as safe as possible during the week, Klausing and his assistants limited full-contact drills in practice. They insisted on proper hitting and blocking techniques, excoriating boys who dropped their heads or threw themselves unthinkingly into dangerous situations. They gave the players frequent water breaks, and encouraged them to eat before practice.

But no matter the precautions, football at the Tigers' speed and competitiveness was dangerous business, and Klausing could only hope to mitigate the risks. A believer in a higher power, he ultimately fell back on praying ardently for the safety of the boys in his charge.

On Friday, the Braddock faithful followed the team bus to Latrobe, Pennsylvania, where Derry Area played its home games. An hour east of Braddock, Latrobe was steeped in football history. In 1895, the Latrobe YMCA had sponsored a team of local mill workers to play amateur teams from nearby towns. Sensing an opportunity, the manager of the Latrobe team, a newspaper editor named David Berry, began stirring up hype to spur ticket sales. But when Latrobe's quarterback bowed out before the opening game, it looked like the local boys were in for a spanking. Frantic, Berry approached a young athlete named John Brallier, who knew the position. Brallier said he wasn't interested, so Berry did something novel—he offered the kid ten dollars and cakes to play for him. Brallier accepted, and would later be recognized as the first professional player in the history of American football. In the 1930s, the National Football League gave the claim an official stamp of approval by offering the original pro player a lifetime pass to NFL games. Though earlier claims of professional status would later emerge, the Brallier story remained the best known.

This Friday night, no amount of sepia lore could help Derry Area out of its slump. Under the lights, in front of three thousand fans, Braddock put on a clinic. Vick opened the floodgates with a fifty-six-yard run straight up the middle for a touchdown. Powell intercepted a pass on the following series to give Braddock another go, and Klausing rewarded the defensive effort by calling a pass play in his direction. Jacobs hurled a long spiral, and the deerlike senior hauled it in for a fifty-nine-yard score. To the dismay of Derry Area's crestfallen fans, Powell intercepted the ball yet again on the following series. With a new possession, Vick scored up the middle for a second time. The Tigers had scored three touchdowns in their first three possessions.

Derry Area threatened in the second quarter, moving the ball in spurts to the Tigers 5, but Stanfield, Grudowksi, and Mudd held the line. The Trojans went for it on fourth down, and the Braddock front wall converged on the runner at scrimmage for a turnover on downs.

The second half began much like the first, with a long bomb from Jacobs to Powell. The running back caught the ball in stride and ran untouched for an eighty-yard score. It was officially a slaughter. Klausing called for the subs early in the third quarter. Derry Area scored late in the game, which eased some of the home crowd's suffering, but the Tigers had trounced their opponent. All told, Jacobs completed four passes out of seven on the evening for 185 yards and three touchdowns. Vick and Powell each had two touchdowns. At the whistle, the final score was 32–7.

"Buddy, you got a phone call!"

It was Saturday, and someone had tracked Ernie Vida down in a betting parlor on Braddock Avenue. A call had come through on a pay phone outside. Vida made his way to the pay phone and picked up the dangling receiver. He listened intently, though for the sake of negotiations pretended not to be overly interested in what he was hearing. When he finished the call, he hurriedly dialed Klausing. He couldn't wait to tell him the news.

Rumors spread quickly in Braddock, and it didn't take long for players and their families to hear that *Sports Illustrated,* the sporting magazine of record, would be sending photographers. The photojournalists would be in town for an entire week, attending classes, going to practice, and maybe even visiting players' homes. The Tigers knew they were regional celebrities, and the boys had some notion that their unfaltering march toward the record was being discussed throughout the country. But *Sports Illustrated* was the big time, a higher pedestal than even the most self-assured among them—Jacobs and Doughboy included—had dared imagine.

Sports Illustrated had only published its first issue in the summer of 1954, just before Klausing's inaugural season at Braddock High, but it had quickly become required reading for the sports-loving masses. The rise of televised athletic events had made spectator sports phenomenally popular in the United States in the previous decade and a half. With its big gorgeous photo spreads and in-depth weekly coverage, *Sports Illustrated* catered to and helped promote the country's growing infatuation. For a high school team to be included in its pages was unheard of, an honor topping any trophy or banquet.

Klausing was ambivalent about Vida's news. He read *Sports Illustrated* every week, and he was thrilled the magazine wanted to give his boys some well-deserved recognition. His own stock would surely get a bump in coaching circles, and that could only help with the next phase of his career. But Braddock, with all its wins, hadn't broken any records yet. Reporters were distractions, and his players were far from immune from outside interference. He thought back to Henry Furrie, the old Braddock High coach who'd had so much trouble getting his players to cooperate. High school kids liked to show off, and letting two cameramen follow the team around seemed to be inviting trouble. Ultimately, Klausing decided the coverage was well deserved, too special to pass up. But he would keep a sharp eye on his boys over the coming week.

On Monday, the picketers in front of Edgar Thomson were out in force. Their numbers had been growing as bored union men joined fellow workers who were scheduled to walk the line. With well-worn signs in hand, strikers cheered passing cars. They socialized, smoked cigarettes, and nipped communal hooch donated by thoughtful sympathizers. Though united in common cause against the steel companies, Braddock's workers weren't so overtly radical as Homestead's steel men. Braddock's labor history was more subdued than Homestead's, and its ties with Andrew Carnegie—the town's patriarch and historical benefactor—were tighter. When supervisors showed up for work in the morning, workers busted their chops and harangued them playfully, but there was no violence or ill will. Many of the supervisors were well liked in town, high school buddies of the men who worked under them. It was more fun to talk Tigers football than to slip into testy debates with old friends.

Elsewhere, Braddock was quiet. The usual traffic slogged down Braddock Avenue, much of it from out-of-town travelers cutting through on their way to Pittsburgh. It had rained earlier in the day. With the sidewalks deserted and many stores empty, the passing cars seemed to be hurrying out of town. When school finally let out, children spread over the hillside like locusts. Games of touch football sprouted in alleyways and church parking lots, and admiring kids laid claim to their favorite Tigers stars: *I'm Curtis Vick; I'm Jacobs; I'm Ben Powell*. In a recent past that now seemed like a different era, Klausing had had to send his team out to recruit players. After the Tigers' incredible success, every boy in town wanted to wear the red and white.

It was on this rain-glazed afternoon—while strikers chatted, children played, and Braddock's business owners lunged one day deeper into their retail despair—that two men, unknown in town, whooshed along Braddock Avenue and turned up Library Street. Robert Huntzinger and Robert Bender were freelance photographers on assignment for *Sports Illustrated*. Bender was in his early thirties and Huntzinger in his late twenties. They were babies in the world of magazine journalism, but they were excellent shooters who knew the region well. Bender was an Ohio native who had been working in a photography studio in Pittsburgh for the last few years. Huntzinger was from

Coraopolis, Pennsylvania, a small town twenty miles west of Braddock. Each understood what high school football meant in Western Pennsylvania, and each knew what was at stake for the boys playing the sport. Though they were accustomed to covering professional athletes, both men approached the Braddock job with due seriousness.

The photographers crossed under the train tracks into North Braddock. This was a plum assignment for them. *Sports Illustrated* paid photographers between $100 and $125 per day. Multiplied out over a week, it was a dazzling fee for a couple of freewheeling young men. Unlike advertising shoots, which were lucrative but required hours of elaborate staging and setup, a news story for *Sports Illustrated* required only instincts and patience. "F/8 and be there" was the dictum du jour.

The Bobs parked across from Edgar Thomson Field. Klausing left his players to greet them. Ernie Vida, who had been watching the Tigers practice, hurried forward to facilitate the introductions. Though he had never met the photographers before, he was proud of his role arranging the article and wanted to make sure things went smoothly.

From the practice field, the Tigers watched the photographers with a mix of eagerness and trepidation. They viewed the men as emissaries from the world of big-time sports. Even Doughboy, the Tigers most outspoken player, didn't utter a sarcastic word. In that moment, the full weight of what they were playing for—a national record—hit them square between the eyes.

Klausing returned to the field and the players returned to practice. With their kit bags over their shoulders, the photographers began surveying the area for interesting angles. This was a workday, and they would soon lose the afternoon light. Both men used thirty-five-millimeter Leica range finders, and both carried three lenses—a wide-angle lens for sweeping scenes, a telephoto lens for action shots and portraits, and a fifty-millimeter lens for candids. For the duration of the week, the boys would scarcely see either man without a camera pressed to his face.

Klausing needn't have worried about his Tigers acting out. They were intimidated by the photographers. As steel-town boys, they didn't have much contact with the wider world—and *Sports Illustrated* was as wide as it got. And there was another thing. The players had heard rumors about a *Sports Illustrated* curse. According to trustworthy sources, it was bad luck to be featured on the magazine's cover. An abundance of selective evidence could be offered to support the theory. In August of 1954, the magazine's twenty-five-cent debut featured a cover photo of Braves third baseman Eddie Mathews taking a walloping swing. One week later, Mathews broke his hand and was forced to sit seven games. In 1955, female skier Jill Kinmont struck a tree and was paralyzed the week her photo appeared on newsstands. In 1956, Notre Dame star Paul Hornung was featured on the cover, only to have his Fighting Irish finish 2–8 on a season that included devastating losses to rivals Oklahoma, Navy, and Pitt. Hornung ended up winning the Heisman Trophy that year, so his curse was a matter of some dispute. But the 1958 death of driver Pat O'Connor in the Indy 500 days after the magazine ran a picture of him on its cover seemed to lay the issue to rest. It hardly mattered that editors at *Sports Illustrated* had no plans to put the Tigers on the cover. This was Western Pennsylvania, where superstition was taken seriously and even a story tucked deep inside the book would be tempting some powerful juju.

School board president Mike Sullivan, for one, wasn't sweating any curses. The *Sports Illustrated* story was going to be big for Braddock, and he wanted to be associated with it. Getting his name in the article—*and hell, maybe even his picture!*—would be a political windfall. Vida may have set the story in motion, but Sullivan would do everything in his power to put his stamp on it.

On Tuesday afternoon, Sullivan and athletic director Dan Rice met at the Carnegie Library to shoot pool. It was a weekly tradition for the close friends, who enjoyed betting on the games. Near the door leading into the billiards room, a sign implored passing patrons to keep their chatter respectfully subdued: QUIET! Sullivan and Rice had commissioned the eighteen-by-twenty-four-inch poster from John Zuger, the Tigers assistant coach and a junior high art teacher. Their pool games had often been interrupted by interminable favor-seekers, an occupational hazard for someone like Sullivan, who peddled favor for a living. Wherever he went, he attracted a line of obsequious hangers-on. On more than one occasion they had upset his leisure. Zuger never did anything half-cocked, and the sign was no exception. Each letter had been carefully shadowed and shaded in two colors. The result was a bold exhortation that no one had yet dared to challenge.

Sullivan and Rice traded turns on the table. Each felt he had been invaluable to the Tigers' success. They had both offered Klausing the support and political cover needed to build winning teams. Sullivan was keenly aware that hiring Klausing had been the most intelligent political move he'd ever made. For six years, the Tigers had been sterling proof of his sharp vision and leadership. His popularity had risen as a result. Klausing and the Tigers were his own private reelection campaign, the best possible argument to reelect him to his seat. But memory—especially political memory—was fickle; Sullivan didn't want to let an opportunity to take indelible credit on a national stage pass him by. He planned to insinuate himself into the article through sheer persistence, if necessary.

Dan Rice also wanted to be mentioned in the article, but his style was more subdued. In this case, he decided to turn to his favorite catchall—a party. He'd invite a few boys from the team, along with their dates, to a friendly evening at his house. The photographers would be invited, too, of course, and they'd be more than welcome to take pictures.

As the two talked amid the clacking of pool balls, a steady stream of men passed outside the door to the handsome, wood-lined room in the Carnegie Library. Many of the passersby had business to discuss with Sullivan, but all lost confidence at the sight of the sign and moved along. Zuger was talented, and his art rarely missed its mark.

When *Sports Illustrated* commissioned two photographers, the magazine was looking for two distinct points of view. With two styles, two visions, and two interpretations, a skilled editor could give depth and dimension to a piece, create visual tension, tell a story. It was as much art as journalism, and *Sports Illustrated* did it better than anyone.

Robert Huntzinger had an eye for the region's topography. Like his hometown of Coraopolis, Braddock sat beside a river on a steep slope. The brick and stone buildings, railroad tracks, and ambitious vegetation that crept over each unpaved patch were as familiar to him as rows of corn would be to a Midwesterner. Huntzinger knew more than a little about the working culture of Braddock, as well. He had done his time in a finishing mill after high school, and he understood what it meant to make a living the hard way. He remembered the blazing-hot torches and the shrill bleating of the pneumatic press as it stamped sheets of steel into car bumpers. Every minute in that plant had felt like a minute in a war zone. Like so many of the Tigers players he was now shooting, he knew early on that that life wasn't for him. He left Coraopolis for college and studied photography. Most of his friends stayed behind, and the luckiest had taken steady jobs in the mills. It was a good bet that the same fate awaited most of the Braddock High boys.

Before school on Thursday, Huntzinger accompanied Klausing on his route to pick up the North Versailles players. At one of the stops, he got out of the car. As he waited, a well-groomed young man dressed in slacks and a three-quarters-length coat came walking up the hill. Smirking ever so slightly, Curtis Vick looked like a kid who knew he would go far in life. Behind him, at the bottom of the hill, the silent mill loomed like a counterpoint to that vision—so grand, even from above, that it seemed capable of toppling over on top of him, or of pulling him by sheer force of gravity into its corrugated jaws. Huntzinger snapped the shot. Then they piled into the full car and Klausing drove off.

On Friday, the photographers accompanied the Tigers to Dickson Field in Swissvale. A victory would bring the streak to fifty-one, just one game shy of Massillon's record. As darkness fell on the stadium, the honey light of the setting sun vanished behind into a glare of field lights. Word had leaked out that *Sports Illustrated* was covering the Tigers, and turnout at the game was higher than usual. Swissvale fans dreamed of upsetting Braddock's run. To do it in front of *Sports Illustrated* cameras would be sweeter still.

The home crowd wasn't made up entirely of die-hard fans. People with little allegiance to football or local teams had been coming to watch the Tigers in droves. After all the media coverage, it was a treat to spend an evening watching the best high school team in the state play for history, and to watch the famous Braddock High coach adjust his Notre Dame hat, size up the field, and call dazzling plays. Tigers football had been a powerful crutch for the region, a reliable thrill in a time of uncertainty.

Klausing's boys put on a show for the *Sports Illustrated* cameras. On the opening play, the Braddock defensive line forced a fumble. Ben Powell recovered the ball on the Tigers' 41-yard line, which brought Jacobs and company to the line of scrimmage for the first time. After a few solid Tigers runs, Jacobs hurled a tight thirty-three-yarder to Elbow Smith, the offensive end. Smith caught the ball in stride as he crossed the goal line for the first touchdown of the evening.

The Tigers stopped the home team again on the following drive. Swissvale's punter made one of the best plays of the game when he belted a kick from midfield that landed on the 1-yard line. It was standing-room-only at Dickson Field, and the home crowd cheered unrestrainedly at the beautiful punt. Taking over near their own goal, Vick and Powell managed to move the sticks twice with long gains on the ground. With the ball past midfield, Klausing picked up the phone.

"John, where are they weak?"

In the stands, Zuger had been watching the defensive ends. They were playing far outside, hoping to push the Tigers receivers into the middle of the field.

Zuger was happy to oblige. "Right up the gut," he said. "They're giving us the middle."

Jacobs threw a thirty-four-yard sizzler to Powell, who turned quickly and advanced the ball to the 13-yard line before a gang of Swissvale tacklers jumped on him. There was no need for Klausing to call Zuger on the next play. This was Curtis Vick's specialty—a hard run straight up the middle. Jacobs handed the ball off, and Vick, staying low to keep his balance, pinwheeled off four defenders. He was built like a brick, and incredibly difficult to tackle. The Tigers had needed just seven plays to cover ninety-nine yards.

Braddock didn't get through the first half scot-free. As if to ensure that Klausing would have something to complain about, Jacobs fumbled in the second quarter while attempting to pitch out to Powell.

"Hellfire!" Klausing screamed from the sideline.

Players grimaced at the thought of the wind sprints coming their way.

Swissvale recovered the fumble Braddock's 27-yard line, and on the next play the home team brought the crowd to its feet with a touch-down run. Though the game had seemed lopsided a moment earlier, the score was now 14–7. Braddock maintained the lead, but it no longer felt comfortable. As if to make up for his error, Jacobs threw a forty-three-yard touchdown pass on the following series. At halftime, the score was 21–7.

It was all Braddock in the second half. Jacobs struck again in the third quarter, breaking loose on a rollout and running it in himself from the Swissvale 36-yard line. A final passing touchdown in the fourth quarter made it three in the air for Jacobs on the evening, plus his long scramble. He finished the night eight for ten with 163 yards passing. Still, all Klausing would remember was the fumble. The final score was 34–7. Vick had run for 157 yards on the night, earning him accolades in the locker room and a pounding headache on the bus ride home. Roland Mudd, the placekicker, hit an impressive four extra points in five attempts.

"That's what *Sports Illustrated* is going to be writing about," he assured his teammates. "You don't see that kind of accuracy too often."

On the bus, the players talked openly about which photos would make it into the article. After the solid win, the curse no longer seemed to bother them. At the front of the bus, Klausing overheard their excited chatter. He was glad he'd let the cameramen follow the team. His boys deserved the attention, and it had meant the world to them to be treated like the stars that they were. In one week they would play Monaca. If they won, they would be co-owners of the most coveted record in high school football.

Chapter Nine

HISTORY

High on the hill overlooking Braddock, members of a gang of youths calling itself the Posties, so named because the boys lived near the town's old post office, were hard at work looking for treasure. Braddock's Field, a steep grassy loll where British general Edward Braddock met disaster in the eighteenth century, was dotted with trees. A commemorative cannon, fixed in place and aimed out over the town, spurred the imagination of local children. They believed it had been abandoned during General Braddock's retreat, and they marveled at the thought of what else had been left behind. Legend told of two boxes of treasure: a pay chest to cover soldiers' salaries and a personal chest belonging to the general himself. Using imaginative reckonings and creative historical interpretations, local children had been combing the fields around Braddock and North Braddock since the area's first homes went up. The Posties were the latest in a long line of treasure seekers, though with the strike entering its fifteenth week, and with life at home strained for steel families, they may have been more desperate to find the hidden cache than all who'd come before.

Directly beside the grassy patch where the Posties searched, a

plume of dust and coal soot rose over ET Field. The Tigers were practicing. The proximity of the two fields—one the site of a general's
disgrace, the other an incubator for a team's hopes—seemed deliber-
ately arranged to remind headstrong young boys of the folly of over-
confidence. After three weeks on the road, the Tigers would play at
home on Friday. Their streak stood at fifty-one. They could tie the
record before a massive home crowd, or they could come up one
game short. Eight years earlier, a high school from Abilene, Texas,
had threatened Massillon's streak by going forty-nine straight games
without a loss. When Abilene lost its footing in the fiftieth game, it
also lost its chance at history. It was easy for Klausing to imagine
what it would feel like to come so close only to fall short.

No one talked about the record at practice. The boys sensed that
it wouldn't have gone over well. With the whistle in his mouth,
Klausing controlled their fates, and wind sprints appealed to no one.
At six o'clock, the tired, soot-caked players left ET Field through the
spectator-lined gates. Most refrained from talking until after they
had crossed back underneath the train tracks. Then, cautiously, they
resumed their boasting and swagger.

"I bet they'll hang my jersey up," Doughboy said. Curtis Vick
laughed, and Doughboy shot him a quick glance. "Curt, they might
keep your jock around. Or some socks. Don't expect much."

"How many yards does Curt have this year, anyway?" called Roland Mudd, overhearing the exchange. "I lost count."

Doughboy took the ribbing in stride. He had come to accept the
inevitable. His offensive production this season had been respectable,
vital even, but Vick was churning out over a hundred yards each game.
There was nothing Doughboy could do to catch up.

Players changed at the high school and then spilled out into the
cool evening. Most hurried home for dinner and homework, but a
few, like backup halfback Mike Pratko, lagged on Braddock Avenue.
Pratko spent idle hours at the United Candy Shop, where his best
friend, Charlie Mikolajczyk, worked evenings. There was a jukebox

at the back of the candy shop, and a soda fountain, and Mikolajczyk was always good for a free milk shake. He used double ice cream and made his shakes so thick that it would have been easier to suck wet cement through a straw than that first frosty sip.

As Mikolajczyk wiped down the counter before closing, he and Pratko exchanged stories. Mikolajczyk had been a trombone player in the Braddock High band before graduating the previous year. He liked music, but he had hated playing during home games. While he was stuck performing, the real fun was going on in the stands. Longingly, he had watched his fellow students laughing and flirting, sneaking pulls of hooch. Braddock High students paid the bums that slept along the railroad tracks to buy alcohol for them, and it flowed freely at Tigers games. Mikolajczyk had even faked an injury once to participate in the communal rites of a Friday-night home game.

"I broke my finger," he told the music director, Mr. Ferber, while brandishing a perfectly healthy digit adorned with a homemade spint. "I can't play my horn."

"Carry it, then," Mr. Ferber responded.

With nothing better to do, Mikolajczyk ripped off the homemade cast and oompahed his heart out that evening.

"Boy, you healed quick," Mr. Ferber said after the game.

Mikolajczyk loved telling that story, and it was well known to his customers. Memories like that one swirled in the firmament above Braddock and became part of local lore. Everyone knew everyone else in town—if not intimately, then by reputation. Walking down the street, residents who passed one another but had never spoken would harbor secrets bits of overhead gossip, clarifying windows onto strangers' lives. Stories knit the town together and created a community out of what, in practical terms, was little more than an overgrown labor camp.

The two friends talked into the evening. Then Pratko left to eat and sleep and prepare for another day of classes and football. He was part of the town's lore, too. The story of the Braddock High Tigers was playing out in real time, but everyone could easily imagine a day not long in coming when, sitting on a barstool or in a break room, they would comb through six immaculate seasons, embellish details, and relive the stunning run when the Tigers challenged history during the steel strike of '59. Residents would draw comfort from the retelling, and it would further strengthen the bonds of their riverside community.

After practice, and after dropping his North Versailles players off, Klausing drove to his home in Monroeville. Turning into his driveway, looking at the manicured bank that abutted his front yard, he thought of how much time had passed since he took over at Braddock. When he'd moved into the Monroeville house, Klausing asked Joe Reaves to recruit a few players to help landscape the bare bank. Reaves showed up with four sophomores. The crew spent two days carting topsoil back and forth, killing themselves in the heat. Joann cooked for the boys and offered them bottomless mugs of lemonade. At the end of the second day, Klausing gave Reaves twenty-five dollars to distribute evenly among his workers. When he ran into one of the sophomores later, he apologized that he couldn't give each boy more.

"Coach, we didn't get a nickel!" the player responded.

Reaves had kept every cent. That memory was well worn now, recounted often at team meetings and coaches' banquets. The landscaping outside the Klausings' house had thrived, and it was difficult to envision the bank as it had been when it was bare.

After climbing out of his car, Klausing retrieved his bag from the backseat. During practices, he was usually too wrapped up in details to think about food. He sometimes skipped meals during football season, so consumed with a thousand menial tasks that he forgot to eat. Now he was starving, and the thought of eating a meal with his family made him happy. The season sometimes felt like a prolonged absence from his wife and children. More than the pressure, that was the hardest thing about coaching. Tired, he entered through the front door.

Joann was in the living room with the children, and she came out to greet him. "How was practice?" she asked before leaning in for a kiss.

"Fine," Klausing said. "This is a big week."

"Dinner should be ready soon. Why don't you go and change?"

In their bedroom on the first floor of the split-level house, Klausing retrieved a T-shirt from the dresser. He walked to the bathroom to wash his face and hands. Inside, he caught a hint of the delicate perfume that Joann wore on special occasions. A picture of the couple hung from the wall. He had met his wife fifteen years earlier at a Polish dance in Wilmerding, Pennsylvania. Joann was a marvel on the dance floor, and the nineteen-year-old Klausing hadn't been able to take his eyes off her. Their first run-in was brief and well supervised. Joann's mother was a strict woman with many rules; she was chaperoning her daughter that night, and Klausing managed only a few words before Joann was whisked away. But the image of her stayed with him. She would ever-after be a laughing beauty twirling on the dance floor.

Joann was the daughter of immigrants. Her parents had been raised in Poland in the same small town, though they hadn't known one another in the old country. They'd met years later on Long Island, New York, after both had moved to America. Joann's father was a taciturn, hardworking man who'd joined the exodus of Eastern Europeans in the aftermath of World War I. It was a time of upheaval and transition in Europe. The newly independent Republic of Poland was searching for stability, the Russian Revolution had brought communism to the region, and America seemed like a haven for new beginnings. Joann's father found work as a butcher in his adopted country, and then set about searching for a wife.

Joann's mother crossed the Atlantic at sixteen, her passage paid by a well-to-do Long Island family that needed a servant girl. She cooked and cleaned for the family, looked after the children, and worked herself to the brink of exhaustion, paying back her ocean voyage. She was sitting in Mass one day when she spotted a young butcher. Their eyes met, and she saw a way out of her indentured servitude.

After a short engagement, Joann's parents married. They had a son, Chester, Joann's older brother. When word arrived that the booming steel mills of Western Pennsylvania were offering respectable wages to men who could work long shifts, the budding family immediately booked tickets on a Pittsburgh-bound train. Joann's father asked his Polish acquaintances in New York which town would have the best prospects for him. Cradling their infant son in the cramped car on the trip west, husband and wife rehearsed the name of their new home: *Braddock*.

In 1941, novelist Thomas Bell, a native of Braddock and the son of Slovak immigrants—"Hunkies," in the pejorative parlance of the region—published his masterpiece about immigrant life in Western Pennsylvania. Early in *Out of This Furnace*, Bell described a family's bumpy arrival in a mill town in the late nineteenth century. Allowing for a few decades, he could have been writing about Joann's parents.

> *The day had been uncomfortably warm; the evening was stuffy and windless, the air so acrid with smoke that even Kracha coughed. Elena, clearing her throat and holding the baby away from her face as she spat, asked if it was always so smoky. Francka replied that it was no worse than usual, and added, "During the strike there was no smoke. But no money, either."*

After transferring in Pittsburgh, Joann's parents arrived at the train station in Braddock. Sending up a prayer, they left their possessions unguarded on the platform and went off in search of lodging. They found a small apartment and paid the first month's rent with the little money they had brought with them. Their furniture and tattered valises were still on the platform when they returned, and they said a second prayer of thanks. Though their new apartment had just two rooms, the family took on four boarders. Joann's parents and brother slept in one room, and the boarders, all of them mill workers, shared the other. Two men at a time slept in the lone guest bed. At shift changes they rose and set off, replaced in slumber by the returning pair. That was the precise rhythm of life in the mills, which turned workers into moving parts.

Joann's father got work at Edgar Thomson, and the young couple had another boy, and then two girls—Joann and her sister. A fifth and final child, a boy, completed the family. Though they'd moved to a small house in Braddock by then, the late addition nearly crowded them out of their tiny living quarters. To make room, two-year-old Joann was sent to live nearby with a family friend, whom she called her aunt. Joann lived apart from her parents and siblings until she was fifteen, when her mother had a falling out with Joann's caretaker. The falling out was over a dance. Joann's aunt thought it would be unseemly for a teenage girl to attend a mixed-sex social function, but Joann's mother was in favor of it. She had bettered her own life through marriage, and she wanted to see her daughter engaged to a good Catholic boy. But to her mother's dismay, when Joann started going to dances, her independence and free spirit always kept her a step ahead of any serious suitors. Why settle down when you can dance and laugh? Joann became an expert dancer, the kind a nineteen-year-old heading off to Basic Training wouldn't soon forget.

After their brief meeting in 1944, Klausing shipped out to Parris Island, South Carolina, for Basic Training. He then got sent to Quantico, Virginia, for Officer Candidate School. He graduated in the summer of 1945, and he was given a fifteen-day leave before starting active service. With a buzz cut and a veneer of discipline, he traveled home to Western Pennsylvania. His first evening back he went to Kennywood amusement park, the hub of the summer social scene for area youths. Skirting the outdoor dance floor, he spotted the woman he'd been thinking about since he left for Basic Training. She was gliding to the music of a live brass band, and though more than four hundred couples were dancing on the huge floor, all of them illuminated by strings of glowing bulbs, a spotlight seemed to be trained on Joann. She was a gifted dancer, unhindered by her clumsier partner. Klausing waited at the edge of the floor, and when he saw an opening, he marched over and asked if he could cut in. She smiled when she saw him—his boyish face and plump, smiling lips were easy to remember—and held out her hand.

Every evening over the next two weeks, the two met at Kennywood. They danced in the warm July air while other young men grumbled about the marine who was taking the best girl. At the end of each evening, Klausing would walk Joann home along quiet streets clasping her hand. In the final days of his leave, he would kiss her good-bye at the top of the last hill, stopping short of her house so her mother wouldn't see. Klausing wasn't Catholic, which meant she would never approve.

When his leave was up, the future coach shipped out to North Carolina to take charge of a group of recruits at Camp Lejeune. He and Joann sent letters back and forth, and their flirtation soon carried suggestions of an engagement. Joann asked if there was a good reason for her to learn to cook his favorite dishes, and she mentioned her stuffed cabbage in particular. In those letters, she also fretted about her mother, who had been trying to put an end to their correspondence. They sent letters through intermediaries, enlisting an army of secret messengers. The secrecy gave their budding relationship added sweetness, more delicious for being illicit.

The war ended before Klausing could be deployed to the Pacific. When he returned to Western Pennsylvania to finish college, he redoubled his ardent courtship. Joann's mother wouldn't let him come by the house for dates, so the pair met in secret. Out of love, if not, at first, a devotion to religion, Klausing began meeting with a priest to discuss conversion. Each week, for two hours, he studied at a local seminary. Unexpectedly, he began to see beauty in the lessons and precepts of Catholicism. He converted in a small ceremony in December of 1947. With that barrier removed, and with Joann's mother placated, he proposed at Christmas. At their wedding, to the melody of a cheerful Polish band, the newlyweds danced before hundreds of guests.

Klausing put on the clothes he had laid out. All these years later, he still loved to take his wife in his arms, to follow her lead and imagine that he had something to do with the graceful way she swayed before him. He regretted that he had so few opportunities to dance with her. During football season, nights out were impossible. There were game films and scouting reports, press inquiries and team emergencies. In his mind, though, they were always dancing, two kids falling deeply in love under the soft lights at Kennywood.

Klausing returned downstairs. Joann had taken dinner out of the oven and was setting the table. Klausing kissed her, and sensing his reflectiveness, Joann stopped what she was doing and embraced her partner.

A procession of men in flannel walked onto the damp field. Beneath the blazing lights, and with the home crowd craning to get a look from the packed concrete bleachers, proud fathers took their places beside their boys. Players who didn't have fathers were accompanied by uncles or older brothers. To a man, every Tiger had someone standing beside them. It was Dad's Night for Braddock High, a celebration of fathers and sons.

The hometown fans were more cheerful than usual before the game against the Monaca Indians. Mike Sullivan had coaxed the school board into giving striking workers free tickets to all Tigers home games. Two days after announcing the plan, Sullivan went to the Braddock *Free Press* to convey how touched he was by the hundreds of thank-you letters he'd received from mill workers. Hardly enough time had passed for those letters to be delivered, but no politician as talented as Sullivan ever let the truth get in the way of a good story.

On the field, John Jacobs Sr. stood next to his quarterback son. Facing the crowd, basking in the applause and sarcastic catcalls of a stadium full of friends and well-wishers, everything seemed right between them. Ben Powell and his father, a striking steelworker, stood next to them. The elder Powell was taciturn and shy like his son, but he smiled wide for the cameras now. A few yards away, sophomore defensive end Phil Lucarelli stood with Mr. Lucarelli, a supervisor at Edgar Thomson. The elder Lucarelli barely came up to his son's chin, but with his chest puffed out, swollen with pride, he looked like a giant. The man had eight sons and two daughters, but only one of them played Braddock High football.

The home announcer called off the names of each pair over the address system. Two at a time, the men took small steps forward and gave a wave. Klausing was last. His father, who never missed a game, who was a source of calm and counsel, was on the field as well. When Klausing was just a boy, Charles Sr. had bought him his first football with money won playing the numbers, a local lottery run by wiseguys with the tacit approval of the police. A one-penny bet netted six dollars. The brand-new ball was like a sculpture of finely stitched leather, and the young Klausing slept with it by his pillow after he got it. He wore the ball out scrimmaging with friends on a field near his house. He was his father's son, and he loved football. In eighth-grade Civics, he wrote a plan for his future career that he'd followed to the letter ever since: "My Coaching Career."

On the field, the two Klausings embraced. From the stands, Klausing's children perked up at the surge of applause. They were enjoying the rare treat of a Saturday game, which was the only time they were permitted to watch the Tigers play.

When all the photos had been taken, many of the players' fathers walked over to shake Klausing's hand. Overcoming the emotion of the moment and the awkwardness of being on the field, they muttered heartfelt thanks for all he had done. More than the trophies or the streak, it was the way their sons carried themselves now, the quiet confidence they'd found in their own abilities, that these men appreciated. Many of the fathers had treated their boys roughly, just as their fathers had treated them. It seemed a miracle that Klausing had done so much without ever raising a hand against his players.

When the fathers cleared the field, the two teams began warming up. The Tigers were so accustomed to playing in the mud by now that they hardly noticed the wet turf. During warm-ups, players kicked up sprays of brown water that streaked their red and white jerseys. The Monaca Indians, who'd been patient through the Dad's Night ceremony, took the field opposite the Tigers. The teams ignored each other during warm-ups. No one wanted to give an opponent the satisfaction of an appraising glance.

High above, assistant coach John Zuger looked down over the field. He had a clear view of the teams warming up from his perch in the third story Scott High classroom, which doubled as the press room. A Braddock manager was fiddling with the school's movie camera, preparing to film the game. Zuger settled into his chair with his notebook in front of him and the telephone handset that Al Burton had rigged by his side. He was Klausing's eyes during games, a chess player trained to see the whole board.

When warm-ups ended, captains John Jacobs and Ben Powell walked to midfield for the coin toss. Monaca chose heads and lost.

"We'll kick off," Jacobs said.

Klausing didn't want to risk one of Coach Aldo Bonomi's famous onside kicks. Bonomi was a sneaky devil, and if the Indians recovered the ball, which they well might on a wet field, it would give the visitors a big boost of confidence to start the game. Klausing trusted his defense, which he knew would make Bonomi's boys earn every yard.

The Tigers took the field. In the stands that ringed the stadium, Braddock High fathers were still glowing from their moment in the spotlight. They cheered their boys on with even more vigor than usual. When he was ready, Roland Mudd ran straight ahead and toe-poked a long low kick to the Indians 20-yard line. Braddock covered quickly, bringing the Indian return man down in a wet heap close to where he'd picked up the ball.

Monaca struggled with the damp field. The Indians' offensive end slipped while running a route on the opening play, and with no receiver, the pass from quarterback Sam LeFaso bounced incomplete. The backfield had the same bad luck—twice runners charged the line, only to lose their footing before they met the waiting Braddock tacklers. The heavy Monaca line had trouble adjusting to the speedier Tigers, and in the mud, they couldn't plant their cleats to use their power effectively. Facing fourth down inside their own 30-yard line, the Indians lined up to punt. Quarterback LeFaso was also Monaca's punt man, a strategic personnel decision that allowed the Indians to execute frequent fakes.

"Watch the pass!" Klausing yelled to his defense from the sideline.

The snap was low, and the ball skidded across the ground. Ray Henderson, in on punt defense, put a fast swim move on his blocker and rounded the outside of the line. LeFaso scooped up the ball and tried to boot it away in a single motion, but Henderson hurled his body forward. The collision of the ball, LeFaso's foot, and Henderson's torso created a thud that was heard all around the stadium. The ball fell to the ground almost exactly where LeFaso had picked it up, which seemed like a meager distance after that sensational explosion of energy. By chance, LeFaso fell on top of the ball, and the Indians turned over on downs.

Starting deep in Monaca's territory, Jacobs and the Tigers offense

took over. From Monaca's 27-yard line, Jacobs handed off to Dough-boy, who punched up the middle for seven yards. Vick took the handoff on second down to add five more yards and a first down. Jacobs pitched out to Powell on the outside with a fresh count, and Powell covered thirteen yards in three effortless bounds. He was fi-nally dragged down by a Monaca defender at the 2-yard line. Powell got the handoff again on second down, and he squeezed through to the end zone off a strong block by Mudd. With just over five minutes gone in the first quarter, Braddock had scored first, and with Mudd's extra point, the Tigers led 7–0.

In a designated area of the stands, Mr. Ferber, the music director, led the Braddock High band in a brassy celebration. Far away from the band section, Charlie Mikolajczyk sat with a big group of friends and cheered on his alma mater. He glanced over at the poor saps in the band from time to time while savoring his post-graduation lib-eration.

After a deep kickoff by Mudd, which pinned the Indians inside their 10-yard line, LeFaso trotted out to take over on offense. With the wet ball and the poor field position, Coach Bonomi stuck to power running plays. Seasoned Braddock fans liked what they were seeing. To knock off the Tigers, it seemed logical that an opponent would have to take big risks. Nevertheless, most opposing coaches played conservatively against Braddock High. Klausing coached his teams to exploit weaknesses, so opposing coaches feared showing him their underbellies. That hesitation usually worked out in Brad-dock's favor. Coach Bonomi was in the middle of learning that les-son. To his consternation, his running backs managed only three yards in three attempts, bringing up another Monaca punt.

LeFaso lined up on his 2-yard line to punt away. The center long-snapped a perfect spiral this time, and LeFasso caught it cleanly. But as he wound up for the kick, he saw a tree trunk in red and white closing on him yet again. Ray Henderson, faking the swim move that had worked so well on his blocker on the previous series, had

gotten a clean release inside. Charging the punter, he managed to get his arms up just as LeFaso whipped his leg forward. Coming off Le-Faso's foot, the hurtling pigskin smacked Henderson's wrists, sending a ringing pain down his arms. A brick wall wouldn't have done a better job stopping the ball, which ricocheted into the end zone and tumbled out of bounds. The referee signaled a safety, and the Tigers swarmed Henderson, who was shaking out his sore arms.

"That's it!" Klausing yelled from the Braddock sideline.

It was precisely the kind of special teams play Klausing had drilled so often after practice. Henderson had rehearsed that flying leap a hundred times, although lunging toward the Notre Dame hat had always hurt a lot less.

Two points further in the hole, the Indians completed the ignominy of a safety by kicking off. Now it was the Tigers turn to be embarrassed. From the press box, Zuger watched as Vick caught the kickoff and took it up the middle behind a wall of Braddock blockers. Vick passed midfield with blockers still in front of him, but as he zigged toward the sideline and found a clean lane on the outside, Roland Mudd blocked a Monaca defender from behind. The flag came out a split second later. At the conclusion of Vick's run, which ended deep in Indians territory, the official who threw the marker was standing alone, clean on the other side of the field. He walked an additional fifteen yards off from the spot of the foul and called for the ball. Mudd smacked his hands together and kept his head down as he jogged back.

The penalties didn't stop there. Braddock hammered three solid running plays up the middle for a first down, but an illegal motion in the backfield sent them trotting back once again. The team reset, but before Jacobs could get through his count on the next play, Ray Grudowski jumped offsides.

"Hellfire!" Klausing yelled on the sidelines. "What are they doing out there?"

It was the kind of slop he abhorred, and the next play did nothing

to calm him down. On a Jacobs handoff to Doughboy, Grudowski left his blocking assignment to help center Dan O'Shea. He came in high and grabbed the defender's face mask. Double-teamed, and with his neck wrenched by Grudowski, the Monaca boy went down like a toppled stack of dominoes. The personal foul would cost Braddock fifteen yards. On the bench, the Tigers players stared straight ahead, not risking any unnecessary eye contact with their coach.

Jacobs finally added some forward progress to the drive on the next play by rolling out and darting up the field for nine yards. Just as it looked like he'd run out of room, he pitched to Ben Powell, who was trailing up the sideline. Powell caught the ball and ran thirteen more yards. On the next play, Vick erased all the accrued penalty yardage with a beautiful twenty-six-yard run that ended just short of the goal. Ben Powell finished the drive with a one-yard lunge.

The penalties might have been forgiven after the brilliant three-play sequence, but center Dan O'Shea made sure that Klausing would be on the warpath come Monday. O'Shea botched the snap to holder Mike Pratko during the extra-point attempt. Pratko picked the ball up and desperately tried to run into the end zone, but the Monaca defenders fell all over him.

Even with the mistakes, Braddock was dominating the game. At the half, the Tigers led 22–0. Monaca had netted minus two yards on the ground and minus four yards in the air, for a combined offensive production of negative six yards in two quarters. Coach Bonomi's conservative play calling had kept his team from finding the weak points in the Tigers secondary, and Braddock had shut his boys down as a result.

The Indians played with more fire in the second half. LeFaso opened the third quarter with long passes to two flankers to move his team to the Braddock 16-yard line. But the drive fizzled when the Indians couldn't punch through on fourth-and-two. The Tigers mounted another spectacular drive for a touchdown, and in short order, the subs came in to take over. As if to enact some small retribution for the safety early in the game, the Indians quickly forced backup quarter-back Ron Davis into the end zone on the next drive. Davis went down, and Monaca got its first two points.

Coach Bonomi let LeFaso loose by calling eleven straight passes in the fourth quarter. LeFaso connected on four of his attempts, including an eight-yarder for Monaca's only touchdown on the evening. Like so many of the Tigers opponents, LeFaso had located his daring too late to make a difference.

At the final whistle, the score was 28–8 in favor of the home team. Braddock hadn't been forced to punt a single time in the contest, managing twenty-two first downs to the Indians' eight. Klausing's defense had kept the visitors to a net offensive output of thirty-five yards on the ground and sixty-six in the air—all coming in the second half. It was a command performance, a slaughter, but it felt so routine to Klausing that it took him a moment to realize what his Tigers had done. With two regular-season games left, Braddock High had tied Massillon Washington High with a record fifty-two games without a loss. With one more win, they would become the most dominant team in high school football history.

On the field, Klausing gathered his boys for a prayer. He thanked God that no one had been hurt. He made no mention of the record. When they were done praying, the Tigers went over to greet their smiling families. Many of the players' fathers and uncles were steel-workers. These men had recently passed a milestone of their own. Two days earlier, the strike had hit one hundred days—a long time to go without a paycheck.

The oak tree outside was ablaze with fall leaves. October was drawing to a close. For a few weeks the cool air would balance the heat of the sun, which would brush the necks and warm the cheeks of tens of thousands of hopeful fans in bleachers across the country. It was football weather.

When Joann had readied the children, the Klausings piled into the station wagon and drove to St. Michael's Parish in Pitcairn. To the great relief of Joann's mother, Klausing had maintained his zeal for Catholicism. He confessed his sins weekly and always sat in the front pew with his family on Sundays. They had started attending St. Michael's years earlier, when Klausing taught at Pitcairn High. There was great comfort now in being part of a congregation that was removed, if only by a few miles, from the intensity of Braddock during football season. Klausing knew there were pastors and priests in town who spoke about the Tigers in their sermons. He tried to get away from that on Sundays, to spend a few precious hours with his wife and children in the presence of God.

Then again, he rarely abstained from thinking about football entirely. Flankers and fullbacks danced on the edge of the altar as Klausing lapsed into thoughts of the Tigers previous matchup. Neither did he keep his Sundays outside of church free from work. He had asked Coach Carr for a scouting report on Canon-McMillan, the Tigers next opponent, and he expected to go over it by the end of the day. The Pittsburgh Steelers were playing the New York Giants, and Klausing would be watching at home, jotting notes on the scouting report in between plays. In matters of the Sabbath, he had not followed his father's lead. Charles Sr. had always flatly refused to watch football on the Lord's Day, despite his great passion for the sport. When Klausing had played at Penn State, Charles Sr. had traveled all over the country to see his games. When the Nittany Lions held occasional Sunday matchups, though, the elder Klausing always bowed out. Sunday was meant for long walks and quiet contemplation, he believed, and not competitive indulgence.

After church, the Klausings returned to their home in Monroeville. The Steelers played poorly, losing to the Giants 21–16. Frank Gifford, star halfback for New York, had two brilliant touchdown catches—one of them for a whopping seventy-seven yards. Bobby Layne, Pittsburgh's tough-as-dirt quarterback and placekicker—easily identifiable on the field as the only player who still refused to wear a face mask—tried unsuccessfully to rally his team with the hurry-up-style offense he'd helped innovate, but he had to settle for three field goals and one touchdown pass on the afternoon. It wasn't enough, and the Steelers left the field with a losing record.

Almost as soon as the game ended, the phone rang in Klausing's house. Sitting in his armchair in the living room, a sheaf of papers sloppily stacked on the small table next to him, Klausing listened to Joann answer and tell the caller to wait a moment. She called to him, and he got out of his chair and slinked through a minefield of his sleeping children.

"Hello?"

"Coach, Myron Cope with the *Post-Gazette*," the man on the other end said in a high, nasally voice. "Congratulations on yesterday's win."

"Thank you, Myron," Klausing said to the sportswriter, whom he'd known for some time. "Bonomi has a good squad. They put us through our paces."

"Sure, Coach, a real nail-biter. Listen, I wonder if you'll have time tomorrow for a sit-down. We're doing an article about your historic tilt this Thursday. You're going to be a tough interview to get after you beat Canon-McMillan."

"I don't see any problem with that, Myron." The reporter's over-confidence made him squeamish. "Stop by my office before practice and we'll talk," Klausing said. "Say one o'clock?"

"That's great, Coach. I'll see you then."

When he hung up, Klausing turned back to Joann. His lips tightened and he shook his head in the exasperated way that fans of lousy teams have of expressing their disbelief when their teams play lousy.

On Monday, players accepted a chorus of accolades and "attaboy's" in the halls of Braddock High. It seemed like everyone had a kind word. John Jacobs basked in the attention, breaking out new dance steps in the hall.

Klausing got his share of the congratulations, too.

"Should we do anything special for the pep rally Thursday?" Dan Rice asked, clapping him on the back.

"Better not," Klausing, said. "We don't want to change our routine."

Ray Grudowski, smarting after his foolish penalties against Monaca, passed Klausing with a meek greeting.

"Hi, Coach," he said deferentially, "see you at practice today?"

As a father of five and a veteran coach, Klausing knew a guilty look when he saw one. He wasn't one to punish a player off the field, though, and he let his starting offensive guard pass by in peace. Practice would come soon enough.

In driver's training, Klausing directed his students along the preset course through town. His foot hovered over the passenger-side clutch and brake pedals as he reminded his pupils to keep their eyes forward. They kept turning to him to talk about the game.

Late in the afternoon, Myron Cope arrived at Braddock High for his interview. A short man with a broad face and receding hairline, he popped in at the front office, where the school's secretary had grown accustomed to dealing with members of the press. After signing in, the *Post-Gazette* reporter made the familiar descent into the school's dank basement. Klausing's desk sat in a small office in the equipment room. Sportswriters all over the region had visited that subterranean domain, and often noted that it was at such odds with the luster of the school's accomplishments on the field.

"Hiya, Coach!"

"Myron, good to see you. Have a seat," Klausing said, motioning to a metal folding chair propped against the wall.

Cope dragged the chair in front of the desk and readied a pad of paper. He wanted to hear all about Klausing's early years at Braddock to get a sense of the history the coach was building on.

"Have I told you about Melvin Coburn?" Klausing asked. "Well, Melvin was a peach of a halfback on the early teams. He had some problems with the play calling, but we straightened that out and he became a real asset for us. There was one game early in the 1956 season, though, when he dislocated his ankle. That's a terrible injury, and very painful, so we took him to the hospital. The doctor scheduled a procedure for the next day, and he told Melvin not to worry about a thing because he'd give him a shot for the pain.

"Well, the next day, the doctor called me up. He said, 'Don't ask me how, but when I looked at that boy's ankle this morning, it was perfect.' I ran over to the hospital to get Melvin and I asked him what happened. He said, 'Man, I wasn't about to let that doctor put that needle into me. I stayed up all night jerking that ankle till it just snapped into place!'"

Cope let out a high-pitched laugh as he jotted notes in shorthand. "Sounds like one tough scaredy-cat."

"So then Melvin is back, and he plays great. We're all set to play Carmichaels in the championship, but the day before the game he comes up and tells me he hurt his shoulder. I had him take off his jersey, and sure enough, there was an indentation—an obvious dislocation. The boys took one look at Melvin's shoulder, dropped to their knees, and prayed to God to do something for him. While they were praying, Melvin grabbed himself by the elbow, gave it a sound jerk, and shouted, 'It's okay! It's back in place!' The kids looked at him like he was deranged. It turns out he's double jointed!"

"How about that!"

Klausing understood reporters. He knew that nothing left a news man grinning like a good story, something with a punch line. He kept an arsenal of them at hand for just that reason. By his third season at Braddock, newspaper and radio men from around the region had latched on to the story of the turnaround Tigers. Reporters liked Klausing. He wasn't gruff or brooding, which was the normal pose for coaches in Western Pennsylvania, and he never called their questions stupid. He was protective of his team and he didn't like distractions, but he also knew how to play the game. Publicity was important for the town, for his players—especially those hoping for scholarships—and for his own career. Klausing strung out a few more yarns for Cope, exaggerating here and there, fleshing out details, but mostly hewing to fact. Legacies weren't built on wins, he knew, but on stories.

Since the middle of the 1956 season, reporters had factored heavily into Klausing's weekly schedule. In the lead-up to the record, the attention had ballooned. On Tuesday, Klausing dropped off his North Versailles players at the end of practice, drove home for a quick dinner, and then dressed for his second interview of the week. This time his interrogator would be a legendary coach in his own right, a man whom Klausing admired very much. Dressed in a square-shouldered brown suit, donning a skinny tie, he kissed his children and his wife.

"Good luck," Joann said. "Or is it break a leg?"

Klausing jumped back in the car and drove to the television studio of Channel 13, WQED. The studio was located in the Oakland neighborhood of Pittsburgh. It wasn't far, but Klausing had to speed to get there on time. He had an on-air appointment with Pittsburgh's most famous doctor, and he didn't want to be late.

From 1922 to 1953, Henry Clifford "Doc" Carlson had been the men's basketball coach at the University of Pittsburgh. During that time he'd led the Panthers to Helms Athletic Foundation national titles in 1928 and 1930, and to a Final Four appearance in the third annual NCAA tournament in 1941. Carlson was an innovator. He'd developed the highly effective weave offense, which had been adopted by many teams since, and he was the first coach of a major Eastern school to schedule road games against teams from across the country, including USC and Stanford on the West Coast.

Though a basketball man, Carlson's pigskin bona fides were indisputable. He'd played football at the University of Pittsburgh under Glenn Scobey "Pop" Warner, earning First Team All-American honors as captain of the undefeated 1917 team. When he retired from coaching, Carlson began hosting a weekly television program called *Pitt Huddle*. The show focused on University of Pittsburgh football, but it had been retooling to expand its coverage beyond university athletics. Klausing would be the first guest under the new format.

The Tigers coach made it to the television studio with a few minutes to spare. WQED, which had begun broadcasting in 1954, was the first community-licensed public TV station in the country. It produced innovative programs that reflected the values of the Pittsburgh region. *Pitt Huddle* aired at the desirable 8 P.M. time slot on Tuesdays. It was required after-dinner viewing for the football-crazed metro area. The values of the Pittsburgh region were clear, and football received prime-time billing.

After a dab of powder, Klausing enjoyed a quick handshake with Doc Carlson.

"Coach, thanks for coming," Carlson said.

"It's an honor. You know, we use a lot of your conditioning advice, Doc, and it's really paid off."

A medical doctor, Carlson had spent years researching exercise and athletic conditioning. His work led him to create the "miracle minute," a workout founded on the premise that short intervals of top-speed, all-out exercise could augment or replace more time-intensive routines. Tigers players had Carlson to thank for some of the worst conditioning drills they ran up at summer camp.

Carlson told Klausing he was glad he could help, and then offered a quick rundown of the show's new format. Out on the studio floor, Klausing sat across from the older coach and took a deep breath. He folded his hands on the table in front of him and smiled. Moments later, a red light came on. The program began with clips from the University of Pittsburgh's loss to Texas Christian University the previous Saturday. Then Carlson introduced Klausing. As he did, the Tigers coach raised his right pinkie and wiggled it. It was the same signal he always used when he was on TV. Back at home, his children—who had practically pressed themselves against the TV screen—squealed with delight.

There were only a handful of men in the world who understood how Klausing felt before Thursday's game against Canon-McMillan, or what it was like trying to sleep the night before. Although Paul Brown had left Massillon Washington High before the school captured the current record of fifty-two games without a loss, he knew all about pressure.

The happiest years of Brown's life were the nine he'd spent coaching at Massillon Washington High. The liveliness and verve of high school players had inspired the soon-to-be-storied coach into a frenzy of creativity. During his years at the high school he developed the idea of diagramming plays in an organized playbook, an approach that hadn't been used elsewhere. He created intricate hand signals to communicate with his quarterback from the sideline, which amused his opponents at first but would soon be emulated by teams across the country. Aware that high school football at the highest level could attract enormous crowds in a steel town like Massillon, he led the charge to build a nineteen-thousand-seat stadium to replace Massillon Washington High School's already impressive seven-thousand-seat facility. When the new field opened in 1939, it was instantly recognized as one of the most spectacular high school sporting venues in the country.

Brown was just twenty-four years old when he took the Massillon job in 1932. Massillon Washington High had been awful before he arrived, posting a 2–10 record the season prior. Brown turned the team around by emphasizing discipline and personal responsibility. In his first season, his boys improved to 5–4–1. The young coach bucked convention by recruiting heavily in the surrounding area. He pursued exceptional black players, many of whom had been ignored elsewhere. Coach Klausing would have a remarkably similar approach more than twenty years later.

The legendary fifty-two-game streak began in 1937 and continued for five seasons. During that time, Massillon incurred just one blemish—a 6–6 tie in the thirty-ninth game of the streak. Although he was knocking on history's door, Brown left Massillon Washington High in January 1941 to take over as head football coach at Ohio State University. The team he built posted another undefeated season the following school year, but lost to rival Canton McKinley in 1942, putting an end to the incredible streak.

Brown had great success at Ohio State, and he had since become recognized as one of the NFL's preeminent coaches. Still, when he looked back, the Cleveland coach considered his time in Massillon the high point of his career. Klausing understood this perfectly. Perhaps even more than his nerves, it was that bittersweet realization that kept him from sleeping. He had done all he could at Braddock, and the time had come for him to move on. But facing a game that, should the Tigers win, would coronate him as one of the country's great coaches, he felt the melancholy of a comfortable life slipping away. He would soon leave the place he loved and the community that loved him to start over. Whatever successes awaited him on future gridirons, nothing could ever compare to the feeling of taking the field on Friday nights to add one more tally to the Tigers improbable streak.

Football weather. Darkness had fallen. In the bleachers at Scott Field, the breath of thousands of spectators billowed beneath the bright stadium lights. Fans were bundled in scarves and coats, but the chilly evening hadn't kept anybody away. It was Thursday, a school night. Braddock High teachers stood near students. Both groups would be celebrating long into the night if the Tigers won. This was for the record.

"Who are we?"

"Tigers!"

"Who are we?"

"Tigers!

Cheerleaders led the call-and-response through large conical megaphones that amplified their voices. Outside the stadium, the chant of "Tigers! Tigers!" flooded the valley like a war call, which could be heard far below on Braddock Avenue, and even across the river in Whitaker and Duquesne. Fans clapped their hands red as the Tigers took the field for warm-ups.

John Smonski, the Braddock *Free Press* sports reporter who'd been covering the Tigers since long before the streak began, was making his usual pregame tour of the stadium when the applause broke out for Klausing's boys. Having observed enough atmosphere, he made his way toward the field. From the bleachers, he ducked under a chain blocking a short staircase and walked out to the Tigers' bench. His long history covering Braddock High gave him special privileges that other media men, who had positioned themselves all around the stands and in the classroom overlooking the field, would have killed for.

John Jacobs, Ben Powell, and Ray Grudowski came walking back from the coin toss. The Tigers had won the call and would receive the kickoff to start the game. Klausing called on his return team, led by Curtis Vick. This was just another game, he told them.

The Canon-McMillan players had never been in front of a crowd so large or so loud. The noise on the field was daunting, and it swallowed up every word that players spoke. The Big Mac, as McMillan's team was called, lined up for the kick. Though there was almost no wind, the ball fell off the kicking block before the whistle. It seemed possible in that moment that the crowd's loud cheering had been the culprit. The McMillan kicker reset the ball. The head referee signaled to proceed. McMillan kicked off, and the game was under way.

Vick caught the short kick and ran it unmolested for twenty yards before meeting a line of defenders. He went down at the Tigers'

46-yard line, and the crowd redoubled its cheering at the end of the play. John Jacobs ran out onto the field with the full force of the seven-thousand-plus Braddock fans at his back. He had a beautiful ability to believe it was all for him. Klausing had sent him in with a passing play. Braddock was going to set the tone on the opening drive.

Dan O'Shea snapped the ball and Elbow Smith exploded out of the left end position. Coming off the line like a runner off the blocks, Elbow got a jump on the linebacker. Sprinting into no-man's-land, he charged past the safety, who had no chance of recovering. Jacobs took a three-step drop behind a strong Braddock line, and then he unleashed an arcing spiral that traced Elbow's arrow-straight run from above. The ball came down seamlessly into Elbow's sure hands and he was gone, galloping the last nineteen yards of the fifty-four-yard touchdown.

Though out of character, it was then that Klausing knew the game was in the bag. The anxiety leading up to that moment suddenly departed, and he felt pure joy to be on the field, to watch Jacobs run over to Elbow and wrap him in a hug. Klausing turned and looked into the stands, and for an instant he knew nothing but the serene and celebratory moment. In a way he would never quite know how to describe, he felt embraced by the sport that he loved.

What could Canon-McMillan do against fate? After three fruitless attempts on the visitor's opening series from scrimmage, the team punted away.

Before the Tigers' offense took the field for the second time, Klausing walked over to Jacobs with a quizzical look on his face, almost grinning. "How about another touchdown?"

Jacobs ran onto the field. At the snap, he rolled out to the right, pretended to look for an open man, and then ran straight at the line. He held the ball in one hand. It was foolish, dangerous, but under the lights, it was also stunning, as if Jacobs were reenacting some storied play from a game already completed. The home fans were on their feet, screaming. Jacobs sprinted up the sideline off a powerful block by Ray Henderson. He dodged a tackler and zipped into the open field. Forty-nine yards later, he crossed the goal line and ran clean through the end zone, finally veering off toward the pompom-waving Braddock High cheerleaders.

It went on like that. Roland Mudd fell on a Canon-McMillan fumble and Jacobs ran it in from scrimmage on the following play. The Tigers offense had snapped the ball three times and scored three touchdowns. Braddock had nineteen points with just nine minutes gone in the first quarter, and they nearly scored again when backup running back Tony Thompson broke free and jetted into the end zone. The play was called back for an illegal block, but the penalty didn't slow the Tigers down for long. Lining his boys up, Jacobs kept the ball again and broke for five yards. As tacklers converged, he pitched back to Doughboy, who rumbled in for the Tigers' fourth touchdown of the quarter.

Klausing sent the subs into the game. He wanted to make sure that every player on the Tigers had a piece of this win. At halftime the score was 38–0. The home crowd was having a ball. Students weren't the only ones who had sneaked alcohol into the stands. A party had broken out on the home field side.

On the field, Canon-McMillan's coach came trotting out to confer with Klausing.

"Coach, your boys are too much for us. What do you say we cut the second half short?"

"That'd be fine," Klausing said. "It's not your night, but you'll get us next time. Why don't we run eight-minute quarters? That way I can get all my players in the game."

"That sounds good. And Chuck, congratulations. This is one we'll all remember."

The Big Mac fared better against the Tigers' third- and fourth-string players during the truncated second half. McMillan scored on a fifty-eight-yard draw play in the third quarter, and then forced three Braddock fumbles, all of them leading to touchdowns for the visitors. McMillan also managed a safety after a booming punt from quarterback Larry Verchak pinned the home team deep in its own territory.

The Tigers subs played well. The only pall came near the end of the shortened fourth quarter. Phil Lucarelli, the sophomore, was in on defense. He went for a tackle, but as he went down under a pile of players, someone's knee bashed his helmet. Klausing diagnosed a mild concussion and sent the boy to the hospital.

Braddock High scored one more time in the second half, bringing the final score to 45–27.

When the shortened fourth quarter ended, players mobbed their coach. A group of boys hoisted Klausing onto their shoulders, and as flashbulbs popped around them, they marched him around the field. Chuck Klausing and his Braddock High Tigers had broken the national record. The game had been broadcast on the radio, and news quickly spread through the Mon Valley. Out-of-town well-wishers drove to Braddock to join in the party that would take place in the streets that night. There were parties all over Braddock, and cheerful bartenders stood drinks for half the town.

Though it was their night, Klausing and Zuger drove over to the hospital after the game and waited with Phil Lucarelli and his father until the boy could be examined.

"Gee, Lucarelli," said Zuger, "if I had known you wanted to make a tackle so bad, I would have put you in the game a long time ago!"

Chapter Ten

PRIDE

ERNIE VIDA ARRIVED at the newsstand early Monday morning. "*Sports Illustrated* come yet?" he asked.

The proprietor was just dragging the last bundle of newspapers inside. "Yeah, I got it. Gimme a minute to open up."

When the man reappeared in the doorway, he gave Vida a once-over. Robberies had been on the rise since the strike began, and Vida—in his too-long coat—looked suspicious lurking along Braddock Avenue in the early morning. Eventually the man stepped aside and motioned to a tall stack near the counter. Anticipating a run on *Sports Illustrated,* he had stocked dozens of copies.

Vida opened the top copy and began flipping through the pages. He sped past articles on harness racing and golf before something familiar caught his eye: a page-tall photo of the Edgar Thomson Works. The picture had been taken from high on a hill in North Versailles. The fender and one headlamp of Coach Klausing's station wagon jutted into the right foreground of frame. Between the car and the mill stood Curtis Vick, frozen mid-stride. Though he was wearing street clothes, his upturned chin and confident smirk, the attitude of his gait, hinted at the extraordinary power that made him such an effective fullback. Beside the photo, the title of the four-page story stood out in bold letters: A TOWN AND ITS TEAM.

Vida bought ten copies and then scurried back out to Braddock Avenue, which was still empty at the early hour. Now and then he stopped to shove his face into the article, admiring what his probing phone calls had made happen.

By midmorning, the entire town was reading *Sports Illustrated*—or trying to; the newsstands were cleaned out, and those fortunate enough to land a copy weren't eager to share. Enterprising residents made a killing. Tony Wincko, a former Tigers manager who'd graduated from Braddock High a year earlier, had the foresight to buy as many copies as he was able. He spent half the day hawking them for a markup. Even striking workers were happy to turn out their pockets to see the Tigers in print.

The *Sports Illustrated* photographers, Robert Huntzinger and Robert Bender, had done a marvelous job capturing the small, telling moments leading up to a Tigers football game. Taken in succession, the photos told a story. Opposite the image of Vick was a photo of Ray Grudowski, the starting guard and Braddock High student council president. He was wearing a striped long-sleeve button-up, which was cuffed handsomely at the forearms, and he was standing at a desk in front of a copy of Gilbert Stuart's famous portrait of George Washington. Grudowski was leading a student council meeting, according to the caption, and though his posture and countenance were convincingly stern—with his square jaw and thrown-back shoulders, he looked like a young corporal—his eyes and tight lips betrayed the self-consciousness of the boy lingering on beside the emergent man.

On the next page, a stark profile of Klausing sitting alone in the disused bleachers at ET Field carried a caption that began: "Thoughtful moment comes to Coach Klausing as he sits in stands of grimy, stony practice field where quarterbacks shout signals over the roar of passing freight trains."

Something in his pensive, distant gaze suggested that the shot had not been posed, that it was an authentic moment of inwardness captured by an alert photographer with a ready lens.

Several copies of *Sports Illustrated* were circulating the halls at Braddock High. Each photo drew careful scrutiny, but none prompted giggles like the image of John Jacobs dancing. Dan Rice had had his party, and Jacobs had been invited, of course. In a dull moment, the quarterback had sprung out of his chair and crossed the invisible threshold in Rice's living room that was keeping the girls separate from the boys.

"You wanna dance?" he asked the girl opposite him.

She hardly had a chance to say yes before he yanked her out of her seat. Grinning ear to ear, Jacobs did the Mashed Potato, a gyrating, energetic combination of steps that looked like an improvised version of the Twist. The photographer had lined up the double image in his range finder and snapped the photo.

"When they mention his name, the girls swoon," the caption read.

Reading that quote, Jacobs smiled. As he walked through school on Monday, groups of laughing girls called out: "Swoon! Swoon! Swoon!"

Two large pictures taken on the day of the Swissvale game spanned the vertical fold of the magazine. One captured the pep rally in the gymnasium. The entire student body looked on from the balcony seats as the Tigers sat in folding chairs on the basketball court below. Two rows of cheerleaders flanked the court like a security detail. In the middle of it all, Klausing stood before a skinny microphone stand in his Friday suit looking every bit the professional crooner.

Below, another photo taken just before the game captured the Tigers huddled together in prayer. The players wore ardent, serious looks, and in their faces there was no trace of the boyishness that the photographers had captured in the photos of Grudowski or Jacobs. In Tigers red and white, the players were young men with purpose.

Before long, Principal Stukus got his hands on one of the copies circulating through school. As he read the article accompanying the photo spread, he scowled. A quote from Mike Sullivan, who had succeeded in getting his name in the article, made him especially angry.

"We had a broken-down town," Sullivan was quoted as saying. "We started with a football team and we're going on from there."

Stukus, who loved Braddock and had dedicated his life to serving its young people, took no joy from that depiction of Braddock. The further he read, the more upset he became.

"Once a town of 20,000 but now smaller," the article continued, "Braddock has few formal recreation facilities to offer its teen-age youngsters."

Further along: "With many players from slums, the coach often aids boys' families."

There were poor neighborhoods in Braddock, Stukus knew, but *slums*? For a man who prided himself on his immaculate suits and coiffed hair, who commanded discipline and tried to instill a deep sense of pride and personal responsibility in his students, he felt the magazine's portrayal was injurious. Though many Braddock High students were quick to call their home dirty or used up, and though some boys hoped to escape the region after graduation, members of an older generation still thought of Braddock as the gleaming tower of commerce and industry that it had been in the first half of the twentieth century. A knock against that ideal was a knock against a vision that guided civic-minded residents.

Stukus spent the rest of the day confiscating every issue of the magazine he could find. Later that afternoon, he took a large stack to the basement and incinerated the contraband in the school's furnace.

Late in the afternoon on Wednesday, Tigers gathered outside the Burrelli Transit Service bus. The scene approximated a similar gathering two and a half months earlier, when uncertain boys had milled about in front of Braddock High before leaving for summer camp and embarking on a new season. This time, instead of street clothes and sour stomachs, they donned jackets and ties and affected the jovial bravado of champions. They were regional celebrities, national record holders. Across the country, professional athletes, college coaches, and an uncounted many high school football players were reading about their journey to greatness. Life was good at the top of the heap.

Players hadn't stopped grinning since Thursday's record-breaking win. The weekend had been all plaudits and celebration. Braddock had held its annual Halloween parade on Saturday, and though replete with the usual mask-wearing children and ghoul-themed parade cars, the Tigers were the biggest draw. The high school band played fight songs throughout the afternoon, and the revelry didn't end until drunken husbands and drunken high schoolers slinked off into the evening to compose themselves before dinner.

With *Sports Illustrated* hitting shelves on Monday, and with reporters hounding Klausing at every turn, the record was all anyone could talk about. Now the boys were off to Downtown Pittsburgh for a swanky banquet in their honor. The Variety Club of Pittsburgh, an association of show business personalities known for throwing galas to benefit children's charities, would be rolling out the red carpet for Klausing and his team.

Ernie Vida, high off his success with *Sports Illustrated,* helped arrange the Variety Club banquet, and Klausing had reluctantly agreed to participate. The Tigers coach wasn't eager to let his team become even more distracted than they already were. The Tigers still had one game left in the regular season—and it was *the game*, the all-important matchup with North Braddock Scott. The Tigers may have broken Massillon's record, but a loss would mar a perfect season and keep them out of the WPIAL championship. Worse, it would give North Braddock bragging rights for a full year. The very thought of it made Braddock fans squirm.

Up until this point, the Tigers had been playing for history. The

North Braddock Scott game was about something deeper: pride. Tickets had gone on sale early Monday morning and sold out almost immediately. Each team had been preparing for the matchup all season, keeping a watchful eye on the horizon for the inevitable battle ahead. So intense was the rivalry that Klausing had even received an unsigned death threat in the mail a few days earlier.

"If you show up to Friday's game," the note read, "we're going to kill you. To prove we mean business, we're going to smash your car this week."

Klausing chalked it up to a harmless prank. Fans were rabid, he knew, but not homicidal. Klausing's father wasn't so sure. Thousands of dollars were at stake whenever Braddock High and North Braddock Scott met. With the media attention from the record, big-fish bookies from Pittsburgh were getting in on the action.

Being the mayor of Wilmerding came with certain perks, and Charles Sr. insisted that Klausing let two of his police officers shadow him during the game on Friday. Klausing understood that his father's position was nonnegotiable. His only condition was that they wear plainclothes. He couldn't risk letting North Braddock Scott—or his own players, for that matter—think he was going into the rivalry fearful.

Klausing had finally agreed to let his players attend the Variety Club banquet. The evening affair would take place at the Penn-Sheraton Hotel, the fanciest digs in Pittsburgh, and it would be a treat for his players. Though ten miles apart, Braddock's steel culture and Pittsburgh's high society set existed on separate planes. Rich people could get in the car and drive through a steel town whenever they wanted, but this would be the last time most of the Braddock players would ever see the inside of the ballroom at the Penn-Sheraton. Klausing wanted to show his boys that they could hold their heads high in any crowd.

When the time came, the waiting boys filed onto the bus. When they arrived in Downtown Pittsburgh twenty minutes later, the players craned their necks to gaze up at the hotel's three tall towers that loomed over Grant Street.

"That's more like it," Doughboy said, breaking an awed silence.

"Coach, what are we having for dinner?" asked Grudowski.

"Anything you want, I guess," Klausing said.

Built in 1915 and expanded in the 1920s, the seventeen-story Penn-Sheraton boasted close to six hundred rooms. It was the first choice of heads of state and wealthy industrialists passing through Pittsburgh, in part because the kitchen made the finest food in the city. Hungry Tigers players were looking forward to confirming that rumor.

Led by Klausing, Zuger, Teitt, and Carr, the team walked into the marble-lined lobby, which was lit overhead by crystal chandeliers. A bellboy greeted them, practically bowing before the lost-looking bunch. He led them to the entrance of the hotel's ballroom.

If the lobby had been an opulent spectacle, the sheer scale of the ballroom cowed the players. As they entered through wide double doors, the guests, who had already arrived, burst into applause. Players wilted under the attention of the well-heeled group. Variety Club representatives converged, shaking players' hands and ushering them toward the four tables that had been reserved at the front. Klausing and the assistants would have their own table, though it took them several minutes to pass through the smiling crowd and sit down. Everyone wanted to congratulate them, and a double line quickly formed. In their fancy clothes, and wearing broad boozy grins, the guests looked like subjects at the coronation of a king.

A handful of Braddock dignitaries had also been invited to celebrate the Tigers' success. Among these were Mike Sullivan, the school board president, and Principal Joe Stukus. Both were known to be fussy about their wardrobes, and each was giddy at the chance to dress to the nines and mingle with Western Pennsylvania's elite. If Stukus was displeased with Sullivan for his comments in the *Sports Illustrated* article, he tried to be amicable now. There was no point airing private grievances in public.

The Variety Club had invited an assorted cast of local sports personalities. John Michelosen, the head coach at the University of Pittsburgh and a former Steelers coach, was sitting near Bob Prince, the Pittsburgh Pirates play-by-play announcer. Prince, the night's emcee, was known miles around for his soothing drawl and pleasant, gravelly voice—partially a product of his lifetime as a smoker. He used his instrument to great effect as a guest speaker all over the state, where his colorful personality and occasional irreverence commanded top dollar.

When the time came, Prince strolled to the podium at the head of the ballroom. He welcomed the team that had made all of Western Pennsylvania proud. The Tigers couldn't help but glow. Representatives from the Pittsburgh Steelers, the Pittsburgh Pirates, and the University of Pittsburgh Panthers were on hand, but Prince was talking about them. From the first summer practice of 1959, each boy had understood the significance of the record in an abstract sense. But the reality of what they had accomplished had to be experienced in waves of pride and deep emotion.

Though unable to avert his mind fully from game preparation, Klausing allowed himself to enjoy the evening. Waiters came bustling out of the kitchen and took orders all around. Most boys were at pains to choose between tenderloin and chicken, but no one was disappointed when the piping hot plates emerged. A few members of the Variety Club gave speeches extolling the Tigers' brilliant performances over the last six seasons, and Klausing gave a short talk in which he thanked his assistants—without whom, he assured the audience, he wouldn't have won half as many games.

During dinner, Klausing and Bob Prince began talking about Pirates baseball, which they each followed feverishly. As frequently happened during encounters with interesting people, Klausing had a feeling even then that he and the announcer would become close friends. Each man had a magnetism that the other responded to, and each projected a rare combination of honesty and bravado. A big part of Klausing's success came from the people he drew around him. Of his many talents as a coach, the most important might have been his ability to consistently draw the good ones.

After dinner and more rounds of congratulations, the Tigers left the ballroom to look for their bus. It was well past bedtime for Klausing's players, though sleep was far from their minds. The coaches did a head count to make sure none of the boys had decided to stay at the Penn-Sheraton.

"Where's John?" Klausing asked jokingly, referring to Doughboy. "Make sure he doesn't jump out when we pull away."

On the fifteen-minute ride back, Klausing met with his assistants. Wednesday was drawing to a close, and very little time remained to prepare. North Braddock Scott was better this year than they had been in 1958, when the Tigers eked out a 9–6 win off Rutkowksi's interception and Roland Mudd's thirty-seven-yard field goal. Both teams were undefeated in league play, and handicappers on Braddock Avenue were laying even odds on the outcome. Joe McCune, head coach of the Purple Raiders, had further fanned the flames in recent newspaper interviews.

"We're not a fancy team," he told the Pittsburgh *Press*. "We run hard and play hard, and our only big trouble so far has been looking ahead to this game ever since they beat us last year. As for their streak, it has to end some time. We have a good chance to beat 'em."

North Braddock Scott's roster was deep with talent. Anchoring the defensive line as right and left tackles were Lynn Zinck and Kenny Sockwell. At a muscular 180 pounds, Zinck had the closing speed of a sprinter and often racked up a dozen or more tackles per game. Sockwell was a power man, a 220-pound bruiser who, according to one reporter, "looks like two guards inside the same suit." With Roland Mudd in the game for Braddock, Friday's game would feature three of the best tackles in the state.

At quarterback, Paul Stanek was Scott's missile-thrower. His accuracy had prompted comparisons to Mark Rutkowski—the former

Tigers quarterback would long be the yardstick against which all other high school quarterbacks in the region were measured. Offensive end Harrison Bradford was Stanek's favorite target. Bradford was tall, with quick legs and excellent hands.

The Purple Raiders had something else going for them: Like the Tigers, they were trying to live up to a long legacy of greatness. While Braddock High had struggled on the gridiron in the first half of the twentieth century, its neighbor to the north had risen to national football prominence.

Under former coach Johnny Reed, who began his career at Braddock High before jumping ship in 1927, the Purple Raiders had captured WPIAL titles in 1933, 1934, and 1935. The 1934 team participated in a widely publicized interstate matchup in Florida. On Christmas Day, Scott High faced off against Miami Senior High in a contest that reflected the growing desire among football aficionados to pit the best squads from around the country against one another. North Braddock won the game easily, beating a Miami High team that hadn't lost in fifteen straight contests. To celebrate, the Pennsylvania boys went deep-sea fishing. To a player, every one of them lost his lunch.

Reed left North Braddock Scott after the 1935 season after he was tapped to coach powerhouse Canton-McKinley High School in Ohio. Even without their storied coach, North Braddock Scott continued to dominate, capturing another WPIAL title in 1937. Reed fared less well at Canton-McKinley. Though he led the well-known Bulldogs to an impressive 39–7–2 record in his five years with the team, he eventually got sacked by a frustrated school board. They had hired him for one purpose: to beat Massillon Washington High School, the prep pigskin juggernaut coached by a determined young man named Paul Brown. Reed never managed to pull off the upset, and so ended up contributing five losses to the Massillon unbeaten streak that would eventually become a national record.

Klausing and his assistants talked about Scott's offensive threats as the rattling bus lumbered along Braddock Avenue. A few all-night bars were open, spilling puddles of stale light onto the sidewalk, but otherwise the town was asleep.

As the bus turned up Sixth Street and made a right onto Lillie Avenue, one of the players jumped out of his seat. "Coach! Look what they did to your car!"

The team crammed to one side of the bus. Every window in Klausing's station wagon, which was parked in front of the school, was broken, smashed to hell. The fenders and side panels were bashed in, and the hood looked like someone had beaten on it with a sledgehammer. Just like that, the death threat seemed credible.

Even with his life in danger, there was too much to think about on Thursday to spend time worrying. Klausing brought his assistants to the gym during the day to pore through Scott High's game film. Against the whir of the sixteen-millimeter projector, the coaches huddled in a small side room off the main gym and watched grainy footage of the Purple Raiders for the tenth time. Any signs of weakness, any tics in Scott's execution or coverage, might be the key to a Tigers victory.

In the five years since Klausing had taken over at Braddock High, film systems had become standard equipment for competitive high school teams. Nevertheless, the etiquette for exchanging films was new, and pregame negotiations demanded diplomacy. Braddock coaches often found themselves in the uncomfortable position of wiping the floor with opponents, only to come back the following season to ask for recent films—all so they might wipe the floor with their opponents again. Most teams obliged, but sometimes Klausing had to get creative. He'd developed a strong network of local coaches over the years. Whenever an opposing team refused to cough up film before a game, Klausing looked for a friendly coach who'd played that team earlier in the season. He used film from the earlier matchup to prepare his boys, a practice he termed "bootlegging." Klausing never liked running the score up on an opponent, but he kept his starters in just a little bit longer than usual against uncooperative rivals.

With the coaches strategizing in the gym, Braddock High students who had P.E. at the same time knew to keep their distance. Disregarding that unspoken dictum, a renegade junior named Tony Buba sidled up to eavesdrop. Slouching against the wall outside the door to the film room, Buba disguised his interest by affecting the look of a slacker.

It wasn't a stretch. Buba was a negligent student, the kind of willful wiseass that most teachers assumed would drop out and drift off by senior year. A highly intelligent young man lurked beneath that blasé exterior, however. Fueled by worries over warmongering leaders, nuclear arms, and the inevitability of mutually assured destruction, the teen had entered a prolonged period of existential tumult. The Berlin crisis had set the Cold War in motion a decade before, and as routine air raid drills made clear, the bomb could drop any day. The Korean War, the Suez Crisis, and growing unrest in Vietnam had all contributed to a bleak outlook for a happy future. A recession had killed the U.S. economy a year earlier, and now, with half Buba's family out of work and the strike nearing its fourth month, the whole idea of American prosperity seemed on the verge of collapsing. Why try hard in school, Buba wondered, when the apocalypse seemed to be lurking around the next corner?

"There, run that back," Klausing said inside the film room. "The safety jumped again. He bites on that fake every time he comes up. I think we can beat him on the back."

The prying junior understood the lingo. He had played defensive lineman on Coach Zuger's ninth-grade team. He'd been so nervous in his first game that he lined up on the wrong side of the ball. His dad got a laugh out of that. The old man had played for North Braddock Scott under Johnny Reed in the 1930s and was part of the championship 1934 team that made the trip to Florida. But the apple fell far from the tree, and not just where football was concerned: Buba's father and uncles worked in the mill, which held little appeal for the high schooler. He had seen the fear on his mother's face whenever Edgar Thomson's whistle shrieked against the valley walls. Like the bellow of a war conch, the whistle alerted townspeople that an accident had occurred. Mill work was hot and dangerous. If four months of eating government cheese had proved anything, it also wasn't as steady a sector as people thought.

Buba detached himself from the doorway after a while. He wasn't crazy about football, but as a teenager in Braddock, he would never miss the rivalry game. For a kid who felt tossed around by the whims of history, it felt good to have a small nugget of inside information. He would be watching the Scott High safety on Friday, looking for one of Klausing's receivers to go deep on him after the fake.

November 6, 1959. A clear sky held over Braddock. Reflected in the Monongahela, that clean, bright blue still seemed like a miracle. One hundred fifteen days after the mills stopped, the soot-free sky hadn't lost its novelty.

Superstitious residents read the week's gossip like tea leaves. It was game day, and every gust of wind seemed to carry some implication for the evening's outcome. Klausing's son Tommy would turn six on Saturday. The Tigers were attempting to capture their sixth straight season without a loss. By anyone's superstitious calculus, that had to be a good sign.

But not all the gossip was promising. A resident named George Lelich had carried an ominous trophy back from a hunting trip earlier in the week. Lelich had fired at a shadow in the underbrush. He thought he had shot a cat in his haste, but when he looked closer, he found a jet-black rabbit. No one in Braddock could recall ever having seen a black rabbit, and word soon spread about the bad omen. Residents who knew about the threat against Klausing's life were especially anxious.

There were more significant issues for townspeople to be thinking about than high school football. A Supreme Court decision loomed, one that would have huge implications for the region's striking steelworkers. President Eisenhower had taken the first step toward invoking the Taft–Hartley Act a month earlier. With strike negotiations stalled, a fact-finding board had set out to determine whether a settlement between the USWA and the major steel companies was still possible. On October 19, the board returned its findings: There was no chance that the disputing sides would reach an agreement. The following day, at the president's urging, the Department of Justice asked the U.S. District Court in Western Pennsylvania for an injunction ordering the steelworkers back on the job.

The union was understandably frantic. If USWA members returned to work for the eighty-day "cooling off" period allowed for under Taft–Hartley, the resulting boom in steel production would refill the industry's coffers. The union would then be at a strategic disadvantage if members decided to continue the strike after the cooling-off period. David McDonald, president of the steelworkers' union, had been betting that lost revenue would eventually force a schism in the alliance of the major steel companies, but Eisenhower seemed to be signaling that he would never let the industry languish without revenue for long.

With no alternative, the union's general counsel recommended going after the constitutionality of Taft–Hartley. The USWA lost its first challenge in district court, but adjudicators stayed the injunction until higher courts could weigh in. The Third Circuit Court of Appeals again upheld the government injunction on October 27, which meant the union would have just one more chance. Union lawyers argued their case before the U.S. Supreme Court just three days before the Tigers were set to take the field against North Braddock Scott.

Now Friday morning, workers were still awaiting the court's decision. With the longest steel strike in the nation's history hanging in the balance—and, to some people's thinking, the very principle of a worker's right to strike—Braddock residents were grateful to have the game to distract them.

Klausing needn't have worried about his Tigers taking the matchup with North Braddock Scott lightly. The boys knew it would be the toughest game of the season, and they also knew what a loss would mean. Local feuds ran deeper than national glory. Attendance would be higher that evening than at any other game during the season, and the potential for heroism—and embarrassment—was huge. A loss would also prevent Braddock High from defending its WPIAL Class A title. A complex point system determined which two teams played in the WPIAL championship game, and the Tigers needed to go undefeated to get a spot.

Before school, Braddock High football players dressed in their nicest clothes. Boys from different neighborhoods, disparate social classes, brushed their teeth, combed their hair, and checked the mirror to be sure their faces betrayed none of the butterflies that were tumbling around in their stomachs.

Starting right end Ray Henderson left his house in Braddock's Bottom neighborhood and set out toward the high school. His father had died years earlier and Henderson lived with his mother in a small home tucked behind a barn that held the borough's idle streetcars. The Bottom was the poorest quarter in town, a few blocks skirting the steel mill and extending to the polluted Monongahela River. People from elsewhere in Braddock usually called the area "the Bottoms," forcing the plural. But it was just the Bottom to its inhabitants, singular, the lowest point by any measure.

As Henderson walked, the mill grew slowly smaller behind him. It was so silent and immutable now that it could have been a painted backdrop in a Hollywood set. The senior loved football, loved being on the Tigers. He had worked hard at it. In the off-season he ran up and down the streets to stay in shape. But football seemed to be drawing to an end for him. Though his team had captured the national record, and though he had played an important role on Braddock's offense, he hadn't received any interest from college scouts. He was a good player, a masterful lineman, but he didn't have the hands to be a top pass receiver. For a black kid to attract attention in Western Pennsylvania, he needed to be a standout in every respect.

Now Henderson was looking ahead to the final game of the regular season. If the Tigers lost, he would walk back to the Bottom, back into the shadow of the giant steel mill, knowing he would never play organized football again. If they won, he would have the WPIAL championship game to look forward to. To prolong the season even one game would be a blessing.

Henderson crossed Braddock Avenue and started up the bank toward Braddock High. The valley spread out behind him in the clear day. The slow, powerful river pushed toward its meeting with the Allegheny, where the two combined to form the Ohio. Everything had to come to an end. If this was Henderson's last game, he would make it count.

At school, all but the most stubborn teachers gave up trying to teach. Students were busy making plans for the evening, cheerleaders were preparing for the pep rally, and band members were looking over the night's songs. Football players had receded deep inside themselves and were concentrating on the game. There was little chance of capturing anyone's attention with a dusty lesson plan.

During seventh period, the entire school flooded into the gymnasium for the pep rally. Klausing's boys sat on folding chairs as seven hundred students cheered them on from the balcony above. It was a scene straight out of ancient Rome—the Tigers were like gladiators receiving plaudits in the Colosseum before battle.

Klausing gave a short speech. "We've had a strong season," he started out, "and there are a few players I want to mention by name."

He talked about John Jacobs, Ben Powell, Curtis Vick, Roland Mudd, and Ray Grudowski. It was the honor of a season to be called out by name in a pep rally. Klausing, the master strategist, hoped it would have an energizing effect on his stars.

At three thirty, the Tigers walked out of Braddock High. Dressed in street clothes and falling in behind their celebrated coach, they displayed their well-earned swagger. They hadn't lost in fifty-three straight games—one better than the legendary Massillon Washington Tigers. Klausing had set out to build a legacy at Braddock High. As players repeated six seasons of accomplishments to themselves to help calm their nerves, he could be sure he succeeded.

The Tigers headed toward Library Street, and fans shouted well-wishes along the way. As usual, the boys filed into the Elks Lodge for their pregame meal. Even with jangled nerves, the food went down easily. Klausing's players lived by routine. After a season of reinforcement, they fell automatically into the gustatory motions of game day.

After the meal, the Tigers marched to Braddock Avenue. Traffic slowed to a crawl as motorists craned to see Klausing's boys parade. The team entered the Paramount Theater half a block down. Inside, players took their seats in the upper balcony. Then Klausing, Zuger, and Bobby Williams returned to the lobby to set up taping stations. When everything was set, they started calling the boys out by position.

Klausing grabbed Ray Henderson. The boy's confidence was low, he knew, and he wanted to give it a boost. With Scott's defensive line threatening to shut the Tigers running game down cold, Klausing anticipated going to the air. He'd need his left end ready to catch the ball when that happened.

A month earlier, Klausing had read an article in *Sports Illustrated* written by Baltimore Colts offensive end Raymond Berry. A favorite target of quarterback Johnny Unitas, Berry was considered one of the best pass receivers in the NFL. His sure hands had been the deciding factor in the Colts' 1958 NFL Championship victory over the New York Giants. *Sports Illustrated* asked the catching great to share some of his tips with readers. In the article, Berry explained a few of the more technical aspects of receiving, such as hand position and proper route execution. He also mentioned some tricks he'd picked up. One of these was to wrap his wrists in towels on hot days to keep sweat off his hands.

As Klausing leaned forward to tape Henderson's ankle, he baited his player by mentioning the article. When Henderson asked what Berry had written, he told him about the wrist wrap. It was early November and the weather had turned chilly in Western Pennsylvania, so Klausing tweaked Berry's tip just slightly.

"You know," he said casually, "Berry swears he can catch the ball better if he tapes his wrists. Just a little added pressure makes his fingertips relax, and the ball stays put."

Klausing didn't mind fibbing a little to help a player gain some self-assurance. Henderson was intrigued. He proffered his arms, and Klausing applied a light wrap to each wrist.

By late afternoon, the air above Braddock was electric. In advance of the game, out-of-town crowds had descended on Braddock Avenue. Savvy shop owners, praying for relief after months of lousy sales, put up signs advertising deep discounts.

The Famous, a five-story department store, hawked clothes, toys, and household goods—all of it modeled by the happiest mannequins, the friendliest-looking cardboard cutouts that had ever vacuumed a rug or tended a grill. Inside, as if to accentuate the state-of-the-art decor, a network of pneumatic tubes sent money and backroom orders flying high overhead. For many small children, their heads turned skyward, these whooshing, space-age tubes were the highlight of otherwise tedious excursions with their parents.

Not that a trip to Braddock was such a chore for small children. For those who managed to escape, an afternoon became a blur of color. Packs of boys swarmed down the street. Trolleys on the old 55 line shuttled shoppers from one end of town to another. Children latched on to the backs of the trolley cars, and conductors, overworked and overwhelmed, gave up trying to shout them down. The boys jumped off after a time, their attention piqued by the shiny hard shells of the latest cars in the Braddock Avenue showrooms.

The dealership at the end of town was a favorite—a huge brick building with concrete ramps and a thousand places to hide. If a kid kept cool, didn't attract attention, he could get to the rooftop display. There, three stories up, he could look out over the town, peer down at the swell of people, and gaze across the street into the frowning maw of Edgar Thomson. A kid was a king on that rooftop, until a salesman, sensing there was fun afoot, pumped his fists and gave chase. Then it was down the ramp, over the railing, and back onto Braddock Avenue, where waiting friends, high on a wild spirit, hooted their congratulations, the whole pack slipping gaily into the crowd.

Fans started their exodus into North Braddock early, and Scott Field was packed before the sun had set. Mounted police had been brought in for crowd control—a riot was never out of the question when these two teams faced off. The horses paced both sidelines while their hawk-eyed riders looked for signs of trouble in the growing crowd.

Joann Klausing rode to the game in a Wilmerding police car with Charles Sr. At their seats in the stands, Joann turned and spotted former Steelers player Bill Priatko. Priatko had played offensive end for Scott High from 1946 to 1948. Beside him in the stands were two large men that Joann didn't immediately recognize. One was Jimmy Orr, the talented Steelers receiver, and the other was Gary Glick, the Steelers safety. Priatko had been telling his friends that the Braddock–North Braddock matchup was like no game they'd ever seen. As fans streamed into the stadium and new arrivals took to standing or squishing between perfect strangers, Jimmy Orr's eyes got wide. He was from the South and had played college football in Georgia, but had never seen a high school game so well attended. Joann and Priatko exchanged friendly waves. They were rivals tonight, but before the opening whistle they could still be friendly.

Though tickets had been closely meted out, and though security was high at the gates, legions of ticketless hopefuls successfully sneaked into the stadium. Some fans had searched the fence for weaknesses, but others were far less subtle. A crowd dozens thick had gathered at one entrance. By brute momentum it had begun surging past the ticket takers. Security guards ran toward the breach to staunch the flow. When the guards had regained control, they quickly swung the gate closed.

Fans stuck outside the gate, some of them legitimate ticket holders, began hollering to be let in. But the guards wouldn't risk it. They directed the crowd to walk around to the main entrance. A standoff ensued, and it was exacerbated a few moments later when a short man in a Notre Dame hat pushed his way to the front of the crowd.

Bystanders leapt to the side when they realized it was Coach Klausing. Fresh from the movie and dressed for the game, the Tigers had to get onto the field. This was their usual entrance, the closest point to the visitors' locker room. But the security guard in charge wouldn't budge. Apologetically, he explained that he couldn't risk opening the gate with so many fans hoping to elbow through. The Tigers would have to walk to the other entrance like everybody else.

Incredulous, Klausing narrowed his eyes at the guard. This was the rivalry game, the most heated high school matchup in the state. He wasn't in the mood to dither around. The man had left Klausing two options: The Tigers could hump to the opposite side of the stadium, or they could make short work of the seven-foot gate by climbing over. The Tigers coach turned and signaled to his players. The curious masses parted as the team came forward. The boys had carried their cleats on the walk up, and now they tossed them over.

Hooking their fingers through the chain link, they started climbing two at a time. Successive waves of Tigers followed, throwing their legs over and then gingerly lowering themselves to the other side. No one wanted to turn an ankle before the game had even started.

The crowd was beside itself, laughing and clapping Klausing's boys forward. It was the kind of thing that could only happen in Western Pennsylvania. Klausing was the last to climb over. When he made it safely to the other side, he walked by the dazed security guard without a word.

The mutual enmity between Braddock High and North Braddock Scott was made all the more intense by the fact that the teams shared a field. Whenever they met, Scott Field technically became neutral territory—neither squad could claim home advantage. But North Braddock Scott used the home field locker room and Braddock players never forgot where they were. After wins in each of the previous five seasons, the Tigers had hightailed it out of the stadium as a group. Until they crossed under the train tracks, they were in enemy territory.

Under the lights, North Braddock was already warming up. Balls thudded off chilled hands. It got cold in Western Pennsylvania in November. Before the 1958 WPIAL championship, Tigers offensive end Jim Hux had barely been able to feel his fingertips. Worried that his best receiver wouldn't be able to catch the ball, Klausing gave him a pair of fur-lined leather gloves that Joann had brought with her. Hux tried the gloves during warm-ups and found he could catch just fine. He decided to wear them in the game. On the third play of Braddock's opening drive against Waynesburg High, the offensive end hauled in a beautiful over-the-shoulder pass from Rutkowski for a touchdown. He finished the night with four receptions to help Braddock to its fifth straight WPIAL title.

Klausing's boys disappeared into the visitors' locker room. The crowd outside was massive, even bigger than it had been in the 1958 matchup. Estimates would put the number of attendees at between ten and fifteen thousand people. With so many gate-crashers, it was impossible to say for sure. Outside the stadium, fans had climbed onto the roofs of several houses that overlooked the sunken field. With people in the tightly packed throng below jockeying for a good viewing angle, these rooftop lookouts might have been the best seats in the house.

The din of the crowd was intense, even from the locker room. Klausing wanted his boys to sit a moment, out of sight, to prepare themselves. This was the last game of the regular season. For seniors, it would be the last chance to step onto Scott Field as Tigers.

When the players finally left the locker room, the crowd exploded. If there was any booing coming from Scott High fans, it was completely drowned out. The dense wall of people ringing the field was breathtaking, even for Braddock players accustomed to fanfare and big crowds. Klausing was so taken aback that he decided not to send his players straight out for warm-ups. Instead he ordered them to go sit on the sideline bench. When they had complied, he walked in front of his seated players like an officer inspecting his platoon.

With a single gesture, he ordered them to their feet. "Let's go," he said.

Flanked by his assistants, Klausing began to walk. The Tigers followed in single file. Skirting the outside of the field, they kept their heads high. They didn't acknowledge Scott's players, even as they passed directly in front of them. It was a victory lap before the game had even started. Klausing was taking back home field advantage, and Braddock fans went wild. The Tigers coach had always known how to work a crowd.

When the team finished its lap, Klausing sent them out for calisthenics. A few minutes later, the referees called for the captains. Scott won the toss and chose to receive the kickoff. The moment both teams had been preparing for all season was upon them. The national record holders took the field opposite the team that many predicted would put an end to their long streak.

One thing was apparent on the opening kickoff: North Braddock Scott wasn't cowed by the hype. Mudd's kick bounced to the 29-yard line. With room to run, the return man advanced the ball to the Scott 42. Joe McCune's offense trotted to the line for the first time of the evening with excellent field position.

Scott opened with a run straight up the middle. Halfback Sonny Thomas fumbled on the opening play, but it worked to his advantage. A North Braddock offensive lineman jumped on the ball near midfield for a gain of seven yards. Starting near midfield, Scott couldn't break free on the next two plays. Braddock's defense had held firm, and the Purple Raiders set up to punt.

The kick was short and wobbly, and the ball shot backwards when it landed, careening into a Braddock player. Luck seemed to be on Scott's side. The Purple Raiders recovered the fumble, and the offense came right back onto the field with a fresh set of downs.

Hoping to catch the record holders snoozing, McCune called a double reverse on first down. The astute Tiger line read the misdirection perfectly, and Vernon Stanfield broke the play up for a loss. After two more unsuccessful running attempts, Scott was forced to punt again. Klausing was pleased with his defense's performance early in the first quarter.

Doughboy caught the ball cleanly at his 9-yard line. Off balance and tripping on his own feet, he handed off to Ben Powell. Powell streaked laterally, crossing from one side of the field to the other before breaking into a dead run for the end zone. Ninety-one yards later, it looked like Braddock had scored a tremendous first touchdown. But the merriment was cut short by a referee all the way on the other side of the field. He was waving his arms and blowing hard on his whistle to try to overcome the crowd noise. Doughboy's knee had touched the ground right before the handoff to Powell. Six points came off the scoreboard, and the air went out of the celebration in the stands.

Starting over deep in its own territory, Braddock couldn't move the ball at all. Three plays later, Vernon Stanfield punted away. It was clear to everybody watching that it was going to be a long, hard night.

North Braddock wasn't having much luck with its ground game, but McCune's boys were making an art out of fumbling forward for nice gains. After a quick run, Sonny Thomas coughed the ball up again. Players from both teams tripped over themselves trying to pick it up, but at last it was Thomas himself who recovered it, netting sixteen yards on the ugly play.

The good luck inspired an offensive burst. North Braddock broke for fourteen yards, which brought them inside the Tigers' 20-yard line. Klausing needed his defense to get tough, and Roland Mudd obliged. The tackle broke through on first down, creaming the North Braddock quarterback for a loss of twelve and forcing the Purple Raiders out of field goal range. Three plays later, the Purple Raiders were forced to punt once again.

The first quarter ended with fans from both teams feeling uneasy. Klausing's offense hadn't had a chance to get going, and North Braddock Scott hadn't been able to convert on its excellent field position.

The old Tigers spark seemed to return for the start of the second quarter. Powell gained nineteen yards on a sweep. Vick followed with hard runs for three and eleven yards. Suddenly, Braddock was inside Scott's 10-yard line. Smelling points, fans began to celebrate. Powell took the handoff on first down for an inside run. But Powell was more accustomed to breaking out wide than lowering his shoulder and punching the ball through the middle, and Scott's huge defensive line surprised him. He took a hard hit, and the ball bounced out of his hands on the 2-yard line. North Braddock Scott recovered.

"Hellfire!" Klausing yelled on the sideline, the closest he ever came to cursing.

The Tigers halted a promising Scott High drive on the next series, but soon Klausing's offense gave him another reason to rip off his hat. A clipping penalty moved the Tigers back to their 37-yard line.

Jacobs managed a first down with a quarterback keeper, but on the next play, running up the middle, it was Vick's turn to fumble.

Klausing's team was demonstrating none of the discipline or talent that had won it national recognition, and the hits kept coming. Braddock managed to stop a Scott drive with good coverage and a batted down pass, but the Tigers offense had come completely unglued. Vick managed a first down off two hard runs, but Doughboy fumbled on the next series and Scott recovered yet again.

All three starting running backs had now fumbled, and the Tigers ended the half in an unfamiliar position: Tied 0–0 with almost no bright spots after thirty minutes of play. The team's legacy, its brilliant momentum, hadn't been worth a damn in the first half.

As Klausing walked toward the locker room, the death threat was the last thing on his mind. His team wasn't performing, and for a championship-caliber coach, there was little else worth thinking about. It had not escaped the players' notice that two men in street clothes had been trailing their coach. The Wilmerding officers stayed close on Klausing's heels, alert for anyone brash enough to make good on the anonymous threat. Klausing had forgotten all about them, but suddenly he found himself in the middle of a fracas.

Just as the coach was leaving the field, a man leapt out of the stands. Blocking Klausing's path, the man raised a dark object. The plainclothesmen leapt forward and wrestled the man to the ground. Fans just above the scuffle looked on in disbelief. In the stands, Joann and Charles Sr. felt a cold chill run up their spines. The officers slapped handcuffs on the would-be assailant and jerked him to his feet. Hearts pumping, they quickly scanned the area for accomplices.

After a confused moment, and with the suspect pressed helplessly against the railing in front of the bleachers, Klausing saw the microphone. Then he looked at the man's face. It was Sir Walter, a reporter for WAMO, a popular black radio station in Pittsburgh. Sir Walter was covering the game, and he'd been looking for some halftime commentary. Klausing shook his head. He apologized to Sir Walter for the confusion and instructed the officers to do the same. On top of everything else, the Tigers coach had now angered a member of the press.

With his boys playing so poorly, Klausing tried to be positive in the locker room. For the past six seasons he had been telling his teams to consider the score tied going into the second half. They were well prepared for this moment, he assured them.

"Come on, y'all," Roland Mudd said, trying to rally his crestfallen teammates. "We're playing like a bunch of sissies, and they still can't score on us."

John Jacobs prowled the locker room, slapping his team's shoulder pads. Did they want to win tonight, he asked, or did they want to cry about losing?

Braddock fans were supportive when the Tigers came out of the locker room, but men with big bets riding on the outcome were tense. It was impossible to say exactly how much money had been staked in all, but individual bettors with deep pockets had won thousands on high school games in the past. Former Pittsburgh Steelers fullback Fran Rogel had played for Scott High in the early 1940s, and he never forgot the night he ran off the field after scoring every point in a big win over Turtle Creek. Grateful bettors had stuffed three hundred dollars into his helmet by the time he reached the locker room. He later bragged to his Steelers teammates that he'd been the first high school player ever to go pro.

Despite encouragement from fans, Braddock's offensive troubles had carried over into the second half. The Tigers received the kickoff and set to work on their 30-yard line. Vick had a nice run up the middle, netting sixteen yards, but Doughboy and Ben Powell couldn't do anything on the ground in their next attempts. John Jacobs ran the ball on a quarterback keeper, but carrying it in one hand, he dropped it before he crossed scrimmage. As the pigskin tumbled by his feet, he pounced on it for no gain.

Scott scored first. Nearing the end of the third quarter, passer

Paul Stanek hurled a thirty-four-yard missile to Sonny Thomas, who ran the rest of the way for a touchdown. Scott failed to convert on the extra point. The score was 6–0, marking the first time all season that the Tigers had been behind.

Scott's touchdown lit a fire under Ben Powell. After the kickoff, Powell caught the ball on his own 20-yard line. Displaying his signature speed and agility, he faked a handoff to Doughboy and then bolted upfield. Sidestepping Scott defenders, Powell covered eighty yards on his way to the end zone. After a nail-biting defensive battle, fans had now seen two touchdowns within fifteen ticks of the game clock. Mudd drove the extra point home, and the Tigers found themselves in a more familiar position—leading 7–6.

Braddock fans had every reason to believe that momentum was now on their side. In previous games, Klausing's boys had typically run roughshod over the competition once the floodgates opened. But when Mudd kicked off, the Scott return man threw a wrench in that thinking. Dodging tacklers, the swift player made it to his 44-yard line. Two plays later, Stanek threw a high, floating pass for thirty-eight yards, putting Scott High inside the Braddock 20. Stanek was proving every bit equal to the comparisons with Mark Rutkowski.

Running back Sonny Thomas ran around the right end on the following play, out-sprinting Elbow Smith and zipping into the end zone untouched. For the second time of the season and the second time in the game, the Tigers found themselves trailing. Scott missed the extra point once again. The score was 12–7, heading into the decisive fourth quarter.

Jacobs hadn't been accurate all evening. Scott standouts Lynn Zinck and Kenny Sockwell had bulldozed the Braddock line, collapsing the pocket and forcing Jacobs to throw before his targets could get free. Early in the fourth, the Tigers mounted their most convincing drive of the evening, with Powell and Vick trading strong runs to maneuver to the Scott 8-yard line. The next three running attempts failed, and Klausing sent in a passing play. On fourth down,

Jake tried to find Elbow Smith in the end zone. It was a rushed pass, and a Scott defender leapt out at the last minute to intercept it in almost the exact spot where Mark Rutkowski had intercepted Scott's pass a year earlier to end the game. North Braddock Scott fans let out a boisterous whoop. The dispassionate pendulum of history seemed to be swinging in a new direction.

The North Braddock Scott celebration lasted exactly two plays. After a run on first down went nowhere, quarterback Paul Stanek tried to advance the ball himself on second down. On defense, Dan O'Shea and Ray Henderson converged. Stanek tried to escape into his own end zone, but the duo tackled him for a safety. With the score now 12–9, Braddock had pulled to within a field goal. Fans of both teams recalled the previous year's game, which had tilted on points scored off the foot of Roland Mudd.

It wasn't Ben Powell's night. The Tigers received the kickoff after the safety and marched to the Scott 38-yard line, but on a pitchout from Jacobs, Powell bobbled the ball. He dropped it, and a Scott defender scooped it up, running to the Tigers' 48-yard line before being brought down.

Powell was devastated. This was the biggest crowd the Tigers had ever played in front of, and the quiet boy wanted to make his family proud. He had scored Braddock's only touchdown, but he had now fumbled the ball twice. In the bright lights of the stadium, it was clear to players on the field that tears of frustration were forming in Powell's eyes. If the Tigers lost, he would carry the defeat on his shoulders for a long time to come.

With the chance to extend its lead, Scott's offense got hot. The Purple Raiders moved the ball to the Tigers' 26-yard line. With less than four minutes to play, and with the Tigers demoralized, a touchdown would be devastating for Braddock. Responding to the pressure, Mudd broke through for a sack on the next play, pushing Scott back two yards. Then it was Powell's turn. Backpedaling while tracking Stanek's eyes, the senior leapt in front of a tight spiral. No force on earth could have kept him from catching the ball. He pulled it to his chest, and with room to run he advanced to his own 17-yard line—and to redemption.

Braddock trailed by three with three minutes and forty-four seconds to play. Jacobs lined up under center. At the snap, Zinck broke through the line and mauled him for a loss of eight. Fazed, Jacobs climbed to his feet and huddled his players. Klausing sent in a play, and the Tigers jogged back to the line. Starting on his own 9-yard line, Jacobs dropped back. Zinck broke through the line again, and the quarterback misfired to Elbow Smith to avoid being tackled. The ball fell incomplete, bringing up third down.

Klausing believed in his quarterback. Though the Tigers were deep in their own territory and turnovers had plagued his team, he sent in another passing play. The Tigers again took the line facing the larger North Braddock front wall. O'Shea snapped the ball, and the Tigers line dug in to give Jacobs time. The quarterback set his feet and fired to Smith in the flat. The sure-handed left end caught the pass and fell to the ground at the 32-yard line.

Jacobs had room and a new set of downs, but he threw incomplete on the next play, misjudging Powell's route. On the following play, defensive tackle Kenny Sockwell broke through the line. Jacobs scrambled, but Sockwell got to him before he could locate a receiver. The play pushed the Tigers back to their 26-yard line.

In the stands, Braddock fans could hear their hearts thumping in their chests. Joann Klausing, who had been on her feet through the entire game, began to see stars.

She turned to Charles Sr. "I feel dizzy," she said.

A Braddock fan standing behind Joann leaned forward. "Try this," he said, handing her a hip flask.

Joann grabbed the flask and took a quick drink. She wasn't accustomed to hard alcohol, but her nerves had never been so jangled.

In the classroom overlooking the field, Zuger picked up the phone. "They're giving Butch space," he told Klausing.

Scott's defenders hadn't been paying much attention to Ray Henderson. Klausing hoped his right end was still feeling confident about the wrist tape. He sent in the play.

At the snap, Jacobs took a quick drop and zipped a nine-yard pass. Henderson grabbed it cleanly as he got tackled.

"That's it!" Klausing yelled.

With Zinck's sack on the first play of the drive, Braddock still needed seven yards for a first down. Braddock faced a dire fourth down with less than two minutes to play. Jacobs took a deep drop. Again, the coverage on Henderson was soft. The end slanted inside, and Jacobs hurled a twenty-six-yard pass. The tape worked its magic as Henderson hauled in the ball. The crowd was on their tiptoes in the stands. For the first time all night, Braddock fans felt that momentum was on their side.

Down 12–9 with a minute and a half to play, the Tigers were on the Scott 39-yard line. Klausing called a running play to Vick, who was quickly stuffed for no gain. On second down, Doughboy tried to break loose. The North Braddock line proved too strong, and the halfback got stopped cold. On third down, Jacobs pitched out wide to Powell. Fighting to make up for his earlier blunders, the senior fought through two tacklers to advance the ball to the Scott 26-yard line. Jacobs hurried his team to the line and tried a quick pass with under a minute to play. The ball fell incomplete.

In the stands, Joann Klausing felt the whiskey going to her head. The next thing she knew, she was being propped up by Charles Sr. A ring of spectators were huddled around her, and their faces registered concern. She had passed out.

"Did we win?" she asked.

"Not yet," Charles Sr. said.

On the field, Klausing picked up the phone. Zuger knew what play to call. The Scott safety always bit on an outside fake.

"Sixty-eight pass, tight end screen left," he said.

Klausing sent in the play. The clock showed thirty-seven seconds.

O'Shea snapped the ball. Coming off the blocks, Henderson threw a quick fake to the outside. The safety jumped. In the stands, Tony Buba recognized the scenario he had overheard the coaches discussing in the gym.

Henderson streaked upfield, leaving his defender half a step behind. The Tigers wall kept Scott's powerful tackles at bay. Jacobs tossed a high, clean pass. Time stopped and hair on the arms and necks of fans from both teams stood up as the ball made its slow arc. At a full sprint, Henderson stuck his hands out. The tape on his wrists formed two white bracelets under the bright stadium lights.

EPILOGUE

On saturday, klausing walked outside his Monroeville home and picked up the paper. Braddock High had defeated North Braddock Scott 15–12. Ray Henderson, a blocking end with boards for hands, caught three passes on the final drive, including a brilliant over-the-shoulder grab for the winning touchdown. Fans mobbed the field after the final whistle, overwhelming Allegheny County's mounted police officers. Braddock players hoisted their coach onto their shoulders in celebration.

Klausing put the paper under his arm. He would read it later.

Inside, Joann was setting the table for breakfast. "It's a big day," she said.

"I'll say," Klausing said. "Where is he?"

Tommy Klausing was still asleep. It was the morning of his sixth birthday. After he woke, the family would spend the day celebrating. At the end of a long regular season, there was nothing in the world the Tigers coach would rather do.

In Braddock, fans were jubilant. The Tigers would play for their sixth WPIAL Class A title in two weeks. The team had gone six seasons without losing, extending their improbable streak to fifty-four games. With a new season on the horizon, residents were already wondering how long the run might continue in 1960.

But even as the victory over North Braddock Scott was being rehashed in barrooms and front porches up and down the Monongahela Valley that Saturday, a more somber story leaked out in radio and television reports. On November 7, 1959—one day after the Tigers' monumental victory—the U.S. Supreme Court issued its ruling in *Steelworkers v. United States*. Voting 8–1, the justices sided with the government. After 116 days on strike, workers were being ordered back on the job.

No one knew exactly what the Taft–Hartly injunction would mean for the union, but steelworkers understood well enough that they were defeated. Half a million strikers had spent four months picketing in front of steel mills across the country. Many had burned through savings and taken on debts. Their families had endured every hardship with them, as had the shops and restaurants in the towns where they lived. Now the men would be returning to work, and negotiators would sit down to hammer out the terms of a new union contract—exactly as they had before the strike began. Workers felt powerless, ineffectual.

Two weeks after the dispiriting news came out, and with the mills back online, the Tigers gave their bruised fans a reason to smile once again. Braddock High trounced Waynesburg High 25–7 to capture a sixth WPIAL Class A title. Shortly after the game, Chuck Klausing made an announcement. He would be stepping down as head coach of the Tigers. Bob Teitt would take over the program, and John Zuger and Harry Carr would stay on as assistants.

Teitt's Tigers did well by almost any measure the following season, but they still fell short of their own expectations. On the second game of the season, Braddock lost 7–6 to a strong Hopewell squad coached by former Braddock High assistant Bill McDonald. When the bus carried the teary-eyed boys back into Braddock that night, the streets were clogged with supportive fans. Braddock residents gave their Tigers a minutes-long ovation. The team finished the season a respectable 6–2, dropping the last game 19–12 to Joe McCune's North Braddock Scott Purple Raiders. The streets of North Braddock had never seen a party like the one fans threw that November night. North Braddock's long drought had finally ended. But the celebration didn't last long. The Tigers were back on top in 1961, finishing 8–0 on the season.

From the last game of the 1953 season to the second game of the 1960 season, the Braddock High Tigers played fifty-six games without losing, which was believed to be a national record. Klausing's team buoyed spirits and inspired hope throughout Western Pennsylvania during one of the region's most difficult hours. It turns out the Tigers broke the record in name only. Before efforts to compile a national high school athletics registry had taken root, claims to scholastic records were based on the best available knowledge, and bragging rights often went to teams that managed to get national press—like Braddock High, which was credited with the national record by *Sports Illustrated*. Until better information came along, history belonged to those who wrote it.

Longer unbeaten streaks are known to have existed before the Tigers' impressive run. The Black Bears from Tuscaloosa High—an all-white school in Alabama—posted sixty-four consecutive games without a loss from 1925 to 1931, predating the streaks of both Braddock High and Massillon Washington High. From 1941 to 1947, another all-white team from Alabama, the Tallassee Tigers, went fifty-eight straight games without a loss. Blowing away the field, the all-black Bedford County Training School in Shelbyville, Tennessee, played eighty-two football games from 1943 to 1950, winning seventy-eight of them and tying four. Bedford's streak also included a hard-to-conceive fifty-two consecutive shutouts.

The historical record remains spotty, and with school mergers and closures blurring the lens, it's possible that other teams deserve mention. The National Federation of State High School Associations maintains the most comprehensive registry of high school athletic records in the country, and the organization's Web site makes an excellent jumping-off point for anyone interested in learning more.

In writing this book, I've hewed to what residents of Western Pennsylvania believed to be true in the late 1950s—and often still say is true for the sake of a good story. The emotional stakes for Klausing's boys and for the region's out-of-work steel-men were real. Much of the power of sports lies in the narratives we build around them, and my allegiance here has, where I've deemed prudent, tipped toward barstool retellings.

The current record holder for the longest unbeaten streak in high school football is undisputed. From 1992 to 2004, De La Salle High School in Concord, California, won 151 straight games. The legendary Bob Ladouceur coached every one of them. It is a pleasant exercise on a dull afternoon to imagine how Klausing and his 1959 Tigers would fare against one of Ladouceur's teams. It's easy to default to modernity in that scenario, but I'm not so sure. The backfield of Jacobs, Powell, Vick, and Doughboy was a force to be reckoned with.

Chuck Klausing went on to a storied college coaching career. After leaving Braddock High, he served as an assistant coach at Rutgers and then at the United States Military Academy. He became head coach at Indiana University of Pennsylvania in 1964, and he led his 1968 IUP team to the Boardwalk Bowl in Atlantic City. From 1970 to 1975, Klausing coached alongside Bobby Bowden as an assistant at West Virginia, where he specialized in recruiting—he had a knack for spotting the untapped potential in high school seniors. Klausing took over as head coach of Carnegie Mellon University in 1976. With a career winning percentage of .821, he ranks as the fifth-winningest Division III head coach in history. As he was being inducted into the College Football Hall of Fame, reporters asked for his favorite memories.

"Some talked about playing in the Rose Bowl in front of a hundred thousand or the Army–Navy game. I got up, and it was my turn, and said playing Friday night against North Braddock Scott was the greatest for me."

Klausing returned to high school coaching in 1987, taking a job at a private all-boys school in Western Pennsylvania. At the time of this writing, he is eighty-eight years old and retired. He still vividly recalls his days at Braddock High, remembering every player, along with every bonehead mistake they ever made. It's a safe bet that his players remember those mistakes also.

Joann Klausing passed away in 2011 after a battle with dementia. Though Klausing always maintained that the Braddock High streak was his greatest accomplishment as a coach, he amended that assessment after Joann got sick. Summoning lessons he learned over his four and a half decades leading football teams, he became a caretaker, trainer, and daily encourager to his wife of more than sixty years. Though painful, the role was a natural fit. He considers it the most important coaching job he's ever had.

Mark Rutkowski, the sensational Braddock High quarterback, lost his battle with German class and left Dartmouth after freshman year. Klausing helped him get a scholarship to Dayton University in Ohio, but his knee never fully recovered. Dayton allowed him to keep his scholarship by serving as an assistant coach. He now lives in the Washington, D.C., area, where he is a psychiatric social worker.

After graduating from Braddock High, John Jacobs accepted an offer from Arizona State, following in the footsteps of Tigers alumnus Larry Reaves. Jacobs earned first team All-Western Athletic Conference honors in 1962, passing for what was then a school record 1,263 yards. After a year of semi-pro ball with the Canton Bulldogs after college, he came close to playing in the NFL, appearing in an exhibition game with the Dallas Cowboys and making the practice squad for the Washington Redskins. After hanging up his cleats, he started a career as a probation officer in Maricopa County, Arizona, where he has helped countless offenders get their lives back on track. He retired in 2009.

John "Doughboy" Gay stayed in the Braddock area. He became an influential minister and church elder, touching many lives before passing away in 2008. Ben Powell played football at the University of Oklahoma for a year and half before joining the army. He moved home to Western Pennsylvania when he got out, where the quiet Tigers running back raised a large and loving family. He passed away in 2013.

Curtis Vick went to Purdue University, where he lettered as cornerback for the Boilermakers in 1962. Tragically, he died from a drug overdose before the 1963 season. His death was wrenching for all those who played with him, and it broke Klausing's heart.

Ray Henderson, who made the winning touchdown catch against North Braddock Scott, served in the navy before going to work in a steel mill outside of Pittsburgh. As Klausing would later lament, his biggest regret as a coach was not being able to give his black players the same opportunities at college scholarships as his white players. Henderson became an effective grievance man in the mill and a dedicated community organizer. He served as board president of the local chapter of the NAACP and now holds a seat on the board of the Braddock's Field Historical Society.

Tony Buba eventually emerged from his prolonged existential tumult to become an acclaimed documentary filmmaker. Buba and Henderson got together in 1995 to produce the film *Struggles in Steel*, which follows the experiences of black workers in the mills of Western Pennsylvania. The movie received critical acclaim. Both men still live in the Braddock area.

The 1959 strike proved to be a turning point for the American steel industry. With 85 percent of production offline, American corporations located suppliers in Germany and Japan. Imports of steel doubled in 1959. Over the next decade, the American steel industry went into a free fall.

Braddock's population declined with it. Younger generations left in search of work. With the arrival of strip malls and the proliferation of the automobile, established workers settled in nearby suburbs; un-knowingly, Braddock's car dealers had sold their customers one-way tickets. In 1950, Braddock had 16,488 residents. By 1980, that num-ber was down to 5,634. The decline persisted. The big stores closed down or moved on, and the smaller shops simply dwindled. Many residents walked away from their buildings, from the town, leaving empty storefronts and vacant houses in their wake. Today, Braddock is unrecognizable as the center of commerce and industry that was once the envy of towns across Western Pennsylvania.

As I was writing this book, another high school football team from a steel town in the Mon Valley did something extraordinary. From 2009 to 2013, the Clairton High Bears won sixty-six consecu-tive games, besting the Pennsylvania state record of fifty-nine straight wins, which was set in 2000. Like Braddock, Clairton is in shambles. Football can't change a region's economic outlook, but during that thrilling streak, the Bears gave their community something great to root for.

"If the town's industrial glory days ended long ago," a *New York Times* reporter wrote of Clairton during its streak, "they are renewed weekly on the football field."

INDEX